Telling It like It Is

To Linda,
Thank you, and I
hope you enjoy!

Telling It like It Is

J.W. Blackwell

Copyright © 2017 by J.W. Blackwell.

Library of Congress Control Number: 2017906530
ISBN: Hardcover   978-1-5434-1939-9
        Softcover   978-1-5434-1938-2
        eBook   978-1-5434-1937-5

All rights reserved. No part of this book may be reproduced or transmitted in any form or by any means, electronic or mechanical, including photocopying, recording, or by any information storage and retrieval system, without permission in writing from the copyright owner.

Any people depicted in stock imagery provided by Thinkstock are models, and such images are being used for illustrative purposes only.
Certain stock imagery © Thinkstock.

Print information available on the last page.

Rev. date: 05/03/2017

To order additional copies of this book, contact:
Xlibris
1-888-795-4274
www.Xlibris.com
Orders@Xlibris.com
738852

Introduction

THE WORLD THAT WE LIVE IN TODAY is probably similar to the world that people many years before us lived in. So what makes this world any different from the world that people before us lived in? The Bible starts with, "In the beginning, God created the heavens and the earth." Then later on, "he created man and woman to oversee the world that was created to be the greatest thing since sliced bread." Soon after the creation of human beings, God discovered that they were not the obedient creatures whom he had imagined or hoped for them to be. Why? Because the first thing that human beings did after God gave them strict instructions not to eat the fruit from one very particular tree or maybe two in the Garden of Eden was eat the fruit anyway.

If God had himself a "mouthpiece" back then such as he has in me today, I would have told those two wackos that they were forbidden to eat from the Tree of Life and Death, period! Now go find another tree to mess with! As we all know, there was another kind of mouthpiece back then, and he is still running around on Earth today. But he is the wrong kind of mouthpiece for God or anyone else for that matter. And I can say this because every Commandment that God sent forth, the devil has twisted around and used to fit his own evil agenda.

Therefore, lo and behold, I had to step forward to say the things that God won't say. To me, it is apparent that the Bible is not doing enough to convince people that God is real and that he is not a myth or some kind of boogeyman, horror tale, or even "God concept" that was written for the purpose of telling the perfect bedtime story to put the people to sleep.

One day, I had a dream that God was talking to me, and he said, "You've got a big mouth for someone so young! But you talk a lot about the right things, and I like that! And it is something that the world needs to hear in the way that you say it. And you could just be the one I've been looking for. How about coming to work for me?"

Naturally, I asked God, "What's in it for me if I go out here and speak for you?!"

And naturally, God replied to me, "Eternal life in heaven with my son, Jesus Christ."

"Listen, God, I know to some folks, that might sound all well and good, but I ain't looking for no pie in the sky when I die. Whatever you gonna do for me, I want it right now!" I said.

"Okay, so what can I do for you right now?!" God replied in a loud, thunderous voice.

I thought for a moment . . . and then I thought about it some more . . . but a funny thing began to happen after I tried to think of something that only God could give me. When I began to look at my situation, I suddenly realized that God had already given me everything that I could possibly want in life and then some. So I asked God sharply, "Did you just do that?!"

"Did I just do what?!" God responded just as sharply.

"I can't think of one thing that I want from you that you haven't already done . . ." I paused for a moment before I continued. "Okay, I'll do it. . . . What do you want me to do?"

"Very good, my son . . ." God replied in another loud voice. "Now this is what I want you to do and say for me to the people of my world. Do you think you can handle it?"

When I woke up from my dream, it seemed so real that I immediately began to write what I believed God wanted to say to the readers of this book. And now I call myself the spokesman for God because this is what he said to me, "Somebody's got to say this, and I need somebody to say it in a way that people will understand. I need someone who has the guts to tell it like it is!" Of course, that was when I knew that I had to write this book, *Telling It Like It Is*.

JWB

Message from the Author

Telling It Like It Is: In the Beginning

WHEN I WAS GROWING UP, my mother would get on about me speaking my mind. She would say something like, "You say whatever comes into your mind, like it or hate it!" And I would say to her, "Mama, why should I lie about something or somebody when I know what I'm saying is the truth?!" She would shake her head as she walked away, smiling because she knew me better than anyone, and she also knew that someday, my mouth was going to either get me in a whole lot of trouble or make me a better man for speaking the truth.

Nevertheless, today, I don't always say what I am thinking, but I can still see things and people for what and who they really are. Now the reason I do not always say what I am thinking is because people have such tender feelings, and they hate to be told the truth even when they know that they are wrong about something. Some people still do not want to be told that they are wrong about something. Well, in my new job for God, I am not holding anything back. I am telling it like it is, point-blank. You can love it or hate it! It doesn't matter. Someone may say, "Why do you always think or assume that you are right?" Oh, I know that there are many times when I am not always right, but the problem is, of course, the people who are asking the question, "Can they prove that I am wrong?" In most cases, they cannot. I have an old saying that I have lived by for many years: "I may not always be right, but I am never wrong."

"Telling it like it is" is an old saying that gets right down to the nitty-gritty about most things. And I am not one for covering up the truth. But wait! Does anyone actually know what the truth really is? Okay, these are the things that I know for certain may or may not be the truth.

The number one question in the world is, "Where do we go when we die?" According to some folks, we are all going to a holding place—or purgatory—especially the ones who are destined to go to heaven. Now purgatory is a place for purification or getting our souls cleaned so we can then one day meet Jesus on our way to heaven.

The number two question in the world is, "What is going to happen to the ones who are not fit for heaven?" And trust me, there are going to be millions upon millions who will not meet the criterion that is required to get through heaven's gates. According to the Bible and a few other believers, if we don't go to heaven, we'll be waiting to be judged by God for all the wrong things that we have done in life. And then we'll be shipped off to hell to become brothers and sisters of Satan.

The number three question in the world is, "If God sent Jesus to die for our sins, why must we go to hell for the sins that we have been forgiven of?" The short answer to that question is quite simple: because we have not been forgiven for the sins that we committed in the world. And the long answer is that Jesus only died to give us the right to be forgiven for our sins. There is no guarantee in his death that we would be automatically be forgiven for our sins. In the real world, if we commit a crime by man's laws, we have a right to an attorney to plead our innocence or guilt in a court of law. But in the case of sin, Jesus only gave us the right to plead our case before God as to whether we are guilty or innocent of said charges.

Think about hell this way: why do we imagine that God created hell in the first place? Do we automatically assume that hell was created for Satan along with his rebellious followers or his used-to-be-angels? Yes, of course! But hell was also created for rebellious human beings who have done evil things, which are products of Satan. Let's not forget there are some human beings who could actually be Satan themselves. And how did these human creatures become so evil minded? They were influenced by the likes of Satan and some of his angels.

So the number four question in the world is, "How do we avoid getting trapped by the evildoings of Satan?" The short answer again is quite simple: just say no to whatever he is offering! Say no to anything that might look like, smell like, feel like, or even taste like it is evil and wrong. That will also include a lot of people whom we might know or come in contact with. But let's not fool ourselves; none of the things that I am talking about are easy to do or stand firm on. You might say, "Yes, it is!" And I will say to you, "No, it's not!" And if anybody else tells you that Satan is as easy to avoid as saying no to him, they are lying, and the truth is not in them.

The number five question in the world is, "If Satan is such a difficult spirit to deal with or avoid, why in the world did God ever allow him to exist?" And many people have gone on to say, "God must have known what Satan is capable of doing. . . . I mean, God's first clue was in heaven when Satan felt like he was way too smart and much too pretty to take orders from the likes of God. This is old news, for heaven's sake!"

Okay, as the mouthpiece of God, I can say this: "Yeah, God knew from the very beginning what Satan was and the things he would do to his people many years down the road. And the answer to the question as to why God would allow Satan to exist that dates all the way back to the days of the Garden of Eden is no big mystery. It's all about us, his people."

Telling it like it is is not as easy as it might seem to be. People today—and I am excluding those of yesteryears because I don't know what to say about people in the past— hate hearing the truth. Not only do they hate hearing the truth about themselves, but they also hate hearing the truth about life, period! For instance, if I want to talk about the inevitable, the fact that we all are going to die one day, no one wants to talk about dying until they are almost dead. And as far as I know, people have been dying since the very beginning of the world. So what is it about dying now that makes people so uncomfortable? Is it the fact that they are going to leave this land of the living and that no one will ever see or hear from them again?

Quite frankly, I do not get it, but it is a fact of life that many people fear having a conversation about.

Telling it like it is is a quality that God obviously appreciates me having. And I am proud that God found something in me that is worthy of sharing with the world, whether the world likes it or not. And I am sure throughout this book, there are going to be some things that I am going to say and write that are going to piss many people off the most. But who am I here to satisfy? God? Myself? Or other people?! Although I have to live with myself and share this world with other people, my primary focus is to please God. And as long as I am comfortable with knowing that God is satisfied with what I am saying, me, myself, and I will tell the rest of the world to just sit back, relax, grab a smoke, a Coke, or a cup of coffee and read.

Telling it like it is is something that I have always wanted to do simply because people have become so "politically correct" nowadays that everybody is afraid to say what is on their mind because it might hurt someone's feelings or offend them. To be perfect honest with you, that is exactly why God gave us feelings: for other people to hurt them. If we did not have feelings, how would we know when someone else has done us wrong? Our feelings tell us when we have been hurt, dogged out, stepped on, pissed off, or insulted. Therefore, it is not my intention to do any of these things to my readers, but I am going to tell it like it is whether it hurts your feelings, makes you smile, or just downright causes you to break out in a cold sweat.

It is a natural fact that the truth hurts! No one wants to hear the truth, especially when it is about them. But of course, as long as the truth is about someone else, it is okay! But here in this book, I will tell the truth about the world as it really is and about the people who are now occupying the earth that God created with his own two hands. We have tried for millions of years to make this planet our own making, but it is not ours. It has never been ours and will never be ours to own or keep. To tell the truth, God is doing all of us a favor by allowing us to live here for a few years, just to see what we can make of ourselves. Once we have done all that we can do or not do, it is time to move on and get out of the way to make room for a bunch of new folks.

But then you might be wondering, "How is God doing us a favor by allowing us to live for a few years on this planet, where we might become rich and famous, and suddenly, the lights go out, and we are no more?!" Well, by God's way of thinking, he never promised anyone a car in every garage, a chicken in every pot, and a million dollars in every bank. Whatever we get in this one life that we have is not ours to keep. Everything that we have on this earth is on borrowed time, including the lives that we seem to think are our own. In other words, we have nothing! This is the truest of all truths: we came into this world as naked as jaybirds, and we will leave here the same way. No one, regardless of what they may have gained in life, cannot take anything with them when they die. You may not be able to add it all up, but it is simple math! You live a few short years, and then you are suddenly gone forever.

Telling it like it is dates back to hundreds of years; when people were fed up with the way things were going, they simply stood up and said what was on their minds. Today, people are fed up with the way things are in local, state, and federal governments, but it seems that no one is saying what is really on their mind. And if they are saying what is on their mind, no one who is in a position to do something about their complaints does anything or pays attention.

How long can the world continue with the way things are going today? We have wars that seem to never end, and we have politicians that grow weaker and dumber with every new election. So what should we do?! Don't even think about trying to find more qualified people, for that is not going to happen. Why? Because every time we elect a new bunch of whoever-they-might-be, they are dumber or worse than the ones we've had before.

Therefore, somebody has got to say it like it really is from point A to point Z . . . which leaves me as the only survivor of the "truth." Do you want the truth?! Okay, let's see if you can handle this kind of truth!

Chapter 1

THE CHURCH IS PROBABLY THE BEST PLACE to start because the church is next in line after Jesus Christ. But then there are those who will question me by asking, "Why the church?! What did the church ever do to you?" Well, let me say this about the church first of all: my father was a Baptist preacher, and my brother is a Baptist minister, and I have several cousins and friends who are ministers and preachers (not that I know the difference between the two), but they are good people who were called by God to deliver his words from the Bible.

But let me tell it like it is: everybody who is standing in the pulpits, calling on the name of the Lord, is not doing it for all the right reasons. There are just as many whoremongers preaching the Word of God as there are out there in the streets. And these same preachers are swearing on the Holy Bible that they were in fact called by God to preach his Word. Okay, so God called them to preach, but to preach what? And what is even worse than these so-called preachers of God is that their congregations have totally missed the boat. No human being can declare himself worthy to be praised. And that is exactly what some church members are doing, praising the pastors.

I had the pleasure to meet a woman one day who is a highly dedicated member of a particular church where I personally knew the pastor as being a gambler, a liar, a whore-chaser, a drug dealer, and anything else that I can think of if I really wanted to. As a police officer in one of America's highly political and religious cities, I got to know a little something about people in all walks of life. And many of those people will do whatever it takes to get what they want.

On this particular occasion, I was talking to a woman who was a friend of mine; she was thought to have been very religious or a very Christian-minded individual. Our conversation came about initially because her pastor had been arrested the previous day for drug possession. Although he was not personally caught with the drugs, a friend accused him of sending her to pick up a suitcase containing a few pounds of cocaine from the airport, where she was arrested as well. The Feds decided to padlock the church where they believed that the drugs were about to be delivered by a friend of the pastor who was waiting there.

"Listen, tell me what happened when the people got to church on Sunday morning and found that the church had been padlocked by the Drug Enforcement Administration officers."

"What do you mean, tell you what happened?!" she snapped at me. "There was nothing we could do but go back home and wait for the pastor to get out of jail."

"So he did get out of jail and return to his church the following Sunday . . . but what did he say to the congregation, especially with everybody knowing that he had been arrested for the drugs that his friend claimed she went to the airport to pick up for him?"

"Look, we love our pastor, and it didn't matter what he said!" she sharply said in response to me. "But since you're asking, I'll tell you what he said." She paused for a moment. "He told us that it didn't matter what anybody was saying about him. People talked about Jesus Christ, and for the people to talk about him, that's nothing!"

"And you really believed what he had to say?" I asked her sharply.

"Why wouldn't I believe him? Look, his friend is a coldhearted bitch, and she will do anything to get even with him for what he did to her, I guess!"

I stopped her right there. "Wait! Are you telling me that this friend picked up the drugs for someone else, but instead of telling the agents whom the drugs actually belonged to, she told them that the drugs belonged to the pastor?! And what did he do to her?" I asked curiously.

"No, I'm not saying that! And I don't know what he did to her!" She was angry now.

"Okay, then why did you make the accusation that she could have picked the drugs up for someone other than the pastor?" I asked her as nice as I could. "Okay! But how did he explain the drug charges that he had been accused of?"

She smiled as she was about to speak. "He said to us that whatever he did or whatever he was accused of doing, it was none of our business! And all that we needed to know or be concerned with is getting our own souls saved and not to worry about his."

"And to you, that meant what?" I asked her.

"It meant that whatever we had heard or had been told by the police or anyone else was none of our business. It meant that we had nothing to do with what had happened."

"And you, along with the rest of the church members, accepted his explanation for going to jail?" I asked, knowing what her answer was going to be. "I mean, he did go to jail for drugs!"

"Yes, we accepted his explanation. Why wouldn't we?! It doesn't matter what he did! I am sure God has forgiven him for whatever he did. He's a good man, and he preaches the Word. You of all people should know that people do things that we have to forgive them for. . . . I mean, you're a cop, and you should know better than anybody else that nobody's perfect!"

"Yeah, I've heard that old saying," I said with a smile. "But this man is your pastor, and he's the one man whom we should be able to look to for guidance. And if he is going to get arrested for drug possession, what does that say about his character?"

"But he didn't have the drugs on him. It was his friend's. She was the one who should have been charged for drug possession, not him, right?!" she then questioned me.

"Yeah, but the suitcase containing the drugs was in his name at the airport, waiting to be picked up by him. But according to the report, he called his friend and told her that he was busy and asked her to pick up the suitcase for him. . . . Now isn't that the way it happened?"

"That's what she said!" my friend snapped at me again.

"But she was not the one who had been on an out-of-town flight. He was the one who left the suitcase at the airport. . . . Tell me, am I right or wrong about that?!" I snapped back at her.

"Yeah, everything that you're saying is the same thing that I heard. But does that make it true? No, I don't think so!" she said with a smile on her face. "Look, my pastor is a good, God-fearing man. He would never stoop to the level of using or selling drugs to anyone."

"So in your opinion, his so-called friend is telling the lie and not the pastor. Although he didn't deny that the drugs belonged to him, right?" I asked in the most honest way that I could.

She took a moment to reflect on the question that I asked before finally saying, "He's our pastor! And that's the way I see it. Come hell or high water, he is still going to be our pastor."

After having that particular conversation with my friend, I went on to do some more investigation concerning this pastor. I later found out that the DEA did in fact padlock the doors of the church as well as make the arrest on the pastor. However, this so-called National Association of Christian Ministers went before a federal judge and demanded that the pastor be released to continue his duties as a minister of his church. At first, I would have thought that a federal judge would throw the book at the minister, but that did not happen. Instead, the pastor was let go, and he returned to his church to do his business of pastoring as usual.

The congregation of this particular church welcomed the drug-dealing pastor back with open arms as if the incident had never happened. And sure enough, as my friend had said before, his exact words went something like this: "Now I know there has been a lot of talk among yourselves and a few other folks who think they know something about me and what happened a week or so ago. But I promise you, you don't know the half of it! And even if you did know, it's none of your business! You don't come to church to judge me. You come here to serve the Lord and hear the Word as I preach it. . . . As far as anything else is concerned, forget about it!"

The church crowd said, "Amen!" And they all went about their business as usual . . .

However, as I previously said, I knew the drug-dealing pastor from other things that he was involved in, as well as being a huge gambler. When I first had the pleasure of meeting him, I was with another undercover officer who had the occasion to sit in on gambling games with him and several other men who were gambling in the backroom of a local café in downtown Atlanta. Before the bust went down, I observed the pastor, who had lost a lot of money during these gambling games. However, it was not so much about the money that he had lost, but it was more about how freely he threw money that belonged to the church on the gambling table.

Not only was this pastor losing money to other gamblers, but there were also at least two other preachers in the group who were gambling as well. It was mostly obvious that all three men who called themselves men of God were not very good gamblers, for not one of them could win on what was a crooked table. This particular pastor who lost the most money was asked by one of the other gamblers, "Say, preacher, what're you gonna tell your congregation tomorrow when they ask questions about the money you're losing tonight?!"

The pastor only grinned as he rolled the dice and said, "Hey, I'm not losing my own money! And don't worry about what they're going to ask me because every dime I lose here tonight, I'll get back tomorrow from the tithes and offering plate." And they all laughed because it was amusing to see him lose the money that belonged to the church.

We allowed the game to continue without making an arrest simply because it was too embarrassing to arrest three preachers in the same city for gambling. Atlanta is a city that is known for preachers and ministers leading the country through a dark period of racial unrest, riots, and demonstrations during the 1960s. After the assassination of Dr. Martin Luther King Jr., this particular pastor began to stand out as one of the next great civil rights leaders. But like most men who called themselves men of God, he had several weaknesses, and gambling was one of them, next to women.

Moreover, speaking of this pastor's weaknesses, there were more such incidents involving several pastors of Atlanta whom I had the pleasure to be associated with. To me, it was like they were serving God and Satan at the same time. There was one such minister who was involved in the gambling game. He later found himself being sued by a deacon of his church for stealing more than fifty thousand dollars that was donated to the church to build a parking lot. Instead of allowing the funds to be used for what they were intended, this minister stole the money or misappropriated funds from the church treasury and purchased himself a brand new Mercedes-Benz.

Naturally, all hell broke loose in the church about the money from the deacon board concerning the cash and the car. However, after all was said and done, the church members came to an agreement to replace the money, and they allowed their minister to keep the Mercedes. Why? Because he was their pastor, and they loved him regardless of the wrong that he had done. "It is not for us to judge our pastor," the congregation said. "For this, he will have to answer to God, not us."

By any reasonable definition of the church, there are no wrongdoings as far as the church is concerned. The church alone is no more than a building with four walls and a roof. The church cannot sin or curse God to his face. But the people who attend the church or any church for that matter can and will destroy everything that Jesus stood for, as well as every ounce of innocent blood that ran down on the ground from his dead body while hanging on the cross.

People, of course, make the church. Without the people, there is no church; it suddenly becomes an empty building. But there is one question that I have to answer in the next chapter: "Why do we need a church to serve God?"

There is more on the minister who was arrested for drugs. A few years later, after everything seemed to have settled down for him, lo and behold: while I was working an extra job at a downtown hotel, I observed the same pastor ride up in a black Mercedes with a price tag of no less than a hundred thousand dollars for a night of partying with two high-priced prostitutes. The car pulled up to the front entrance of the hotel, and he slowly stepped out while glancing around to see if anyone recognized him. Of course, if anyone did, they did not let it be known to him.

After checking into a tenth-floor presidential suite, he rode the elevator up to his room. Obviously, he did not recognize me as being the same cop who had allowed him to escape getting arrested a few years back for gambling. And if he did, he pretended not to or did not care.

No longer than fifteen minutes later, another expensive Mercedes arrived at the hotel, but this one was white. And in the rear seat were two very attractive women, one black and one white, who also checked into the same tenth-floor presidential suite, the same one that the pastor was in. Was this a coincidence? No, it was not. They were one-thousand-dollars-a-night hookers who there to serve the pastor with all kinds of sexual favors and pleasures.

How do I know that these things happened in the pastor's suite? I was a cop at the time, and it was my business to know all the high-priced hookers in Atlanta. But more importantly, I knew the pimp who sponsored the hookers. Not only was he a pimp, but he was also a drug dealer who supplied cocaine for all three people in the room. Therefore, the price tag for a night of fun and sexual pleasures probably cost the pastor more than three thousand dollars plus the hotel bill that was charge on his church's credit card.

As a normal, everyday man, I would probably not expect better behavior from the average guy, especially if he could afford such a lavish evening on the town. But I would expect for him, a pastor of the church who stands before his congregation twice on Sundays and God-knows-how-many times during the week, to act in a much more godly manner. As God's mouthpiece, I would say that this type of conduct was totally unsuitable for a pastor. And there is no room for argument as to whether he is a human being or not. And being such a creature, he cannot be judged for his actions; only God can do that. This is what most people believe.

Yeah, I know all about the story of David and how he had purposely arranged for a man to die in battle because he wanted the man's wife so desperately. So why would God choose David as one of his favorite servants in spite of knowing that David had gone to great lengths to have a man killed for his wife? I cannot answer that, but I do know that God is terribly disappointed with the way that preachers, ministers, and pastors are conducting themselves in and out of their churches these days, and he will probably be disappointed in many days to come.

Personally, I would say that it is good for all men of God to have their own wives. Hopefully, this would eliminate the desire for other women who are now dominating the pews in the churches. Of course, this is not the case either. Many of these men of God are finding themselves guilty of adultery just as much as other men who are not preaching the Word of God. Why is that a problem?! It is a problem simply because the Commandment says, "Thou shalt not commit adultery." And if the preachers are not going to obey the Commandments, how do they expect for their followers to obey them? But then maybe they do not expect for their followers to obey the Commandments. They are saying, "Do as I do and nothing less!"

Moreover, if their followers are disobedient to the laws of the Bible, that allows the preachers to do so as well. If the followers are willing to commit adultery, there is no harm or foul done by anyone. They also believe that two willing participants cannot violate the laws of God. And if the preachers are not going to uphold God's laws, why should anyone else? Naturally, this is where God is having his biggest problem with people who call themselves speakers of his Word. They themselves are not abiding by the Word, and that is a big problem. "If we can't trust the preacher and the teachers, who can we trust?"

Chapter 2

PREACHERS OF LA (LOVELY ATLANTA) — Although chapter 1 dealt primarily with the shenanigans of a few preachers, it is obvious that is not the end of the story as far as the church is concerned. Therefore, as a semi-mouthpiece for God, I am going to dig deeper into the business of the church and the people who run it. As an employee of the city of Atlanta, and being of the inquiring-mind pack, I personally made it my hobby to learn all there was to know about the religious aspect of the city, as well as dip into the political game along the way.

As I mentioned before, Atlanta is the place where the civil rights movement took root, which included Dr. Martin Luther King Jr. as the "point man." However, for a city that was completely burned to the ground by General Sherman and the Union army, which chased the Confederate troops down during the Civil War until they literally surrendered, Atlanta has never been a location for racial demonstrations or riots during the 1960s. Why was that? It was because black ministers and preachers in Atlanta have always been able to deal with white folks in charge, and they were able to iron out their differences and demands peacefully.

In fact, black preachers in Atlanta had an open-door policy with the city hall and the governor's office to clear any hurdles or obstacles that they were confronted with. There was such a clear understanding between the preachers and the mayor's office that when Dr. King wanted to bring his troops to Atlanta to hold a march for equal justice, he was told by others, "Look, we don't need you to come to Atlanta to hold your marches. The mayor and other city leaders have agreed to anything and everything that we have demanded. So you can save that energy for someplace else where they really need you. You will only mess things up for us here."

Atlanta had been a powerhouse city for black preachers for many years in the past. And even to this day, things have not changed much. And of course, Atlanta has always been a melting pot for corrupted preachers who have found that there is a pot of gold at the end of the rainbow in Atlanta's churches. There are more mega-churches for black preachers in Atlanta than anywhere else. It is a known fact that in Atlanta, the bigger the churches are, the bigger the crowds are. Churchgoers in Atlanta are under this weird impression that there is power in mega-churches, and the power that they find flows out into their communities and business worlds. In other words, if a person says that he or she is a member of a particular mega-church, they are automatically accepted into whatever it is they are trying to get into.

Personally, I would refer to Atlanta's mega-churches as a fool's paradise. Why? Because anyone who joins a mega-church simply because it is a huge church or because other people will view them differently is foolish. The church cannot do anything for anybody but provide seats for its congregation. The preacher, of course, is a totally different story; he or she is there to sell the people a product, and that product costs lots of money. In other words, all churches in today's society are selling religion, which is disguised as tithes and offerings that most people believe are going directly to God. The truth of the matter is—and it has always been a pure fact—God never receives or sees a penny of the money that is being collected in churches.

"Lord God, that's pure blasphemy! You can't say that about the house of the Lord." Many of you are thinking or saying that right now. "You're gonna die and go straight to hell!" Yes, die, I must do. But going straight to hell is a maybe! Maybe I will, and maybe I won't. My chances of going to hell are about as good as any other human being's because it is clear from the day of birth that there are no guarantees in this world. The best thing that anyone can do is be as faithful to God's Word as he or she can be because the final decision will be made by God.

The totally misunderstood idea behind religion—and to some extent, the Bible reinforces it—is that if we, as human beings who without a doubt love God and believe that Jesus Christ was born and died for our sins, pay tithes and offerings, this is proof that we are born-again Christians. Naturally, this belief is another way of hoping that we can buy our way into heaven or buy our way out of hell. Either way, if we pay enough money to the church, God will see that as being obedient and will bless us abundantly. But we totally forgot the preachers are the very ones who are playing God and profiting from the money that we give to the church. The money eventually ends up paying for big mansions, expensive automobiles, and high-powered jet airplanes.

The fact of the matter is that regardless of the amount of money that is being collected in the church, no one can buy their way into heaven or buy life forever. We all must die someday, but after that reality, where we end up is totally a mystery or in the hands of someone else. We can only hope that someone else is God. The mega-churches and expensive-suit-wearing preachers cannot determine or preach our way into heaven. The only person who can get you into heaven is you! And it may come as a shock to you, but it does not take paying your last money in tithes and offerings to get you into heaven; if God so decides, that is where you should be.

Once upon a time, there was a preacher in the city who decided that it was time for him to purchase a new jet airplane that was estimated to cost around sixty-five million dollars but not with his personal money. Naturally, this was a cost factor that he would not or could not pay for himself. Therefore, he did what most of the "now-generation" preachers are willing to do; he spread a plea for funds all over social media by asking for donations to make his dream come true. But of course, there was so much backlash behind his actions, he backtracked by saying, "If Jesus wants to bless me with sixty-five million dollars, then let Jesus bless me!" However, as far as I know, this LA preacher may be still waiting for his millions.

Naturally, this particular mega-church preacher was obviously convinced that the average believer in God is a complete idiot. And I must admit most of Jesus's believers are idiots. They are idiots because they undoubtedly believe in the preachers more than they believe in God. I firmly believe that if Jesus stepped out of a cloud and began begging for sixty-five million dollars to buy an airplane instead of riding on his cloud, the cops would be called, and Jesus would be marched off to jail, and he would be facing a judge the very next day for fraud.

First of all, no one would believe that he was, in fact, Jesus in the flesh. Secondly, if he were Jesus, why can't he simply ask God for whatever he wants and have his prayers answered immediately?! Preachers are supposed to be servants of God who undoubtedly believe in the power of prayer. The Bible clearly states that "whoever believes can ask God for whatever they want in the name of Jesus, and it shall be done." Also, preachers are supposed to have a special bond between themselves and God primarily because God called them to deliver his Word to his people. This means that it is not the people's responsibility to supply the preacher's needs; it is God's responsibility. And if God had wanted this preacher to have a new plane to fly all over the planet spreading his message, he would have dropped the sixty-five million dollars right down on top him in the pulpit, which might have killed him.

So why didn't this preacher take his money request to God instead of placing it on social media? It occurred to me that the preacher did not believe in the messages that he so often gives to his congregations. If he does not believe in the God whom he preaches about, how does he expect for the members of his church to believe in God? In other words, if he is constantly telling other people that God is the creator of miracles but is asking people on social media for the sixty-five million dollars he needed to purchase the jet airplane that he desired to have, he then in fact does not believe in the God of miracles himself.

Moreover, there are many preachers today who do not believe in God, but they preach the Word of God daily. You might ask, "How is that possible?" It is possible because they have discovered a secret that most of the people whom they preach to have no idea about. The secret is the same as that of an atheist's. On the surface, some preachers want it to appear that they are Christians or believers in a higher power, but on the inside, they only believe in themselves. "How can an individual believe in himself or herself yet make it sound as if they have all the faith in the world in God?" Atheists are people who think that other people who believe in God, who is a myth to them, are idiots. Normally, it is believed by atheists that the people who believe in God are black, poor, and old folks who are hoping that there is no hell below. This, of course, is where the preachers of mega-churches come into play. They are demonstrating that big churches, big houses, and fancy automobiles are the results of their faith in God. Obviously, it does not take an idiot to realize that God had nothing to do with their riches. It is the people who march into their sanctuaries and dish out their hard-earned money to make the preachers' prosperity messages possible.

Admittedly, there are some pretty stupid people who call themselves Christians. But they are followers of Christ, and they believe in the Word of God. The obvious problem, however, with born-again Christians is they fail to comprehend or understand that God is a spirit, and no one who is alive today has ever seen or touched God personally. They speak of God as if he is a human being and that he is ready and willing to solve all of their problems or difficulties in life. But by no means is this the role of God. It has never been the role of God in our lives, and it never will be. God is the creator of all things, including atheists, although most of them are too stupid to realize it. Nevertheless, God provides each and every person who is born into the world with whatever is needed for them to sustain life as well as wealth and happiness.

Mega-church preachers, as well as smaller church preachers, have no more of a personal relationship with God than an atheist has, except the atheist does not believe in God. Anything beyond those who believe and those who do not is worthless. "Why is this a fact?" It is a fact because every living creature on Earth has to die at an already-determined point and time in life. And this is a question that no one can answer, whether they are believers or non-believers; they are lacking the knowledge and are not mentally equipped to know and understand who makes that determination or decision as to whom or when or how anyone will die.

"Why do you say that preachers have no more of a connection with God than anyone else?" I am asked this on a regular basis. "I mean, these are servants of God whom God has called to preach, and they must have heard God's voice when he called them." Really?! The

Holy Spirit is the only voice that anyone will ever hear from God. And although it is my belief that God wants every human being to prosper financially, spiritually, and mentally, he did not call any particular preacher to stand in a pulpit to speak his Word only for the purpose of robbing poor people of their hard-earned money and using his name to commit the crimes. In a plain, common-sense approach, the preachers are blind to what God really wants them to do, and the congregations are blind to whom they should be following. Or I could simply say this is no more than the "blind leading the blind."

To further state my case or prove my point, once upon a time, there was a certain preacher who was known all over America, if not the world. His message was one that I can identify with, but his action was one of a stone-cold criminal. He obviously preached prosperity, but it would appear that he was the only one profiting from his messages.

This particular preacher sold out churches and arenas all across America. People came by the thousands to hear what he had to say. He had a paid group of assistants who worked the crowds, collecting every dime that was brought into these gatherings. In fact, round metal containers or buckets were placed in the aisles in every arena for the packed houses to place their money into. And his messages were based upon the amount of money that was collected at each of these gatherings.

His primary message to the people went like this: "Don't be waiting around down here, talking about some pie in the sky. That's pure nonsense! There is no pie in the sky! The only pie you're going to get is right here on Earth because God wants you have your piece of the pie right now while you are still alive. The more you give today, the more God is going to bless you tomorrow. That's a promise from God, and he told me to tell you what he said."

Of course, it was a lie, but the people believed it, and that is all that mattered as far as he was concerned. Nevertheless, it gave the people hope. It was something that they could believe in if they kept their faith in God. And when it was all said and done, it appeared that God only blessed the preacher for the things he was doing. In 1976, he appeared in *Ebony Magazine* as one the most flamboyant ministers in the world. He was showcased in the magazine with his twenty-four very expensive automobiles, sixteen of which were Rolls-Royces.

Even back then, the net worth of his vehicles alone was well over one million dollars.

This particular minister was considered or placed in the star category of celebrity status. Needless to say, no one could accuse him of not giving back. He always gave back to every city that he visited. But then one might not wish to call it giving back to the community because there was a designed purpose for his giving away expensive gifts to some people whom he knew were more like an advertising commercial. Therefore, a few weeks prior to his appearing in a particular town or city, he sent some of his assistants out to purchase brand new cars for a few of the people who had sent in "prayer requests," asking God for new cars.

Throughout the cities, some people would awaken to find new cars parked in their driveways with a note attached, saying, "You asked God for a new car, and he heard your prayer, and it was answered," signed by the minister. The news would soon spread like wildfire in every city across America. From that point on, people would pack every place that he traveled to to speak his message. Millions upon millions of dollars were stacked on the tables in his mansion every year thereafter. But the question is, "Was he a crook or just a clever businessman?"

In my opinion, he was a little of both. Not only was he a crook and a clever business-minded person, but he was clever enough to use God's name to steal millions of dollars from the people who believed in him instead of God. So who do I really blame in this particular situation, which is much like that of all the other crooked preachers and ministers who are doing what they do simply for the money? I blame the people who are gullible enough to fall for the wicked schemes that are being pulled on them. Why? Because if we read the Bible, it is already written that there will be many who will come before us, making false claims that they are speakers of God, but they are absolutely lying. They are called "false prophets."

The problem is, of course, we do not read the Bible like we should to get a better understanding of God's Word. We rather rely on the religious cheaters to tell us or explain to us the meaning of God's Word. The secret is, of course, they are only doing what they do because there are people who are eager to pay a handsome price only to be told that God loves them. Wow! What a crock! We should already know that God loves us, or he would not have created us. To be more precise, I could say if he did not love us, he would not have taken his precious time to be born as a human being and die as a slave on a rugged wooden cross just for our right to ask him to forgive us for the sins we so freely commit without thinking of him.

When we really get down to the nitty-gritty of this whole idea of being saved from the sins that we are committing without thinking twice about what we are doing, who else but God would have given his life for a bunch of people who could really care less about what he did? Or even worse, there are a group of people who live on this planet, a planet that God created for them, who do not even like him or could care less about who he is or what he stands for. And to make matters worse, some of the same people whom I am referring to are the same people who open up a Bible and make claims that they are preaching God's Word. This is a clear indication as to how far the world has turned away from God. And the millions of people who still believe in God are being jilted by those who do not believe in God, only because some of us are too lazy to find out who God really is for ourselves. Instead, we would rather take the word of someone else than to read it for ourselves. However, understanding what we read is the key.

Speaking of people who failed to discover who God really is and instead relied on the spoken word of a flesh-and-blood human being, this takes me back to a well-documented story about an evil man named Jim Jones who founded the Peoples Temple Church that started in Northern California. Now here was a human being who realized that he had the great power of persuasion over the minds of a huge following of people, and he eventually convinced many of them to follow him. They left everything that they owned behind and followed Jim Jones to a place by the name of Jonestown, Guyana, where a total of 913 people died from drinking grape-flavored Kool-Aid that contained cyanide poison.

Just think for a moment: 913 people ended their lives because some idiot who thought he was God told them that dying was their way out of their misery here on Earth. However, the misery that the people found was in Guyana after the so-called minister Jim Jones promised them paradise in South America, where they all packed up and moved to. Instead, the people found out that this place was a living hell in the middle of the jungle. I wondered then, and I am still wondering today, how so many people could become that absentminded of reality that they actually believe a man who could deliver a worry-free paradise located in the middle of a hot, snake-infested jungle with wild animals and no way to get back home. How could they?!

The mind is obviously the weakest link of the human body, which means it can easily be manipulated and persuaded to do almost anything for the person who is doing the manipulating and is telling lies that are convincing enough. Preachers and ministers have discovered the secret to getting weak-minded people to follow them to the ends of the world. Jim Jones had discovered this magnificent power of persuasion, and he obviously used that power to convince 913 people to willingly commit suicide. And unfortunately for those who were not willing participants, they were murdered by the hands of the aides who were working with the minister.

Although this particular massacre occurred way back in November 1978 when Jim Jones himself died along with his followers, the power of persuasion did not die with this particular preacher. It is still very much alive today. The bottom line is this: if the people who are preaching the Word of God only believe in God for themselves, the power of persuasion would not be necessary to convince other people to do likewise. But as I have said before, the very people who preach the Word of God do not necessarily believe in God or his Word. God is simply their methods or means to make money for themselves.

Chapter 3

WORKING AS A COP for many years was a slow process of learning what was most important in my life. I have learned to take my time so that I might see and hear all that I can before this life is over. And being a cop has help me to understand many things that I may not have learned otherwise. Although there were many times when I was not too sure if I was going to make it or not, I was never too proud to fall down on my knees and ask God for his help. However, being in the law enforcement business, I found many cops who said that they did not necessarily believe in God, and I suppose they had their own personal reasons. However, as for myself, growing up as a PK (preacher's kid), believing in God was not an option for me. Therefore, whenever I pinned on my police badge, I also put on the armor of God as well.

So how did that work out for me? In my thirty-seven years, I found out that cops (not all, of course) are some of the worst, cutthroat, backstabbing sons of bitches in the world. There is very little that some cops won't do if there is a promotion involved, to get a woman, or for money, if the price is right. When I first joined the force way back in the late 1960s, in my first interview with a high-ranking police officer, he made it very clear to me: "There are three things in this department that will get you to run off quicker than any other thing in the world. They are the three Bs. We call them booze, broads, and bribes."

What the public sees only tells half of the story about the life of a cop. There is a particular image that cops are trained to portray to the public. That particular image is to tell the public that they are there "to protect and to serve." That is the only image that the general public sees in a cop. However, having been raised and taught by a minister who strongly believed in God, there were many things that I could have done in the line of duty or off duty that I refused to be a part of.

As a rookie, I was assigned to a veteran officer to learn the ropes (sort of). And soon after my first tour on the evening watch with my training officer, I learned that he was a cop who liked to have a drink of alcohol before taking his first call in the evenings. After we departed the driveway of the police headquarters, which was on Decatur Street in downtown Atlanta, we gassed up and made a stop at a fellow officer's home in the Kirkwood neighborhood, which was on our beat. We parked the black-and-white car around the back of the off-duty cop's home, and as my training officer opened the car door, he glanced at me and snapped, "You listen to the radio, rookie, just in case we get a call. Our car number is 40-B." He turned and went into the rear entrance of the home, leaving me staring out of the car windows and listening to the radio.

Being a rookie on any assignment is no picnic simply because a rookie only has the training beforehand that he or she gets in the police academy and that comes straight from books and other recruits. There I sat very patiently, waiting to hear our car number 40-B called over the air. Needless to say, I was ready to go to work, but my partner wanted to get his drink on before going to work. And I supposed he wanted me to blow the horn or run inside to get him if and when the dispatcher called our number, for that is what rookies do.

About an hour had passed before my partner returned to the car, and the off-duty police officer was with him to say hi to me, the new cop on the streets. But as it turned out, I recognized the off-duty cop as being an old friend from my hometown. Naturally, I was shocked to see him, much less know that he was an Atlanta police officer. As I emerged from the vehicle, my homeboy came around to my side and congratulated me for becoming a member of the sacred fraternity, the "Black Atlanta Police Officers Club." This term was often used to let white officers know that we were a group that stood together for equal rights and treatment under the department's rules and regulations, as well as the city's guidelines.

My homeboy ran a "liquor house" for cops who could not work a complete eight-hour shift without having a drink. And it was also for the ones who were getting off duty, and if they wanted to, they could stop by for some group choir practice (police officers getting together for a drinking session). This was also done by the white cops as well, but most of the white officers did their drinking in the parking lot near the police headquarters.

Obviously, this sort of thing was a standard practice among most of the cops due to the tremendous pressure that most cops were under on the streets, as well as inside the department, to make arrests. There was also the pressure that black cops were under primarily because the department was undergoing a new integration policy of white and black officers working together. The department was still trying to deal with the racially mixed department that had been segregated since the first black officers were hired in 1948. Therefore, we were now reporting to the same location for roll call as that of the white cops, and many of them still had not adjusted to the new way of doing business in the Atlanta Police Department.

My training officer's breath was reeking of liquor, for I could smell it even on my side of the patrol car. And as we left the home of my homeboy, I politely asked my partner, "Are you supposed to be drinking on duty?" Of course, it was a dumb question for me to ask a senior police officer, and he immediately let me know it was not my place to be asking those kinds of questions. As most rookies do, they ask dumb-ass questions.

"Okay, first of all, you don't ask me a question unless it's pertaining to the job. And secondly, you're a rookie, and as long as you are sitting on that side of the car, you're not permitted to ask me anything unless it is pertaining to the job."

Naturally, I may have been a rookie, but I was a smart-mouthed rookie, probably one whom he had never dealt with before. I immediately responded, "This is pertaining to the job! But what if I report you to the sergeant, telling him that you've been drinking on duty? What then?!"

He rolled his eyes at me without moving his head. For a moment, he did not say a word. And suddenly, he burst out into loud laughter. "How do you know I've been drinking?!"

"It's because I can smell it on your breath. And if I can smell it, so can anyone else," I answered, trying to be polite about it as I possibly could.

Of course, he begged me not to mention what had happened primarily because I was a black cop, and all black cops stuck together. "We don't run and tell the white supervisors what other black cops are doing on the beat, even if it's wrong," he advised me. Naturally, I disagreed with him, but I was not a snitch either. So I kept quiet about my first encounter with the things that some cops do. The lesson I learned that evening was if I had snitched on my partner, he would have gotten in trouble, but I would have been blackballed by other senior black officers. In other words, they would have found a way to pay me back for what I had done.

It has always been an unwritten rule that cops do not snitch on other cops for any reason. If cops get caught up in something that is unlawful or against police department policy, it will have to be of that officer's own doing. Most police departments are very similar to a secret society, which means that the public and the media will never know the real story behind any police corruption or wrongdoings. The only way a cop will get caught doing something wrong or violating someone's civil rights is if he or she will implicate themselves and not by other cops.

My partner, who loved to have himself a drink before actually going on duty, had a very unique way of dealing with individuals who broke the law. I don't know how many people he had shot or killed. He knew how to put a scare in most people who thought that they could bully the police. One afternoon, we got a call saying a black male was walking along Boulevard NE, and he was armed with a handgun. When we arrived at the scene, the description matched the man standing on the corner in the Kirkwood neighborhood on the east side of town. My partner stepped out of the vehicle first, and we approached the man who appeared to have been in his early forties, short, and very drunk . . .

The man stood still with both hands in his front pockets, which was a clear indication that he had one of his hands on the gun that he was carrying. My partner spoke to the man first, "Hey, fellow, we got a call saying that you are armed with a pistol. I want you to take your hands out of your pockets very slowly with your palms facing me."

The man appeared to have been highly intoxicated as he slurred in his speech. "Why do I have to take my hands out of my own pockets?! Am I breaking some kind of law, officers?!" the man shouted at us as he took a step backward.

"Partner!" my partner said to me. "Tell the dispatcher to send us an ambulance and have Grady Hospital be on standby for one man wounded by a gunshot. He might be DOA!"

I looked at my partner for a moment, and he glanced at me, which said to me that he was serious. As I turned to do as I was told, I heard my partner say again, "Now you have one or two choices. You can take your hands out of your pockets, or I'll be forced to shoot you! And don't think for one minute that I won't kill you where you're standing," he told the man as he pulled his own weapon from his holster.

To my utter surprise, the man immediately but slowly pulled the revolver from his right pocket and placed it on the pavement in front of him as he started to grin and said, "I'm sorry, Mr. Officer! You know I didn't mean you no harm, I swear I didn't!"

I learned a valuable lesson that day from my senior partner, and he said it very plainly. "Listen, to police these streets every day and live to go back home at night to your family, you always have to be one step ahead of the criminals. Not only that," he continued, "but sometimes, you have to put yourself right down on the same level as they are or be as crazy as they are. And sometimes, that's the only thing they understand and the only way you'll survive."

"I was taught in the academy that we are law enforcement officers, and we have to carry ourselves in a professional manner at all times, along with enforcing the laws as they are written in the law books," I said to my partner.

"The academy is where you learn how to be a police officer," he responded sharply, "but out here in the streets is where you learn how to enforce the laws. What you do out here is not always written in the books because the criminal element does not always understand the laws as they are written in the books. Being a good cop is 25 percent books and 75 percent common sense. The academy can't teach you how to stay alive. You have to learn that on your own."

That was when I began to understand that police officers are human beings, just like any other person in this world. They want to go back home to their families in one piece like anyone else. The only real difference between cops and the rest of the world is they get paid to protect and serve the rest of the idiots in the world who could care less about cops until they get in trouble. The police are the only help that the people in trouble know to call upon.

In the real world for the average cop today, he or she has many things to deal with besides the problems of other people whom he or she does not get paid enough to protect. Cops are the lowest paid people on the planet. They ride and walk twenty-four hours a day, looking for trouble. Getting killed by some crazy person or by someone trying to make a name for himself is a constant thought running through a cop's mind. A soldier can serve his country for three years and get discharged to go home. But a cop has to serve a city, county, or state for twenty or thirty years before he can even think about retiring. And when they do retire, their pensions are hardly enough to live on for the rest of their lives.

A professional athlete can earn tens of millions of dollars a year to play a kid's game, entertaining a bunch of yelling, smelly, drunk fans, whereas a cop only gets paid a few thousand bucks a year to protect the drunk fans and sometimes babysit the overpaid jocks. Cops are often called the pride of the city, but when they overreact, they get dumped by the city leaders like hot potatoes.

The lifespan of a cop after he or she retires on an average is only five years. Of course, there are a few leading reasons why cops have short lives after retiring, the reason being most cops have nasty habits during their time on the job. Many cops are smokers, drinkers, and of course, users of dangerous drugs. Most cops believe that substance abuse helps relieve the stress and pressures that they are confronted with on the streets as well in the departments. The pressure of a beat cop normally comes from higher-ranking officers who make cases and arrests to justify their positions and/or assignments. To be on a particular beat or assignment, most cops are put on notice to make a certain amount of cases and arrests on the beats or be reassigned.

Many cops are under pressure to make their departments look good when in reality, the departments are understaffed and run by a bunch of people who cannot hold decent jobs anywhere else. Many police chiefs and command staff are people who should not even be cops, but in today's world, finding qualified, intelligent people to wear the uniform is very difficult if not impossible. Therefore, many departments are forced to hire the few people who are left from a wide range of unfit applicants. And the few people who are left to hire are not always the best and the brightest.

In spite of who and what police officers are in their personal lives, the vast majority of cops are dedicated human beings who serve and protect lives. The pay is usually lousy, and the work environment is even worse. But the way most cops view their situation is shared by most: somebody's got to do it, or the world would collapse under its own evil corruptions. To put their lives on the line every day for the general population who do not deserve to be protected under any circumstances is an effort that is worthy of unspoken monetary values.

The future is never bright for most cops, for their lives are always hanging in the balance. For most men and women, they are lucky to live through an eight-hour shift each and every day. Although life has an uncertain must-die factor for all of God's creatures, for cops, it is even worse. I suppose that is why many cops live their lives on the edge on and off duty. Sex, for the most part, is a pleasure that many cops find as an outlet of frustration that cannot be found in any other aspect of living. However, for many cops, especially male cops, there are no women off-limits to have sexual encounters with. In many instances, women who love cops will have sex with most other cops regardless of the friendships or the coworker status.

This kind of behavior between cops creates ill feelings among the ranks and files of police officers. "Never take a buddy cop home with you to meet the wife and family." These are the words spoken by many cops toward coworkers. Most male cops have the opinion that if a woman will have a relationship or sex with one cop, she will have a relationship or sex with most cops. Needless to say, this is an ignorant opinion. But then no one ever accused most cops of being brilliant individuals. There is an old saying that has been around for many years among cops: if a woman has dated more than one cop, she is normally considered as "police pussy." For obvious reasons, this is not a very flattering term, but it is one that is only known among male police officers.

To say that this behavior is a normal thing among beat cops and investigators would be a terrible injustice to regular officers. It is, however, a common practice from police chiefs down to regular beat cops. High-ranking officers seems to think of it as a privilege that goes with the rank. In the Atlanta Police Department, it was an act of selfish pride for a high-ranking cop to steal a low-ranking cop's girlfriend or wife simply because the low-ranking cop has very little or no leverage against the high-ranking cop. "There is no honor among thieves." But in the case of women, there is no honor among cops. When it comes to women, male cops are probably the worst human beings on the face of the earth.

Chapter 4

RACISM AMONG COPS is probably more common than most people will ever believe, especially for the average citizen in these United States. The shooting of armed and unarmed black people, especially black men, is nothing new in the United States. What is new, however, is social media, as well as camera phones, which can record cops doing things that are illegal. But make no mistake; the idea of cops killing black people is not a new phenomenon, and if anyone believes that this action toward black people is going to cease, they may be safer to believe that lightning will strike in the same place twice.

I have heard it said by many uninformed or uneducated people about the duties of a cop: "Why don't cops shoot to wound instead of kill people?" There is not one police department in America, or probably in the entire world, that will train their officers to shoot to wound a suspect when it becomes necessary to fire their weapons in the first place. In all police academies across America, when officers are trained to shoot their weapons on the firing range, they are trained to shoot to kill a suspect, not to wound the suspect. There are two good reasons for this type of training. The first reason is that when a police officer feels that it is necessary for him or her pull and fire their weapon at a suspect, the idea is not to allow the suspect to return fire, or the officers will find themselves in the same position as the suspects, wounded or dead.

The second reason is that the officers will usually end up being sued by the wounded suspect if the case is dismissed in court. "Bloodsucking lawyers" are always looking for a reason to sue the cops and their departments for large sums of cash when a suspect is wounded. Therefore, the chance of a cop being sued if the suspect is deceased is highly unlikely. And if a case does go to court with a lawsuit, it must be brought on by the families of the dead suspects. Cops have a standing motto: "I'd rather be tried by twelve than to be carried by six!" That has always been an unwritten rule by cops, which still stands today. This is the reality of cops.

There is not a cop today who leaves home without the thought in mind that he or she is going to kill a human being during their watch. However, the thought that he or she may or may not make it back home to his or her family is a thought that stays on a cop's mind. The biggest problem with cops doing their jobs is probably that a Joe Blow citizen has not a clue what most cops go through just to wear the uniform and carry a gun. The average cop always arrives at the crime scene after the fact. Cops can neither read minds nor predict beforehand when a crime is going to take place. They must wait until the dispatcher gives the call out to a particular location, and then they respond to that call. If all hell breaks loose when they arrive at the scene, it is their duty to respond with the necessary force to get the situation under control.

The thing that the average citizen does not know or understand is the fact that a cop does not wear a gun to make love to people who violate the laws. A cop's job is to make arrests whenever possible or feasible. If a cop encounters violence in his response to a call, he or she must take whatever action is required by law, the necessary response to the violence that he or she may encounter. If that response means killing the perpetrator, so be it.

On the other hand of what a cop's job is, there is racism among the ranks now. And there has always been racism within most departments. Racist cops do not necessarily reside in the South. From my own personal experience, the most racist cops that I have ever encountered were in Los Angeles, California. The LAPD has some of the most racist cops in the nation. If Rodney King was alive today, he would probably say the same thing. Nevertheless, if we look closely, we will find and encounter racist cops in every corner, crack, and alley in America. Just because they wear the uniforms and enforce the laws does not mean that they have forgotten their roots.

Without a doubt, white cops or Caucasian cops are probably the worst of all racist cops. The reason why they are the worst when it comes to dealing with other races, especially blacks or African Americans, is because they still have what is known as the "inbred slave owner and master mentality" in them. It is not necessarily a mentality that they themselves developed, but it is an inherited mentality that has been passed down from many past generations. Human beings do not eliminate who they really are just because they become employed by a city, state, or federal law enforcement agency. In fact, they probably become even more aware of their feelings toward race when it comes to enforcing the laws. Why? It is because they have the power and the authority to be discriminatory without anyone really knowing their true feelings.

Needless to say, the cops in LA are probably no different today than the cops in New York, Atlanta, or any other city. Nevertheless, I mentioned the LAPD for a number of reasons, and one of those reasons is particular to the investigation of the O. J. Simpson murder case. I dare make the case that OJ was innocent of murdering his ex-wife and a friend in Los Angeles. But the cops were so set on making OJ their murder suspect, they violated every rule in the handbook for securing a crime scene as their number one priority. The LAPD abandoned the crime scene, leaving the bodies to be contaminated by other cops nosing around, and they all rushed to OJ's home, looking for a known suspect in the murder. The case was lost in court against OJ simply because they had probably failed to perform their police duties at the crime scene.

O. J. Simpson should not have been the cop's primary suspect simply because there was no evidence that pointed toward Simpson. But they assumed that Simpson was the angry black ex-husband, and he suddenly became their go-to guy immediately, leaving the dead bodies out in the open for eleven hours while they searched OJ's home and planted evidence.

Was the O. J. Simpson case an act of racist police investigating a famous black man for murder? It was indeed. If OJ's skin had been white, which he probably wished it was, he would have been the last person on their list of suspects. Why? Under a normal murder investigation, investigators try to establish motives to present to a grand jury to get an indictment. In this case, there was no such motive for Simpson to commit murder. Some might say it was jealousy. Why was he jealous? Or better yet, who was he jealous of? Was it Ron Goldman? Or was it someone else? These are a few of many questions that the cops should have been trying to answer instead of chasing Simpson and trying to make him their number one suspect.

In law enforcement, there is more to crime fighting than the color of a person's skin. Criminals come in all shades and colors, and cops must be able to understand and view their positions in a color-blind manner. Understandably, sometimes being color-blind is very difficult, especially when working in an area where the police are only dealing with one particular race of people. In most instances, black people are the only color that some cops view as a serious threat to their law enforcement duties. Obviously, that is why jails and prisons are filled with blacks.

On the other hand, blacks and other people of color must come to a simple understanding that it is because of them that so many cops are needed in most metropolitan areas. Cops are hired based upon the criminal elements that are operating in any given area or city. If there is no crime in certain areas, there is no need for cops. But due to whatever reason the criminal behavior may have stemmed from, human nature tells us that human beings must act in ways that are violations of city, county, and state laws. For a society to get rid of cops, that same society must cease in its behavior of committing crimes. No society can have one without the other; criminal activities bring about law enforcement officers who are hired by the society for protection from criminal behavior.

In today's society, many people of color fall into the category of being harassed by the police. And the question is, "Is there a certain amount racism that goes into play when a cop pulls over black people?" Seventy-five percent of the time, racism plays a very important role. Why is this so? It is so because based on previous experiences with many cops, they are going to be confronted with opposition from the person or persons whom they have pulled over. People of color will often challenge the officers as to why they were being pulled over rather than to allow the cops to tell them why they were stopped. That within itself is a self-initiated act of racism . . . and it is also because people of color will immediately challenge the police when they feel that they were pulled over simply for their race or color.

Needless to say, the vast majority of the times when cops pull someone over, it is due to the particular violation the person has committed and not the color of his or her skin. To take this situation a step further, many people of color see this type of police action as an opportunity to highlight other situations that have nothing to do with the violation itself. This is a typical reaction from many people of color. "Why are you stopping me?!" "All you cops are alike!" "You see a black person riding around in a nice car, and you just got to pull us over for no reason!" Again, this is a self-initiated act of racism. It is all in the black person's imagination as to why the cop stopped them in first place and has nothing to do with race or color.

But on the other hand, racism does exist in many police departments simply because many white cops grew up in racist households or backgrounds. Their parents and grandparents were racists, which means every generation since the days of slavery has raised their children to be racists and to consider non-white people as inferior human beings.

The Atlanta Police Department in particular was once filled with racist cops, especially during the '50s, '60s, and '70s. Many white cops were also members of the Ku Klux Klan secret society. However, just because we have entered into the twenty-first century does not eliminate racist white cops. Many cops who are on the force today are children, grandchildren, and great-grandchildren of cops who were members of the KKK or a similar racist organization. So what does that mean? It means that the younger generation of cops today fares no better when dealing with other races than the generation of racist cops before them.

In 1948, the first eight African American police officers were hired to patrol the streets of Atlanta. But there was one primary stipulation that the black cops had to adhere to, and that was they could play police as long as they did not arrest white people. The question that was asked by the black cops was, "If we wear the same uniform as whites, carry guns like the white cops, and we wear badges just like the white cops, what's in the rule book that says we can't arrest white people?" Of course, there was no answer in the rule book. But white people on the streets, as well as white cops, considered the hiring of black police officers as no more than a smoke screen to please black people who would eventually burn the city to the ground once again.

Moreover, not only were black leaders asking for black officers to patrol black neighborhoods, but it was also reaching a boiling point in certain neighborhoods on the south side of Atlanta, where young black thugs were creating an unsafe environment for white cops whenever they tried to enter those areas. Cops would come under fire whenever they crossed Georgia Avenue going into the Summerhill neighborhood, south of the city. Some white cops were even attacked in their cars with rocks, bricks, and bottles. The chief of police, as well as the mayor, knew that the black people in Atlanta were no longer afraid of white cops, and it was time to bring in some black cops who knew how to relate to those "crazy niggers," it was said.

For the first eight black cops, racism did not stop with not being allowed to arrest white people; it also went as far as not allowing the black cops to even enter the police headquarters building, where all the other white cops reported for duty. The black cops had to report to the Butler YMCA just off Auburn Avenue, a predominately black upscale business district. This, of course, was a direct slap in the face of every black citizen in Atlanta. But being the first among a totally white establishment is always a difficult task for any minority individual. Cops are no exception!

Having to endure the first two racist requirements, the first eight cops had more to deal with. Each one of the eight men who were recruited was still in college or had already graduated college. This was not a requirement for white officers when they had joined the force. In fact, many of the white officers did not even have a high school education. "So what were their requirements?" someone asked later. The answer was quite simple: there were no requirements as far as education was concerned. They were simply told how to enforce the laws and arrest the people who violated city or state laws.

Today, of course, the requirements for cops to get hired are much different. College degrees are not mandatory, but it is good to have one, for it puts a few dollars more on the paychecks. And as far as racist cops in today's society are concerned, there are still many who probably hate blacks and non-whites just as much as the KKK members did, but they do so in secret.

Recently, we have seen and heard about many cop shootings that involved young black men in particular. On one hand, we all can agree maybe some cops were not justified for using deadly force. But then on the other hand, anyone who has seen a police officer patrolling the streets in any city or county knows that this is exactly what they are paid to do. They also get paid to stop or, if possible, prevent crimes from occurring. And if it takes deadly force to stop a crime in progress, that is what they are going to do. It would take a moron to challenge a cop on the streets regardless of how right or wrong one thinks he or she is. "Never try a case on the streets." That is the golden rule. That is also why we have a court system to hear all cases and an internal affairs unit to hear all complaints on cops. You must take advantage of the rule.

The one singular point that I must make clear for anyone who is quick to blame the cops for acts of racism is cops are not hired to protect law-abiding citizens; they are hired to arrest anyone who believes or thinks that they can commit a crime and get away with it. If there were no crimes committed, there would be no need for cops, jails, judges, or lawyers. The world would be a safe place to live in. But sadly, that is not the case, and society must have cops to lock up the bad guys regardless of how racist some people think they are. If we want cops to stop being "racist pigs" against people of color, then we must learn how not to give cops a reason to exercise their racist authority. Most cops only react when the public gives them a reason to.

Yeah, we may feel that the rights of individuals are violated when cops treat them less than human beings. But when people violate the laws of the land and are arrested by cops, "innocent until proven guilty" is the only right that they have. As far as their treatment by cops is concerned, most people are treated the way they act or ask to be treated. Once a person is approached by a cop for committing a crime, that person is automatically under suspicion and is subject to be arrested for the crime regardless of how minor or major we may think the offense might be.

In a shooting situation, no cop is going to take a chance by allowing a suspect to pull a weapon and fire first, even if the weapon turns out not to be a weapon. There have been cases where suspects are mentally challenged, and cops are blamed for not knowing prior to using deadly force that the individual was insane. The truth of the matter is cops cannot and will not, in most cases, and they are not trained to determine who is insane and who is not. An insane person can kill just as easily as a sane person can. And it is not the cop's job to determine if an individual is insane before using deadly force or not.

Yeah, there are racist cops, but there are just as many people of color who like to cry "race-wolf." To call a cop a racist is one way of getting everyone's attention. Lawyers love it when they get a racial case against a cop. It is an automatic reason to file a lawsuit against the police departments. If the lawyers can cry race-wolf loud enough, the news media will get involved, as well as social media. Then the cases are usually settled in courts. If the race-wolf cry is loud enough, it will suddenly become a "money game" for all who are involved.

Only in a perfect world will we ever find different races of people getting along perfectly. Calling a cop a racist is no more than a figment of most people of color's imaginations when it comes to something that they want to go their way. Oftentimes, crying racism is the only way we can get out of a bad situation, especially when it is dealing with cops. If I say a white cop stopped me because I am black, but the reason that I was stopped was that I was clocked running down the Interstate fifty miles over the speed limit, who is the racist? I may not admit it, but I am the racist simply because I believe that I can get away with being stopped for a violation that I committed for speeding, not because I was black.

The criminal situations in America are the exact same thing when it comes to cops. If the jails and prisons are crammed to capacity with mostly people of color, they were not locked up because they were black or some other color darker than blue; they were locked up because they were convicted of committing crimes. There is an old saying that goes, "If you can't do the time, then don't do the crime." No one forces anyone to commit a crime, to my knowledge. Crimes are committed by people who are too stupid to realize that most criminals do not escape the "long arms of the law." Cops do exactly what they get paid to do, catch criminals. And if the criminals so happen to be black or some other dark-colored race, so be it.

To prove that a particular police officer acted out of his or her official capacity simply because of a suspect's race is a rare occasion, and in a vast majority of the situations, it will be obvious not only to black people but also to white people as well.

But then let's flip the coin to the other side; let's go over to the black cops. Why is it that we very seldom, if at any time, ever see or hear of black cops being found guilty of racism? The reason might surprise most people. Most people in America automatically assume that black cops are not racists or cannot be racists. But the truth of the matter is there are many black racist cops. They hate white folks and non-white folks just like the white folks do. In fact, black cops probably hate their own people more than any other race. Why? Because they know their own kind better than they know other races. However, when a black cop arrests or pulls over a black person simply because that person looks like he or she has done something wrong, no one calls that racial profiling. But in reality, that is exactly what it is, and black cops are as guilty of racial profiling as much as white cops are.

Moreover, speaking of racial profiling, there is no way that any rules and regulations of any police departments can prevent any officer from racial profiling on the streets. Why? Because no one can look inside of a cop's mind to determine if he or she has already made their decisions or made up their minds based on race before an arrest or a traffic stop is made. The truth of the matter is politicians, government officials, activists, or anyone else who can make all the claims that they want to about racial profiling or how to stop it are simply blowing hot air. There is no such measure available to determine what a human being is thinking before he acts or react. And even after a cop acts on any given situation based upon race or not, if there is probable cause for his or her action, racial profiling just flew out of the window. And if there is one thing that all cops know or should know better than anything else, it is "probable cause."

Chapter 5

THE RISING OF A MESSIAH is what the world needs, as well as in America, especially in the black neighborhoods. Now I am saying this with full knowledge beforehand that if such a person would ever come forth or exist, racist white people will find a way to eliminate him or her from the earth. History will verify this statement as being accurate. Black Americans has been at the threshold of breaking free of this notion that white Americans are far superior than they are. This is a lie in the eyes of the Creator, and it is a lie in the minds of a clear-thinking human being. But there is one segment of American society who cannot and will not, for over five hundred years, come to the realization that all men are created equal.

Millions of Africans were sold and brought to this country for their knowledge and hard labor. And because many Europeans knew that the Africans were not going to work and build America for free, an act of slavery was put in place. By doing so, forced labor was mandatory for all Africans, primarily in the southern United States. To build America into a powerful nation, the knowledge of the Africans was ultimately important. African men knew how to use their hands to take different earthly materials and minerals and build everything that America would need to become a strong nation. But to become that strong nation, the white elites of this country had to always maintain a certain amount of ignorance among the black slaves, the very people who were doing the work.

The second Messiah was Abraham Lincoln, who signed into law the Emancipation Proclamation and pushed through Congress the Thirteenth Amendment to the U.S. Constitution, which permanently outlawed slavery. Southern whites hated this whole idea of freeing slaves with a passion, and they did everything in their limited power to place fear in every slave and to eliminate the one man who had made this law possible. And on April 14, 1865, five days after the surrender of Confederate Commanding General Robert E. Lee on April 9, John Wilkes Booth, a Confederate sympathizer, assassinated Pres. Abraham Lincoln.

Abraham Lincoln was a messiah simply because he was willing to put his life on the line to free the slaves. There is no doubt that he must have known that there were white people all across America who did not agree with what he had done for the African slaves. And from that point on to this day, anyone dared take a stand or a position to educate black people to the point of knowing that America is not a "white man's land" but an everyman's land. And the sooner white people can get that simple idea through their small minds, the better off the entire United States will be.

On the Internet, we can google what is known as the "Willie Lynch Letter," which was written by a white man named William Lynch who came from the West Indies to teach a bunch white Southerners to make a slave. As crazy as it may sound to some folks, it is not beyond my imagination that this really did happen. The letter goes on to say to these white Southerners:

> *First of all, to make a slave, we need a black nigger* [what other color would they call a nigger?]. *Then we need a pregnant nigger woman and a nigger boy. Second, we will use the basic principles of breaking a horse.*

In other words, they treated human beings as if they were animals; they would beat them until they learned to obey their masters.

The Willie Lynch Letter, if not real, was a cruel joke that white people could not have played on any other race of people on the planet except black people. But then let's not kid ourselves; the Willie

Lynch Letter is no more than telling us how the welfare system works. The government pays women to stay at home and birth more and more children, and it pays more for every child. The claim is simple: if the mothers cannot locate the fathers, then the government will foot the bill. The welfare system obviously forces women to stay at home, which encourages them to avoid trying to enter the workplace. This allows the government to pay for housing, food, childcare, and everything else that the mothers need for their children. In my opinion, the welfare system is the Willie Lynch who came to this country especially to teach the government how to make slaves out of the women who are undesirable in the workplace.

Jesus Christ was the first Messiah who came into the world to help the poor and the slaves of kings and masters. The basic word messiah means "Anointed One." Jesus's primary purpose in the world was to teach mankind how to become Christians and to love one another just as God loved them. However, as soon as he announced his plan to save the sinful, heal the sick, and rescue the world from a slippery slope to hell, mankind began to turn against him. And eventually, mankind assassinated Jesus just like they have killed many others through the years. There were others who may have seemed like messiahs to the people they were trying to save from racism and lawless acts of racial terror, men such as John F. Kennedy, Robert Kennedy, Malcolm X, Martin Luther King Jr., and many others.

All these messiahs had one thing in common: they were killed by people who did not share their views or ideologies based upon their political correctness. The whole idea of a messiah is to tell the less educated people how to live to make the world a better place for all people and not just the elite few. Unfortunately, there are people who believe wholeheartedly that the color of their skin or the amount of money that they have in banks or even the positions that they hold in their occupations should make them feel more special than other people. They feel that these things alone should give them the privilege to treat other people who have less qualifications as lesser human beings. This is a lie in any manner that anyone may want to tell it.

Perhaps the most profound spiritual work of the Messiah Jesus was his position as the intermediary between God and the people. The teaching of the Bible tells us that God created the heavens and the earth, and then he created human beings. The creation alone should tell us that there is only one who can and does control everything under the sun on Earth, and this was not done by mere mortals. Mankind's only responsibility on Earth is to love God and one another. He is to learn how to protect himself against the invasion of Satan based upon the truth written in the Bible. Needless to say, mankind does not understand that responsibility. That is why someone who understands it must speak it so mankind gets it and will obey it.

The Messiah is someone who gets it from the standpoint of God. The Messiah is a person who gives people hope for a better tomorrow and not the same old pitiful, sad stories that say the world is only for the rich and the powerful. There is a spot on this earth for every man, woman, child, and just the elite few. But as history has shown us very clearly, every single time someone has tried to stand up and guide the weak, the poor, and the uneducated out of the wilderness and the darkness, he has paid the ultimate price for his effort, and that means death.

In spite of what the Bible might say about Jesus Christ dying on the cross for our sins, I am not convinced at all that God brought himself down on Earth as a baby to live like a slave and then to be murdered for a bunch of people who have yet, to this day, to appreciate the price that he paid. And I am not convinced that Jesus is sitting in heaven on the right hand of God just waiting for the day to return to rescue the so-called good folks and take them to place called the "new earth." It is my contention or my belief that Jesus knows better than anyone else that there is no honor among thieves, and 90 percent all human beings on Earth today have no honor when it comes to having a relationship with God. It is always "give me something."

The truth of the matter is, how can we honor God when we despise other human beings who were born by the same processes as we were? What that means is quite simple: no one owns the earth. No one has a monopoly on knowing or being blessed by God. What God has done for one, he will do for millions more. Not only that, but it appears to me that human beings expect the world from God, but most of them are not willing to give up a single sinful act for God. How does that add up on God's calculator? In other words, it simply does not add up.

This is what a messiah does—he tells the people how it is and how it should be done and the right way to do it, not just shouting out a bunch of words that he thinks the people want to hear. Yes, God loves all of us, but make no mistake about it: God will send you, me, and every other sinful person to hell as quick as we say the word. There is no doubt in my mind that God has grown very tired of dealing with people who either believe that he does not exist or simply assume that since he has not shown his face since the days of Moses, he has died like everyone else who has lived and walked the earth. In other words, where did God get the idea of dying?

Naturally, if God has never saved their lives or blessed them in ways that they will never forget, I can understand why some people might assume that God is dead or is just a simple myth. However, the same things happened long ago during Noah's days of living. It was the beginning of the human race becoming evil. It all began when the "sons of God," whom I imagined were placed on Earth, helped make the world grow faster. Nevertheless, they were a wild bunch of men, and they saw normal women who were very beautiful, and they were crazy about them. They did not ask for permission to marry these women; they just picked whoever they wanted and married them.

When God saw what was going on, he said, "My spirit will not remain in human beings forever because of their flesh. I will make it where they will only live for 120 years, whereas I wanted them to live much longer." Back then, the sons of God were called Nephilim, and they had sex relations with the female humans, and these women gave birth to children who became famous and mighty warriors. Not only did human beings become famous, but they also, on the other hand, became very wicked, and everything that they did or touched became evil.

Just like today, the world has become a very evil place, and just like back then, God is very sorry that he even created human beings. Now allow that to soak in for a moment! If God was sorry that he created the human race back then, think how he must be feeling today. Let me say what I think God might be saying right now: "I destroyed the world once before because I was sick and tired of being sick and tired of people doing whatever made themselves feel good and making a mockery of my name. I promised Noah after I destroyed the earth the first time that I would never do it again. But you know what? I lied! I don't have a choice anymore. People are worse today than they have ever been before. And I must do this, or they will destroy everything that I stand for. This, I cannot have, and I will not have it any longer!

"One of my angels asked me, 'Lord, what are you planning to do this time?'

"I looked at my son Jesus Christ, and I stared at the scars that the human beings who killed him like he was nothing but a cold-blooded animal put on his body. See what they did to my son Jesus?! And the only thing that he tried to do was show them love and kindness. He tried to show them a way to save themselves from what I am about to do to them now. Heaven is too good for human beings, and hell is not bad enough. I need to create something worse than hell. I need a place where they will forever remember what they could have done to save themselves."

"'But Lord, tell us what on earth can be worse than hell!' another one of my angels asked me.

"I thought about the question for a moment, and then I said, 'Look, I have given the human race every opportunity that can be given to get themselves right with me. Even my so-called prophets and ministers are only using my name to get rich. But to answer your question, the fires in hell alone are not enough for humans on Earth. They need to be slaves in the fires of hell. I want them to work every day from death until eternity. I want them to work as slaves, and I want the demons of hell to whip them every time someone stands up to take a break.' I glanced at my son Jesus again, feeling the pain that he felt when they led him to the cross. 'And what is even worse, this torture should never end, and every human being will remember the many things that they could have done to save themselves every day of his or her life.'"

It is probably a good thing that I am not God because I simply would not have any mercy on people who do wrong, especially the ones knowing beforehand that the sinful acts are wrong. Based upon what we read in the Bible, or based upon what the so-called speakers of God's Word tell us, God is a merciful God, and he will forgive us of all our sins regardless of how small or how great the sins are. However, I cannot believe for one moment that God will have mercy on the people who shouted more than once to "crucify him!" (Jesus) and forgive them for the wrong that they did. Yes, I believe that Jesus may have said to God, "Forgive them, Father, for they know not of what they are doing!" But I cannot conceive that the people who murdered the Son of God will be forgiven. Forgiveness will never happen if I were God.

The purpose of a messiah is to teach the poor, the dumb, and the destitute how to rise up from where they are and become a people of power. This power will enable the people to change the world like no other people have done before. This is the same power that Jesus brought with him to save the world over two thousand years ago. And of course, this is the same power that scared the living hell out of the same kind of people who wanted Jesus dead.

The Messiah is naturally a person sent by God to do the right thing for the people whom God knows need help the most. That was the very reason why God himself came down to Earth as a human being named Jesus Christ: to see firsthand the real problems that some of the people of this world were facing. God realized that although he has the power to see everything and be everywhere at the same time, it was not the same thing as coming to Earth as Jesus to gain firsthand knowledge and feel the same frustration that the people were experiencing. And after thirty-two grueling years, God found out just how bad the world and his people had become once again. This is the position that we the people have put God in once again.

So now God is upset once again with his creation. But because he made Noah a promise to never destroy the earth by water again, he is now second-guessing himself about the promise that he made. The question is, "What is God going to do? Is he going to come back as Jesus once again to round up the few who refused to do evil and take them with him?" In reality, God is still going to do what he promised Noah he would not do again: he is going to destroy the world and the people who have not done what it takes to go with Jesus.

The proof is in the sweetbread or the Book of Revelation: "the New Jerusalem," as it is called. And it says, "Christ will win over evil!" The message goes like this:

> *This is the revelation of Jesus Christ, which God gave to him to show his servants what must soon happen. It is the Word of God;*

> *it is the message from Jesus Christ. Happy is the one who reads the words of God's message, and happy are the people who hear this message and do what is written in it. The time is near when all these things will happen.*

In spite of what I have said concerning the rising of a messiah, I see a major problem with that idea. It is the same problem that I find with a vast majority of the so-called preachers, ministers, prophets, and whoever give false messages of God; they will never give the true message of the Revelation. Why?! The Revelation is the message concerning the end of all living life as we know it. No one wants to hear about the end of all living creatures as we know it because all living creatures, including human beings, must meet God's revelations.

Moreover, there is no profit in telling the truth! People do not go to church to hear the truth. People go to church to hear the pastors tell them that God loves them and how much he is going to bless them with wealth and all kinds of material things as well as good health. I have yet to hear a minister preach a sermon from the Book of Revelation. Why?! Not only will the Book of Revelation scare the living daylights out of the congregations, but it will also scare the bejesus out of the ministers as well. Here is one prime example of why I am saying this: "Babylon is destroyed!" The city of Babylon is the earth itself, especially America.

> *Ruined, ruined is the great city of Babylon! She has become a home for demons and a prison for every unclean bird and unclean beast. She has been ruined because all the people of the earth have drank the wine of her as well as having the desire of her sexual sin. Babylon has been ruined because of the kings and presidents of the earth that have sinned sexually with her as well. And merchants of the earth have grown rich from the great wealth of her luxury.*

In other words, every good thing that God created the earth to be has been ruined by its people. Therefore, to clean the earth once again, God has to get rid of the people. You cannot clean a house by leaving the very things that messed it up in the first place to stay in the house. Everything and everybody has to go! And when ministers start preaching about cleaning the world of its sins, people become frightened of what God is going to do. Preachers become fearful of what God is going to do as well, which means they will only preach all the good things in the Bible without the conditions that are required to receive the blessings.

A messiah will not omit the very things that will save the people from being hell-bound. As much as the truth might hurt, a messiah has to tell it like it is. America has always lived behind a great, big, fat lie. This is not a nation for all people; it is a nation of a few people. In America, it is not what people know that makes them rich and successful; it is more about who they know that gets them to where they want to go. But then life itself is neither what we know nor how much we know that makes or breaks us or will get us into heaven's gates; it is going to be who we know. In others words, reading the Bible alone will not guarantee us a trip to heaven. The fact of the matter is that we must get to know God, and we must accept Jesus Christ as our savior. And if neither one of those things occurs in our lives, we have a one-way trip to hell.

A messiah will ultimately tell us what we must do to know God. But as I said earlier, the truth hurts, and most people in the world today would rather run through hell with gasoline drawers on than hear or know the truth. However, the truth is out there, and we must find it to make it out of this world in good standing with God. Everything that most people have told themselves about life and this world that they live in has been an absolute lie. Now this is the first truth that they must admit to themselves. After that, all truths will come.

Okay, allow me to give you the first and foremost truth: the world and universe was not created by some "big bang theory." Human beings did not evolve from apes because if they had been, then how do we explain apes? Where did apes come from?! That is why no one can explain the chicken and the egg as far which one came first. If we say the egg came first, must we then explain what laid the egg? We cannot have it both ways and make it add up to just one. The truth is that someone or something put it all together, the universe and the entire solar system. And we can rest assured of one thing: no human being could have been that intelligent. There will never be a human being with such a great mind.

In the grand scheme of all things, there has only been one Messiah, and that was Jesus Christ. With him, he brought a clear and precise message: "Love God with all our hearts, souls, and minds. And after we have done that, then we should love our fellow man like we love ourselves." Of course, that is the "one" absolute truth that no man wants hear or know. Why? Because man is a selfish creature, and he believes that whatever advantages he gains in this world all belong to him. But on the other hand, that is an absolute lie! There is nothing on this earth that belongs to one man. The world was created for all men, and the sooner all men come to understand that one simple truth, the better the world will be for all men.

If and when such a person will come along who can deliver God's message as God intended it to be, it will be the day that the Messiah will rise again. But for the Messiah to rise, the people of this world will have to be willing to listen and want to hear the truth. There is one simple fault with the truth: it is hard to bear if the listeners are not doing what is right. And if evil is in the hearts of mankind, no amount of truth is going to do any good. The evil of mankind was alive and well when Jesus came the first time, and it remained alive throughout his death, and when he rose and went back to heaven, evil was still in the hearts of men.

Finally, the only way or the only reason a messiah will rise again will be when mankind is willing and ready to hear the truth, not a bunch of lies or mere words that are going to boost or stroke his ego.

Chapter 6

A BLACK PRESIDENT WAS THE ONE THING that no American would have ever thought they would see in their lifetime before Barack Obama happened. Not only did he get elected in 2008, but he also did it again in 2012 for a second term. But now that his eight years have passed and gone, we all were able to witness the impossible become possible. So what can we say about a man who simply flew under the white folk's racial radar and right into the White House? And what was even more amazing than Obama becoming the first African American president of these United States was not even his own Democratic party imagined that such a thing was possible. Therefore, never let it be said that a black man cannot do the impossible.

Some people have called the election of President Obama a miracle that only God could have made possible. And then there were others who believe that it was inevitable; it was bound to happen soon or later. However, for some white folks, it just happened a lot sooner than most of them thought it would. As for myself, I believe he was just one nigger who slipped through their fingers, or I could say that he was that one nigger who slipped through the crackers. However, regardless of what happened or how he managed to wiggle his way into the White House, he was good for the nation and the world.

There has never been a president who had to fight the entire white Congress, who dug their heels in and declared they that they would object everything that he tried to do whether it was good or bad, from day one. And sure enough, they made good of their promise.

The Obama administration was dead in the water from the moment he was sworn into office in 2008. And two years later, they dug in even deeper by getting even more hard-nosed resistances elected to Congress. To them, this meant only one thing: he may have been elected to the office of president, but the only thing he would be able to do was occupy the office and nothing else. To make matters even worse, his own Democratic party did not even participate in his effort to make things happen for the country and for the world. Of all the things he got accomplished in his eight years as president, he was forced to do them on his own by executive orders. He received no votes from the Democratic Senate or the Republican-majority Congress.

Needless to say, Barack Obama was a strong president despite all the opposition that he had faced. And among many things that he was able to accomplish alone, the Affordable Care Act was his finest moment or his greatest accomplishment. Not only was he able to get it passed in spite of Congress opposition and fight to the very end, but he was also able to make it the law of the land. Suddenly, the magic word "repeal" became the only occupation for all of Congress, which went before the highest court in the land fifty-five times, trying to get Obamacare repealed with no success. And even after Obama's second term as president, the white-majority Congress was still buzzing about repealing a health care plan that has helped twenty-six million Americans afford health care, something that they could not afford in the past.

The question is, "Why did a pure white Congress fight tooth and nail with the one and only black president who was able to do what was considered to be the impossible?" The Affordable Care Act had been something that several white presidents in the past tried with no success. But along came the one dark spot or a fly in the milk who made it seem like a walk in the park by getting it done. Now how amazing was that?! It is called "Obamacare" today.

We do not necessarily have to call Obama a genius to have outsmarted most white Americans in this country to become president, but we do have to give him the credit for being the man that stood his ground and looked all white men in the whites of their eyes and said, "I'm your president whether you like it or not, and there ain't a damn thing you can do about it!"

It is true they could have tried to assassinate him like they had done to Kennedy and Lincoln, but the time was not right for an assassination in the twenty-first century. Although many threats of killing the president were made, to try and pull it off would have sparked a race war that could completely destroy America. So as much as white people hated Obama, they were more afraid of starting something that they could not finish, and that was a race war in the streets of America. Also, white America realized that Obama was not necessarily elected by black people alone. His votes came from a wide assortment of people, which meant they would be fighting some people who were members of their own white race.

Once upon a time in America, many people were under the impression that we had overcome a racist society. After the riots and demonstrations of the 1960s, some black people actually believed that they had made that most important leap out of that terrible slave-mentality era. But lo and behold, with the election of a black president, race relations suddenly took a U-turn right back to the state of racism that we have seen in the past. White America was suddenly confronted with a situation that they had never been confronted with before: a black man as the most powerful man in the world. Here was a black man as head of state, or as some would say, the HNIC (head nigger in charge), and this very idea of Barack Obama being looked upon as the commander in chief of all armed forces in America was unthinkable. They forced themselves to believe the world was not ready to deal with a black man as president.

Now the question becomes, "Why was it that white America and even some black people were not ready for a black president?" Of course, everybody has an opinion as to why Obama should not have been elected president, but the fact of the matter is Barack Obama has proven to the world that he will probably go down in history as one of the best presidents America has ever had. Why were some black people not ready for a black president? Because for four hundred years, all black people have ever known were white presidents. So what did black people expect from a black president? Nothing! They could not expect any more or any less from Obama than from any other race of presidents in America. Many people forgot the one primary factor about a president regardless of his or her color or race: he or she is the president of the United States, which includes people of all races. Anyone who may have been duped into believing that Barack Obama was going to be the president of black America was totally uninformed or knew very little about the office of the president. They were simply stupid.

History has shown us that only two presidents have ever tried to help black America. The first one was Jimmy Carter, who issued out social programs like crazy, and he barely made it out of Washington alive. Today, he is considered the nation's worst president who has ever held the office. The other president who tried to help black Americans was Abraham Lincoln when he freed the slaves, and they killed him shortly afterward. Today, the only people who still consider Lincoln as president are black people during Black History Month. And I can assure you that Barack Obama made up in his mind that being black was not a reason to be accused of being a black president for black people only. He studied his history well. He knew as soon as he was sworn in that his responsibilities as president were going to be ten times harder than all the other presidents put together. For a black man in charge of a white majority of anything, he has to be twice as intelligent as most white men doing the same job to be successful. He was that!

Speaking of race relations having taking a U-turn when Barack Obama became president, today, racism in America is worse than it had been since sharecropping was in style in South Georgia. And because of what Obama accomplished, race relations will never be same again, the reason being white people have always believed and have had the opinion that if African Americans were ever given a little power, they would take over the country. And African Americans taking over America was their greatest fear during the entire eight years that Obama was in office. There was a rallying cry throughout the eight years of the Obama administration: "We want our country back!"

Now the question becomes, "Will there ever be another black president?" I can unequivocally say no way in hell to that question. There is no way Americans will elect another black president within the next one hundred years. Why on earth would I say a thing like that? As I said before, Barack Obama slipped through the crackers this time. Before anyone could have found a way to stop "the Obama Machine" from becoming president, they would have. And as a result of what Obama did, the entire Republican party has come unglued at the seams again. If anyone cared to pay attention to what was going on during the election at the end of Obama's eight years, they would see that the Republican party has thoroughly lost their way to do anything right for the United States. Today, what we have in Washington is a Republican clown show.

The next black president will have to be three times smarter than Barack Obama and ten times more courageous. He cannot have a fearful bone in his entire body, and he must be willing to wage a war on any country that he thinks has a nuclear weapon. Most importantly, his skin color will be lighter than Obama's. Skin color should not be a part of the qualifying criterion if the candidate is African America, but it is most definitely a piece of the puzzle. If Obama had been a shade darker, he would have never been elected president regardless of his brilliance.

Skin color is a known fact of life in America. And it has always been a factor in politics and entertainment, as well as on most local news stations. It is very seldom that we ever see dark-skinned people reporting the news, especially as anchors. There used to be an old saying that has been around since the days of slavery:

> *If you're white, you're right. If you're light, you're all right. If you're brown, stick around. But if you're black, get the hell back!*

And to make matters worse, these same old skin stigmas are still around today.

Besides being the first black or African American president, Barack Obama accomplished something else that was extremely fantastic, and that was he gave every redneck, backwoodsman, and crackpot the belief that they could become the president of the United States. How did he accomplish that feat? He accomplished it by just being black. As a result, fifteen Republican candidates joined the race for president in the beginning, knowing that they were not as qualified as a fifth grader to be president. But just the idea of a black man being president gave them all a glimmer of hope. And lo and behold, look what popped out of "the rat race"; Donald Trump suddenly became the next "great white hope"!

Needless to say, history has shown us that "great white hopes" do not always win the fight. Back in the early 1900s, Jack Johnson presented himself as an unbeatable fighter in the heavyweight boxing world. Not only was he unbeatable in the ring, but he also walked around like a proud peacock with a beautiful white woman hanging on his arm. This kind of shenanigan infuriated white people to the point of them finding someone whom they thought was big and strong enough to beat some sense into the black man's head and send him packing back to the Negro neighborhood where he belonged. Well, that didn't happen! Johnson knocked him out cold in the second round, and that was the end of the "great white hope."

Barack Obama was an unbeatable black heavyweight champion in the ring of politics, and white folks could not come up with a single "white hope" to defeat him. And after eight years in the ring, taking everything they threw at him, he finally walked away untouched and undefeated. But to take away some of the improvements and impressions that Obama had left in the political world, the best that the white folks could come up with is Donald Trump and a few other losers. But to think that these are the best that the Republican party has to offer the American people! This should be a slap in the face for the American people and politically shameful in the eyes of the world. However, who can we blame for that? We can blame that one and only black man who became president of the United States.

This is obviously one accomplishment the African American people made that white Americans will never live down or forget. This will go down as a date in infamy! One hundred years after Barack Obama departed the office of president, a few white people will still be alive to talk about the one that got away, Barack Obama.

Chapter 7

THE MILLENNIAL GENERATION is a generation in crisis. According to Google, these are the people who are in the age group of eighteen to twenty-six years of age. And this is the age group that has an IQ of less than a hundred. So my next question will become pretty obvious. If this group of mindless individuals are the best that America has to offer in terms of leadership, who will then emerge from this bunch of nitwits to be the next president of the United States?! We have seen what the past and the present generations have been able to produce to lead this country, and they have been absolutely deplorable.

No country as great as America should have to settle for the losers that America has had to tolerate for the past twenty-five to thirty years. And the so-called millennial generation will offer very little in the hope to find anyone from this group of people who is intelligent enough to lead America anywhere besides down a slippery slope to hell.

Admittedly, I am hard on young people, and that is by design. I call it by design because the parents at home and the teachers at schools have all failed to do their responsibilities and their jobs. If we are lucky enough to find a genius in this generation of young people, it is because God has blessed him or her with a brilliant mind and not because the parents or the teachers had anything to do with it. The parents of this generation of kids are no more than a bunch of crazed, incarceration-bound dopeheads who make money any way they can and do not have the time or the skills to raise their kids at home, and the teachers certainly do not have the education to teach the kids properly in schools. So with that in mind, where does the fault lie for an untrained, uneducated, undisciplined millennial generation?

The truth of the millennial generation or the reason why there is such a lack of confidence in them is quite simple. The older generation has come to realize that these young people didn't receive the proper training and guidance that they should have because the only accomplishment that their parents made was to birth them. The "now generation" reminds me of Cain and Abel, who became at odds with each other because Cain was convinced that God favored Abel more than he did him. How could the children of the first two people on Earth become so angry with one another if Adam and Eve had done their duties as parents?

Despite their obvious faults, Adam and Eve can be given a pass simply because we have to assume that they were not mentally equipped to raise their own two children. Perhaps this was something that God did not tell them despite them having broken his first command (do not eat from the Tree of Knowledge). But mankind has been in existence long enough now to know and teach others how to raise their children properly.

Obedience is written throughout the Bible. And it is there for a precise purpose: to obey God and his Commandments. To obey the Father who is the creator of all things is no different from obeying the people who gave birth to children. If the children of God fail to obey his Commandments, there is a punishment waiting for those who have been disobedient. However, the problem of obedience comes in. It has been proven that many people today are refusing to believe the words of the Bible. And it is very difficult for people to be obedient to something that they do not believe in. Therefore, the children in today's world are very similar to Cain and Abel many years ago who were left to raise themselves. Cain killed his own brother because he had a screwed-up mind and believed something that was not totally true. He believed that he was slighted by God because he was too lazy to do the work properly compared to his brother Abel, whose work had been pleasing to God.

Today, children are pretty much raising themselves simply because their parents are clueless as to how to communicate with them. A child has to know as soon as he or she exits the womb who is responsible for them being in the world. And the people who are responsible for them being in existence are in charge of their lives, their well-being, and everything else that may come their way. Also, when children are old enough to understand who are responsible for them being in the world, boundaries and rules that the children must understand and abide by have to be set. There is no such thing as children telling their parents what they want, when they want it, and how they want it. When a child tells a parent what to do, the parent is no longer in charge of that child. Ultimately, that is a disaster waiting to happen.

The days of old when children obeyed their parents are no longer a factor in these so-called modern days of raising children. Therefore, to spare the rod and spoil the child is a biblical passage that is no longer a meaningful scripture to people with children. In fact, spanking a child can easily bring about a criminal action taken against the parent. This is the result of people who have taken child punishment to a whole new level of abusing their children. The abuse of children takes place when the people in charge have allowed their children to take charge of them. Raising children starts from day one after birth, and that duty continues until the children are old enough to think and raise themselves (the law says seventeen years old).

However, the vast majority of today's parents are under the false impression that children can act and think for themselves when they enter the first grade. The reality of children acting and thinking for themselves actually does not start until they have entered college or have moved out on their own. And even then, there are times when the advice of parents can be useful to make the transition from childhood into young adulthood much easier.

So what does raising children have to do with the millennial generation? Everything! It all began about thirty or forty years ago when the "baby boomers" stopped doing the right things that would have prevented their children from going wild. The baby-boomer parents were very strict, for they believed in the punishment of their children to avoid having to visit them in prisons, hospitals, or funerals. However, the baby boomers did not have the same values for taking care of their kids because they believed children should have a say-so in grown-up affairs. This, of course, was the end of parental guidance done the right way. Today, we are seeing the results of giving children a free hand to do whatever they want.

Despite the baby boomers having a bad influence on the next generation simply by not being the proper parents that they should have been, the boomers did, however, work hard to provide the material things that their parents could not afford. And because the boomers did not spend quality time with their children, the next generation fell apart like a wet paper bag.

Today, the jails are overcapacitated. The graveyards have bodies in coffins stacked on top of coffins with the young and the dead. Now everyone is asking why. The answer lies right before us. The parents are the reason why there are so many young people dying in the streets and becoming members of gangs. These same young people have turned the streets of America into a battleground, committing violent crimes in every neighborhood. Why am I blaming the parents? Because there is no one else in the chain of command of the human race to blame. Poor parenting or no parenting at all are the primary reason why the streets of America are filled with crimes and the deaths of so many young people today.

I need not look any further than Chicago's homicide rate to make this call. Five or six hundred people are dying in the streets of Chicago each and every year by the hands of other young people, primarily the African Americans, who are totally ridiculous by any name that we want to call them. But Chicago is not alone in this statistic; they are in every major city across America, and no one is blaming what is happening on the parents of these children. There is no doubt in my mind that if mothers and fathers would take the time to teach their children just the Ten Commandments in the Bible, there would probably be much less crimes in the streets.

I am constantly bombarded with the same question whenever I am having a conversation concerning the crimes that we are witnessing firsthand or through the news media: "When will the senseless killings and criminal activities ever cease?" My answer is very simple and clear as well as to the point: when hell freezes over!

What every decent American is watching each and every day on his or her television set is the monster that older people with children and grandchildren created. It reminds me of a monster movie: an ego maniac creates a monster from body parts of other dead corpses, and he brings it to life. Then he sets the monster free to prey on innocent people. When the killing begins, the maniac suddenly realizes what he has done, and he cannot contain the monster because it is too late; it is on the loose!

The police are powerless to stop this type of violent situation simply because they are never present when these young thugs or young idiots will pull out weapons and start shooting. This type of scene is repeated over and over again in every major city across America. When these so-called millennials are not killing each other, they are patrolling the streets, searching for homes to break into, cars to steal, and people and businesses to rob. There is a sadness to this madness in that they have absolutely no use for the merchandise that they steal and rob; it simply becomes the nature of the monsters' trademark.

When will this madness ever end?! As I said before, when hell freezes over! Or I can give several possibilities that will end it: (a) parents must take responsibility for the monsters that they have created; (b) the police must arrest every parent for every child who is arrested under the age of seventeen; (c) the criminal justice system must put an end to the revolving doors of prisons that allow these jailbirds to be in and out of the system repeatedly for the same senseless crimes; and (d) every tax-funded state prison will authorize the bringing back of hard labor or "chain gangs." I believe these measures will eliminate many senseless crimes.

We are living in what we want to believe is a civilized society, where all its citizens are obedient to the laws of the land. But now! This is America, where its citizens are corrupted and filled with greed and where a large segment of the population are barbarians. It is a known fact that a free society is not free when decent, law-abiding citizens are afraid to walk or drive on the streets after dark. Not only is it unsafe for them to ride or walk at night, but it is also unsafe for them to live inside their own homes. This has to stop immediately, by any means necessary! Or we are all in danger!

Of course, I know that the measures that I named above will never happen in America. But if we are going to survive this senseless madness of human behavior, we are going to have to make law enforcement officials, politicians, and parents accountable for the disease that they are all taking part in. There is no other way to end the madness in this country without taking drastic measures. The crime situation is getting worse each and every day. Why? In my opinion, some human beings are very similar to roaches; where you see one, expect others to be close by. If you get rid of one, ten more will show up the next day or possibly the same day. Most criminals are accustomed to doing the same things that they see other criminals doing. Or I could simply say it is a "human nature" sort of thing (monkey see, monkey do).

When I look at young people today, I have to keep reminding myself that most young minds are emptied of anything that is meaningful, godly, or worldly. In other words, most young people are empty-headed with nothing more serious in their minds than sex. How do I know this? It is because we have all been in the same exact spot as they are today. The only difference between me and probably many of you is our parents were at our side every step of the way, trying to make sure that we did not waste our lives doing stupid things. In the old days, mothers and fathers were very careful about whom their children made friends with, where they went at night, and the time they expected their kids to be home after dark. It seems also criminal today that parents would treat their kids in such a way, but it was a way that turned kids into decent adults.

When I became an adult, and looking back over my life, I saw where things could have gone terribly wrong, but I was saved by the bell because Mama and Daddy were there to make sure that as long as I was under their command and lived under their roof, their rules were my rules, and I had to abide by their rules. Most parents today do not have rules for their children to follow; they simply accept their children as they are and hope they will make it through life on their own. Children cannot set rules for themselves simply because they do not have the minds to do so. The Bible says we, as children, think like children. That is why children need parents to think for them and not the other way around.

Many times, I have heard young people make claims that they have suddenly found God after they have committed a crime and are in prison for the rest of their lives. I find it very strange, also laughable, to hear them say those words. Why? Because it only confirms what I have been preaching all along: no one has to find God, for he has never been lost. God has always been as close to us as the nearest Bible; all we have to do is read it. When we read the Bible, God will practically jump off the pages and into our lives. It is amazing to me how deep of a hole young people have to dig for themselves before they finally realize that the only way to ease their pain of being in Earth's hell is to find God. But again, I am placing the blame squarely in the hands of the parents. The Bible helps us know better about what we should expect from life. And if we know better, we will ultimately do better.

I am going to expose a truth that most people have never factored into their daily lives or into this society. In today's world, the crimes committed by stupid young people are the grease that makes the wheels of many businesses in this country turn. As long as the crimes are operational, the criminal justice system is fast at work, and the people who are employed in this system are paid handsomely for the work they are doing. Think about the cops who sometimes work overtime just to keep up with the paperwork that they have to fill out at each crime scene. Think about the jailers who are hired just to keep watch over the criminals that are locked up in jails. Think about the lawyers who are hired by the state or family members just to represent hopeless cases that they have no chance of winning. Think about the security cameras and alarm systems that are being made and sold just to keep watch on homes and businesses for individuals who are too stupid to realize that there is no way they can hide from the cameras. Millions upon millions of dollars are being made and spent each day in America from catching and arresting young criminals.

And let's not stop there; prisons and private businesses have gotten in on the money-making racket. Private businesses are making tons of cash from the free labor of making the same product that would have cost a lot of money to make in the free marketplace. This is simply slavery by another name or in the name of stupid people who are not smart enough to stay out of the prison system. None of these systems are in place by chance. They are well-calculated, well-studied, and well-thought-out plans done by a bunch of smart, business-minded people who know that a certain segment of the American population will always refuse to do the right thing under man's laws as well as God's laws. Therefore, they are saying, "Why not make a fortune off stupid people?"

There are many things that most people have always failed to realize or come to grips with, such as the fact that there are old, gray-headed men who do nothing else but sit around tables and think about how to make money off the backs of the young and the stupid. It is a known fact that young people are the most unsatisfied or unsuccessful group of people in our society or in the world, for that matter. And because of this terrible uneasiness among the younger generation, they have a tendency to do more drugs and commit more crimes.

The truth of the matter is that regardless of how successful the parents are for their children, there is no guarantee that their children are going to be successful as well. Life does not give out any such guarantees at birth. And no matter how much parents may try to make it happen or wish for such things to be true, they cannot. Life has a mind of its own, and it cannot be changed.

Because of the uncertainty of young people and the fat cats who sit around tables, thinking of ways to make money off the backs of these kids, life becomes one hellhole that many of these kids cannot climb their way out of. This is a reality that most parents will not discuss with their kids when they are young. All mamas and daddies want to believe that their babies are going to be God's gifts to the world. Such a want is a flat-out lie, and reality will not support it.

Knowing the reality of life is the only way to live in this world and be at peace in most bad or good situations. Needless to say—but I will say it anyway—whoever children will ultimately become in their lives, the parents can be blamed directly, or they can be partly to blame. I say partly in this case because regardless how much some parents teach their kids to do the right things, kids grow up with their own minds and will ultimately do whatever they want. However, the Bible does points out one major factor concerning kids: if parents raise their kids in a righteous and upstanding manner, they will oftentimes stray from the Word, but they will eventually see the errors of their ways and return to the correct way to live.

Bases upon what I have seen in parenting, people with kids have come to a place where they refuse to believe or understand that children are like most other creatures on this planet: they have to be trained or carefully taught to do the right things. Very few people do what is right if they are not taught or trained to do so.

That is why when people go to jail or prison, there are supposed to be rehabilitation programs in place to help the inmates reenter society with a much improved attitude toward how they should live among other law-abiding citizens. People are very similar to animals; if they are not trained properly, they will act the only way they know how. And oftentimes, the only way they know is very bad or unlawful. Sadly but apparently, this is an inherent human characteristic that was put in place during creation. Why is this a fact of life? It is a fact of life because apparently, this is God's way of wanting parents to do their jobs of raising their own children before turning them over to the outside world.

The objective for parents to teach their young children to do the right thing is not very complicated. That is unless the parents do not know what the right things are to teach them. This situation is more widespread than most people realize. The world did not get into the condition that it is in by itself. The people who were created to take care of the earth are responsible, and their children are failing in every phase to do the very things that they were created to do. Now I am forced to ask a simple question: "If we are not here to take care of what we have to, such as our children and the planet, what purpose do we serve by being here?" If we are to simply give birth to babies and, as soon as they are able to walk and talk, leave them to raise themselves or believe that it is someone else's duty to raise them, what is the purpose of mothers giving birth in the first place?!

I am sure if there is a God up there somewhere, he is certainly asking the same questions. But what answers do we have to give him? I daresay that we have no reasonable answers to give the Almighty.

Chapter 8

THE BLACK EXPERIENCE is a kind of experience that, for most African Americans who are old enough to have experienced it firsthand or were told stories by their elders, was a time in American history that we will never forget. In fact, those of us who actually lived the "black experience" do not ever want to forget it. And the reason why we wish not to forget it is it keeps us focused on what is real and what the lies being told in today's world are. The black experience is based on the treatment that we received dating back over four hundred years ago, and we still have yet to overcome its realities.

Some young people would like to believe that what happened in the past should be left in the past. Many of these same young people, especially young African Americans, are under an illusion that white people have changed over the past half-century. However, if that were true or a fact that we could believe, then Barack Obama would have been treated just like any other president. But he was not, and that within itself is proof enough to tell those who are not old enough to know that in the world, as well as in America, that black people will never be accepted as equals. Something in the back of our minds keeps telling us, "Once a slave, always a slave." We cannot escape the ugly stigma that is now classified as black history. But in reality, it is no more than a harsh reminder of what the hatred to the core of white people, slave owners, and a wide range of other people did to us, primarily due to the color of the Negro people's skin.

It has always been amazing to me to see and hear white people narrating the experiences of the harsh reality suffered by black people. How do white people know what it felt like being a slave?! How do white people know what it feels like to be turned down for jobs or anything else simply because of skin color? In one quick answer, they don't know! But they think they do.

I was born and raised in a small South Georgia town of Monticello, better known as "Bloody Jasper," approximately sixty miles east of Atlanta. "Bloody Jasper" was given to Jasper County by black people in surrounding counties due to the fact that Jasper County was well known for lynching and castrating black people in the middle of the night. Just outside of Monticello, the county seat of Jasper County, was a small dirt road travelling east that crossed over Murder Creek, the prime location for all the murders that took place in Jasper County many years after slavery had ended. And for whatever reason, the white people of Jasper County could not put aside their slave-brutalizing mentality.

On Murder Creek, hundreds of African Americans were put to their death simply because they were black and for no other reason known to mankind. When the white people of Jasper County were not killing black people, black men in particular, they were riding through black neighborhoods, wearing the traditional white hooded sheets on the backs of pickup trucks, terrorizing black people by burning crosses in churchyards and many yards of black people.

As a kid growing up in Monticello, I was able to witness many nights of cross-burning and foul language. "Burn, niggers, burn!" they shouted from their vehicles. I would often ask my father, "Daddy, what does all of this really mean? Why are these white people doing this?"

My father was a very religious man; I am sure that the words he wanted to say were probably against his religion. But I knew what he meant when he said, "There are people in the world who hate other people who are not like them. [He was referring to people like us, black people.] And I suppose this is their way of expressing their dislike for us."

Murder Creek still stands today. And of course, very few people in and around Jasper County know very little about the past years. And I have often asked myself, how can we forget or not want to know what happened at Murder Creek? However, because of the history of Murder Creek, the white-owned newspaper in Monticello once wrote an article denying that the name Murder Creek was due to the hundreds of black people killed by hanging from a huge oak tree that is still standing with the lynching limb hanging over the creek. The article stated that Murder Creek gained notoriety from a bunch of Creek Indians who were battling it out with only-God-knows-who, and some of those same Creek Indians were killed in the battle. I have always said that a lie does not care who tells it; it just wants to be told. And so goes the history of Murder Creek and the black history in a county known for its racial murders.

The last brutal lynching of black America was reported to have taken place in 1946. Of course, I am sure there were many more that were not reported. Think about that for a moment! The last know legalized hanging of an African American was in 1946, and some of those same white people who lynched black folks back then are still alive today. If they are not alive themselves, their sons and daughters are alive and doing well today. They know well what their fathers and grandfathers did to black people leading up to 1946. And the election of Barack Obama as the president of the United States brought back memories of those days for many old white Americans. And to think that some African Americans today wish to forget the past! If it was left up to some of those same white people who know about and/or took part in the lynching black people some seventy years ago, they would still be doing the same thing today.

There are those of us who lived through a period of time when we were not allowed to sit in the same restaurants as white people. We could not use the same toilets that they used or drink from the same water fountains that they drank from. We could not sit in the same lower section in a movie theater where they sat, and we were not even allowed to enter through the front doors of their homes, but they could walk right through our front doors. For me, the black experience has become a very hurtful period of time to think about. It seemed that we were not good enough to even live on the same planet as they did. And to make matters worse, this was a law made for white people just in case black people were infected with the "mad cow disease."

Finally, the day came when white folks such as Coach Paul "Bear" Bryant for the University of Alabama discovered that black kids had superior talent that was unmatched by their white counterparts. Once upon a time, there was a white coach who coached a football team from Southern California, and there were several African American players on the California team and no black players for the Alabama team. The Alabama team was no match for the California team as the black players outscored, outran, and outplayed the Alabama team to the point of total frustration for the Alabama coach. Later that same day, he called a meeting with his assistant coaches and said, "I've got to have me some of them black boys! They ran over us like a herd of deer!"

In 1970, every segregated black school in the South was forced to integrate. This was the beginning of the downfall of powerful sports programs for all segregated black high schools. And the previously-all-white colleges' and universities' sports programs began to improve dramatically in a very short period of time. Today, the Alabama team is a prime example of what the white coach envisioned his team would be like by recruiting superior black athletes for his team. The Alabama team today has one of the most winning sports programs in college football history.

The tremendous story about the discovery of black athletes is all well and good, but I ask, "What did this discovery do to the HBCU (historical black colleges and universities)?" It ultimately depleted their would-be talent pools. In other words, schools such as Morris Brown, Morehouse, Clark-Atlanta, and many more predominately black colleges are now at the very bottom of the winning chart in sports. Why? Because big-money, predominately white colleges and universities have taken all the premium black athletes out of high schools into their bigger-than-life sports programs.

This idea of offering young black athletes big-time scholarships to attend America's most prestigious schools and a real shot at the professional ranks does not take a rocket scientist to figure out. It is simple math: "We will make sure that your families are well taken care of, and you will have free access to everything that our university or college has to offer, including very pretty white girls," so say the scouts of these white colleges and universities. "And let's not stop there. We will also make sure that your GPAs are at a high level, and you'll never have to study an hour, for you will be too busy playing football or basketball."

When the mentioning of pretty white girls and no studies is thrown into the mix, young black athletes are bought and paid for. They then become properties of a white-dominated sports world called college football and basketball. Some people might wonder how or why these young kids are so influenced or so enticed by such offers from big, powerful white schools. And the reason why is quite simple: in most cases, these young athletes are found mostly to have been raised in poor households where there is only one parent, primarily the mother. The picture is very clear: a young mother with a gifted son or daughter is presented an opportunity for her child to attend a powerful, predominately white school, and she does not have to pay a dime for his or her education. There is no argument there. "Sign him or her up!"

Moreover, the mothers are also presented with a clear picture of the possibility of their children playing in the NFL or the NBA/WNBA when their college careers are over. This is a picture that is presented to the mothers of these young black athletes without ever being given the possibility of failure. And then the question comes to mind, "What happens if or when some kids do fail?" Playing college sports is only one step that might grant them an invitation to try out for the "big leagues." But what if they fail the test? Let's do the math. Thousands of young athletes graduate from college every year with hopes of taking their skills to the next level. There are only thirty-two NFL teams and thirty teams in the NBA. All of the NFL teams together might cut, trade, or retire more than a hundred players each year. The NBA does so much more than that because there are less players on each basketball team. So what does all of this mean? It means there are many college players who will never play a professional game in their entire lives. And what is even worse is they have nothing meaningful that they can fall back on.

Now allow me to add injury to insult. These gifted young college players who did not have to study or take classes while they were playing sports are now on their own without the ability to read or write as civilians. There are no available jobs for "has-beens," dumb jocks who did not make it to the pros and who aren't smart enough to go into business for themselves. So what do they end up doing to make a living? Many of these young people start doing what those who have never seen the inside of a college are doing—using and selling drugs. These are very sad endings for what could have been very bright futures for a few bright young people if they had only taken advantage of the education that had been granted to them.

Speaking of playing the game, there was once a time when the only jobs for black Americans in deep South Georgia were working in the homes of white folks and picking cotton in the hot sun and dusty fields. There were also jobs of hauling logs and cutting pulpwood in the forests. I remember picking a hundred pounds of cotton for three dollars, which would take me all day long to pick. Pulpwood and logging were just as bad. We would work all day and sometimes into the dark of the evenings for five dollars a load. On most days, we only managed to cut and load two trucks a day, which amounted to ten dollars a day.

Naturally, we believed back then that this was good money for the uneducated black man. However, someone from the days of slavery said that if black people wanted to seek and secure the same job opportunities as whites, they must get a college education first. Needless to say, this same ideology is still being passed along to every young black high school kid today. But the question is, "Is it true or false?" Having lived the black experience myself, I can truthfully say it is a lie! Even back in the days of old, it was a lie. However, what a college degree would guarantee most black females is a teaching job or work in hospitals. And later on in the 1960s and 1970s, we moved up the ladder to become doctors and lawyers, which were the good times.

As with everything else in life, the good times did not last forever. There was a time when doctors and lawyers were at the top of the professional game. And if we wanted to be someone important, we would go to college for four years and then proceed to law school or medical school for another four years, and maybe we would hit the big times. But lo and behold! As it turned out, we became too many lawyers and too many doctors and flooded the inner cities' hospitals and law offices. Soon, there were not enough criminals and sick people to go around. The malpractice insurance was costing more than the now-professionals were earning. So what is happening now with all these people running over each other, trying to get to paying clients? The situation has now become worse than first believed because doctors and lawyers are still trying to pay off student loans some twenty to thirty years after graduation.

I mentioned inner cities because these were the locations where everyone with a doctor's or lawyer's degree wanted to hang their shingles. Why? Because the inner cities were believed to be the places where the big money was flowing in hospitals, and a lot of criminals were getting arrested and needed lawyers to represent them. However, the doctors were placed in county-funded hospitals, and the criminals were given court-appointed attorneys, which was free to their clients. As a result, the dreams of being a high-paid lawyer or a high-paid doctor with his or her own private practice was no more than a pipe dream for most black people who were seeking higher education.

Big-money law firms only hire the so-called best and the brightest law students in their class. Doctors are working in both hospitals and private practices to make the best of their education. And in both cases, these individuals are not very good at what they were trained to do. That is why malpractice insurances are through the roof with doctors and lawyers.

Speaking from the black experience, black doctors and black lawyers are low on the request for the service list. Why? It is because black clients and black patients do not really trust black lawyers and doctors. Johnnie Cochran, who came to the rescue to defend O. J. Simpson, put an end to the old black stigma of there being bad black attorneys and put some respectability into hiring black attorneys. Before OJ's trial, black criminals trusted black lawyers about as far as they could throw them, and that was not far. I have seen many court cases where black clients preferred white attorneys over black ones unless they were looking to get the maximum sentence.

In 1921, black educators tried to remedy the lies we had been told that to compete with whites who had no degrees, it was to our advantage to get college degrees. Throughout the South, black educators came up with a brilliant strategy to prepare black high school kids for the outside-world job market before graduating. These educators received grants to build schools that would train kids to perform skilled jobs upon graduation. There were many other jobs in America besides doctors, lawyers, and schoolteachers. These jobs were dealing with building America as the greatest manufacturing nation in the world.

In my school alone, there were young people who were trained to work on automobiles and canned food and repair as well as build homes. Upon graduation, many of these young people skipped college and landed jobs doing the things that they had been trained to do. Most of these schools were named training schools, such as the one I attended named Jasper County Training School (JCTS). Only the people who wanted to be doctors, lawyers, and teachers went on to college to become such professionals. Therefore, the lie that blacks had to attend college to compete had been premeditated by white people to keep blacks out of the job market.

Today, many younger people do not understand the reason why these lies were told to keep blacks out of the job market. The reason why was because most black people were hard workers, and they would work long days and nights to make their American dreams come true. A good example of hard work and a black achievement that was ranked among the best in America was in a place called Black Wall Street. Black Wall Street could have been the Black Hollywood of the mid-western United States. They had a slogan that said, "We are not the Old Black or the New Black. We are All Black!"

In the early 1900s, many African Americans moved to Tulsa, Oklahoma, for a chance at the high life due to the oil boom. And soon afterward, dreams began to come true as many of these same blacks began building their own communities located in Greenwood, Oklahoma. Despite being in the midwestern United States, Tulsa was very much like many towns across America; it was hostilely segregated, and black people there did not feel welcome in the downtown area. Therefore, they began to build their own town that became a site to be seen.

Blacks in the area created entrepreneurial opportunities for themselves, which housed a highly impressive business district that included banks, hotels, cafés, clothiers, movie theaters, and many contemporary homes. The folks in Greenwood enjoyed the kind of luxury that their white neighbors did not have. These things consisted of having indoor plumbing and a school system that was superior to any educational system in the nation for their children.

When the white people saw what was going on in Greenwood, they became very jealous and more hostile than they had been before. The situation became very ugly as the white folks vowed to put these uppity Negroes back in their places (wherever that may have been). This was the very first act of terrorism known to have taken place on American soil.

Of course, they had to make this act of violence against the black people in Greenwood appear legitimate. But in disguise, they blamed it on a black kid who had assaulted a white woman. This is what white people have always done throughout the history of America. To make it appear legitimate in the eyes of the public, they staged this scene by setting up a young white woman to make an accusation against a young black man, saying that he had attempted to sexually assault her while they both were on an elevator. Naturally, this kind of accusation from a white young woman toward a black man brought out the worst in white men toward black men.

On May 31, 1921, a mob of white men posing as their own brand of temporary police officers staged a horrifying attack on an unsuspecting Greenwood community. Some people described the attack as a "race riot," but a race riot could not adequately describe what happened during the two days and nights of terror in Greenwood, the reason being if it had been a race riot, it would mean that both blacks and whites were equally to blame. This was certainly not a race riot! It was plainly a terrorist attack by whites who killed more than three hundred African Americans. Not only that, but they also looted and burned forty square blocks or 1,265 black people's homes to the ground, including hospitals, schools and churches, and over 150 businesses.

The so-called deputized white men and even members of the National Guard arrested and detained more than six thousand black people who were later released upon being vouched for by some white citizen who saw this as a senseless act of terrorism. At the end of the two-day terrorist attack, on June 1, more than nine thousand African Americans were left homeless and were forced to live in tents well into the winter months of 1921.

Telling it like it is can sometimes bring stories such as what happened on Black Wall Street to the point of hatred toward the federal government for allowing the murders of innocent black people, who were simply minding their own business. These murderous white terrorists walked away from it all without even a trial. The year of 1921 has not been that long ago that we should forget what happened. It was a plain and simple act of terrorism on black people who were simply making their own community worthwhile. The white people could not stand the mere sight of such of a thing occurring among African Americans.

Why is it that black people have always got to be the "low man on the totem pole" in the eyes of white people? African Americans built America with their own bare hands, along with blood, sweat, and tears, and yet they are the last ones to get credit for anything except their demise. It is time for the black experience to change into something much more than just another black face in the news for killing our own brothers and sisters.

Moreover, it is a known fact that many African Americans have tried to escape the fact or the reality that they are black by trying to act or look like white people. But the truth of the matter is we cannot be someone that we are not. The truth will always remain inside of us, which is just below the surface of our skin. Therefore, when God created man, he never appointed the white man to be the "superior being" over other men. The last time I checked, we all came to this planet by the same identical process. And we are all going to leave here the exact same way. It is up to the good Lord to determine where we will end up. As of right now, no one knows if that is heaven or hell; it is, by far, still a mystery.

Chapter 9

THE BLACK EXPERIENCE (PART II) is a continuation of issues that are still plaguing the black communities today with no end in sight. Some people are constantly asking, "What is the reason, or why can't we move forward?" When I look at what happened in Tulsa, I wish that I could have told the people in Greenwood, "This too shall not last for long." All they had to do was look back at their own history, and they would have known what was bound to come. Almost every invention that African Americans could think of was always challenged or stolen by whites because getting inventions patented was their only way to get on the market.

Black Wall Street was no different from the many developments and businesses that African Americans had put together two hundred years earlier. Throughout the history of the black man in America, he had always worked hard to develop or invent many things for the betterment of this nation, only to have them taken or stolen by the white man.

There is a recent story about a typical case of how an African American can be swindled out of a lifelong business by nonblack people who are only looking to make a huge profit. A case in point was the famous Motown Records and founder Berry Gordy Jr. who made recording history for fifty or sixty years. Motown was founded back in 1959 in Detroit, Michigan, and the company attracted such artists as The Temptations, The Miracles, The Supremes, Stevie Wonder, and The Jackson Five, just to name a few. During the '60s, the '70s, and the '80s, the Motown sound rang supreme all over the globe. And to think that the demise of Motown went down the exact same path as many other black businesses in the years of the past, and there is no doubt in my mind that it will happen again in the future.

In 1972, Berry Gordy Jr. moved his company to Los Angeles because as some people would say, "Detroit was rapidly becoming the slum that it is today." And in 1988, MCA Records made Gordy an offer to buy Motown for a figure of sixty million dollars. But let me hold it right there! Why did MCA Records want to buy out Motown, which was a predominantly black recording company? Now I can only imagine it was due to the same reason with black inventors back in the seventeenth, eighteenth, and nineteenth centuries. Back then, the black man could not get a patent unless he got it under a white man's name. Gordy, who performed miracles for fifty or sixty years, was forced out of the distribution racket. He could make the records, but he had to go through the white companies to get his material on the market.

Berry Gordy Jr. sold his baby of a company to MCA Records for sixty million dollars, and it was a done deal. MCA Records held on to Motown for a measly three years and then sold it to PolyGram Records for 360 million dollars. Now you do not have to be a mathematician to figure out that Gordy was outsmarted in a business deal that he never saw coming. How could a failing company, or so it seemed, have a profit margin of 600 percent in three years?!

Where is Motown today? I would assume it is operating under the PolyGram Record label. Where is Berry Gordy Jr. today? I would imagine he is still in Los Angeles, kicking himself for allowing a fortune to slip right through his fingers. Needless to say, however, he obviously did the only thing that he could have done under the circumstances that he was facing.

My black experience did not stop with Motown; it travelled all the way to the '60s, the days of "Black Power" and "Black is Beautiful." And even today, I often ask myself, whatever happened to the words of "Black is Beautiful" and the Black Power gesture that was in every raised fist? I have one answer for you: all the old militant black figures who marched across America, demonstrating for equal rights and fairness and justice, are dead and gone. And those who are still alive are hidden away in prisons somewhere. And the ones who are not in jail are too afraid to speak their minds for the fear that young blacks today are no longer interested or never knew what black people did in America fifty or sixty years ago.

Needless to say, "Black is Beautiful" and "Black Power" were the expressions of African Americans who were thought to have hated white people. And due to that fact, it was always in the back of white people's minds that blacks were going to rise up and start a race war within these United States. So far, that never happened, and it will probably never happen, for America is the land of the free and the home of the brave (whatever that means).

Going back to the 1960s, when I was just a rookie at the Atlanta Police Department, just before the assassination of Dr. Martin Luther King Jr., Atlanta was the home of the civil rights movement back in those days, and along with a senior officer, we had the detail of following every movement that was made by black activists such as Rap Brown and Stokely Carmichael. This was a big deal back then because the city and the police department believed that these men were Public Enemy Nos. 1 and 2, although the most harm that was actually caused by either man was burning up a lot of gasoline and following these guys around the city.

Nevertheless, we had a reason to be concerned because many of the white officers were afraid that they would be placed in violent situations where they would have to respond, and that within itself would spark a riot in the city of Atlanta. The riots never really materialized, and a few years later, I was informed as to why Atlanta did not become a Detroit, Los Angeles' Watts section, and a few other cities that were burned and looted by black rioters.

Before Martin Luther King Jr. was killed in the late 1960s, he wanted and attempted to bring his road show to Atlanta, but that never happened either. The reason he could never come to Atlanta and speak to the people like he had done in so many other cities, including Washington, D.C., was because his father Martin Luther King Sr. and several other black leaders in Atlanta told him to stay away. They literally said, "Listen, Martin, we love what you're doing, and we think America needs to hear what you're saying. But we here in Atlanta, we got this! We have an open-door policy to city hall, and we can get the mayor to do whatever we want. Bringing your marchers and demonstrators here will only damage the relationship that we have already built."

On April 4, 1968, Martin Luther King Jr. was shot and killed in Memphis, Tennessee, and the entire nation was in shock. By that time, I was working the morning watch, and I had the luck of the draw to be guarding Dr. King's residence that was located on my beat. I drew the assignment to watch the home for several nights after the assassination. And as I watched the people come and go at the home, I kept asking myself, "Why?" Why would anyone kill a man who was only trying to do good for black people? I kept asking myself this question because it seemed to me from listening to his speech in Washington that he knew something like this was going to happen. And based upon the mission that he was on, he had received many death threats, which led him to believe that one day, someone was going to make good of those threats.

But the question mark was still stuck in my mind. "Why?!" That was when I thought about the mission that Jesus was on when he tried to save the people from their sins. Even as far back as two thousand years ago, people did not want Jesus to go around preaching to the people who needed to be saved or freed from slavery. But lo and behold, we were again going through a similar situation of a man preaching a message of freedom named Martin Luther King Jr.

I remember as time went on from the '60s to the '70s, the message of equality seemed as though it was finally getting through to the white people who had been trying desperately to keep things the way they had been for four hundred years. Although slavery was no longer an issue, we were now trying to gain equal opportunities to what we believed they were entitled to. We thought that their neighborhoods were better than the slums that we were living in, as well as their government projects. We thought their schools were better, and their teachers could teach our kids better than what they were being taught in our segregated black schools. Everything white seemed to have been better than what we had.

We said to the white man, "We just want a piece of that same pie you're eating, brother man!" Eventually, the white man opened the doors to equal opportunity, and we began to climb up that ladder to get our share of everything that white America had to offer by using the great new law called "affirmative action." Until now, that law says we could go anywhere in this land that the white people have gone to, and no one could stop us. Of course, all of this was very good for a little while until the white man realized that everyone in the black community was not taking full advantage of the great new opportunities that had been afforded to them.

Now what?! Like everything else in life, when you ask to be a full partnership in a business, you need to know the operation of the project. You need to know the ingredients of what goes into the wealth-building pie. Otherwise, if we fail to know what is in the pie that we had just received a slice of, when it is all eaten up, we have no knowledge of how to make more pie. A good cook knows what is in the meal that he has prepared. We failed to learn the secret.

So what am I saying? I am saying that affirmative action was only a start or a "feel good" measure to make black people think that they had arrived. The pie that we were so desperately asking for was the beginning of the end to equal opportunity. And as I said before, if you are lacking the ingredients that go into making the pie, how do you make another pie once your slice is all eaten? We could not and we still cannot make another pie the way that we envisioned or believed the white man was eating that tasted so delicious to him. Was it real or just an illusion?

Yes, it was real and good while it lasted. But on the other hand, it was an illusion we believed was going to last forever. When our piece of the pie ran out, we could not make our brand of the pie that was as equally good as the one we had just eaten. So what do we do now? We have to do without simply because we failed to ask for the recipe when we were asking for a piece of the pie. The perfect example of having the correct recipe for success was Black Wall Street before the white man bombed and killed black people for what they knew and for what they were doing in Greenwood of Tulsa, Oklahoma.

Before the 1921 massacre, black people in Black Wall Street had found the formula for success while building a community that was a symbol of pride and of how to rise above the level of poverty by making the dollar bill work for the entire neighborhood. On average, the dollar circulated in Greenwood a minimum of twenty times before it left the neighborhood. How was it possible that one dollar could circulate in one community that many times before being passed on to someone outside of Black Wall Street? It was very simple: they supported each other. Everything that was needed to build Greenwood was shipped directly to the area by the manufacturers which eliminated the so-called middleman in Tulsa. Black people in Greenwood had no reason to buy and shop in Tulsa, for everything they needed and wanted, they made and bought from each other.

What started out in the 1960s as a good gesture by asking the white man for equal access to whatever he was enjoying eventually became a nightmare for black people. We wanted to live, work, and go to the same schools as white people did, not realizing that what we had could have been built upon and made better or just as good as anyone else if we had continued to work for ourselves by doing it for ourselves. But that was not the case; we wanted to be like the white man in every aspect of the American lifestyle, and that was the illusion that I spoke of.

That old saying of "White is right, brown sticks around, and black, get back!" was one of those obvious lies that we were led to believe. Therefore, we automatically assumed that since we, for the most part, were transported to America by slave ships, the white man owned America. That was a lie as well! The Native Americans owned the land, but they were killed off by white people who came here from the European nations, and the land of the Americas was stolen from the Indians just as the black people in Black Wall Street were killed off and their land was taken from them.

My black experience also carried me back to the 1970s, the height of the Vietnam War. This was a dark and bittersweet era for the black man primarily because the Vietnam War took on a whole new image in the late '60s and early '70s. This was when the U.S. government and the draft board decided that the drafting of young black men who may have been involved in marching and demonstrating across America was the best course of action to take. This, of course, was the surest and best way to take the troublemakers off the city streets in this country and place them where they could do some good or be killed. It was like killing or shooting two birds with one stone. And sure enough, it solved America's problems as far as the riots and demonstrations were concerned. But it created a much more serious problem for black families.

In 1975, at the end of the Vietnam War, black soldiers as well as other soldiers were so mentally disturbed and addicted to drugs that when they returned home, they were more like the "walking dead" than actual human beings. If they were not messed up in the head or addicted to drugs, Agent Orange would become the next best thing in killing the Vietnam veterans as the years passed.

If Agent Orange was designed to kill vegetation in the jungles of Vietnam, why didn't the geniuses who came up with this idea realize that this chemical weapon would kill human beings as well? Or did they actually know this and decide that American soldiers were dispensable and that the United States could move ahead without them? Whatever the reason may have been, the damage was severe to black families back home.

The damage was done in many ways. It deleted all the troublemakers who were tearing America apart, and it actually eliminated a vast majority of black men out of the workforce. Then there came the so-called "blue collar" jobs such as automobile factory workers, police officers, firefighters, postal workers, and any other job that did not require workers to wear suits and ties. These jobs, of course, paid decent salaries for a bunch of veterans who only had military experience as a formal education, which was compatible to a college degree.

As I have often said before, in life, good things always come to an end, and so did all the blue-collar jobs that were known to be "made in America." Pres. Bill Clinton signed into law the so-called NAFTA (North America Free Trade Agreement) with Canada and Mexico in 1994, which automatically shut down most plants and factories in America. But somehow, China, who was not a part of the NAFTA, is now producing more "Made in China" goods to the United States than Canada and Mexico combined. And we are asking ourselves today, "How did America allow such a thing to happen when there are millions of people right here in these United States who want to do the same jobs as the other countries who now have a lock on doing business in America?"

Again, I will eagerly announce that this agreement has placed a heavy burden on the black families who are said to be well over the 50-percent unemployed rate in America. But who dropped the ball? Or should I ask, "Who allowed the ball to be dropped as far as pushing African Americas out of the job market was concerned?" Obviously, we did! While black people were parading around, calling President Clinton "the first black president," he is the same so-called black president who sold black people out by signing the NAFTA. Those were jobs that black Americans could have had and should have had, but instead, he allowed Mexico and Canada and now China to perform the same jobs for far less money.

I asked the question as to who allowed such a thing to happen when we thought that we had gained a piece of the so-called economic pie. Well, obviously, this did not start with the signing of the NAFTA. It started years before Bill Clinton became president. It began at the end of the Vietnam War when the discharged soldiers returned home, many of whom were men unfit to hold jobs or go back to the families that had they had left behind. But they did have a trade that was similar to what they had done well in the fields of Vietnam, trading on the "black market."

Now we were facing a new way to trade in the inner cities of America where the "white flight" had taken its toll. The housing projects and the ghetto had found themselves a brand new bag or brand new way to make fast money. That was, of course, dealing drugs, which was better known as "crack cocaine." The drug trade caught the hood and the cops by surprise because neither one had ever seen anything like this in the history of America. There were kids and young men dealing crack cocaine on every street corner in the black neighborhoods across America. And millions of dollars were pouring into the hood like rain. Every major city in the nation tried to combat this kind of crime by organizing their brand of drug squads. In 1984, Atlanta came up with a group called the "Red Dog Squad."

Drug dealing in America gave the black community a new way to make fast money in a short while. And of course, this new way of making money gave young black kids an escape route from attending school to get a decent education or look for a job. "Who needs an education when you can make millions of dollars selling drugs?" they were all asking each other. After all, that is why they were going to school: to learn how to make money.

The job market was steadily slowing down due to a lack of interest from young black people who were rapidly ignoring affirmative action for something that was more exciting and far more lucrative. Drug dealers became the new millionaires of America. There were young men as well as old black men who were rapidly becoming the new black businessmen of a nation that was steadily writing them off as a nonfactor in American society. Today, it is still that way; young and old black men are a nonfactor in American society.

Today, in the twenty-first century, my black experience has brought me to the point of asking this one question: "Who are we as black people?" We have been down so many roads of desperation that we have lost our direction and our identity. We are not really sure if we are white, brown, or black. And a more pressing question that I have to ask is, "Where do we go from here?" Martin Luther King Jr. took us to the mountaintop, but we couldn't cross over it; we fell back to the bottom. Malcolm X said we should succeed by any means necessary, but we were tricked by the white establishment, and we lost our would-be shares in the economic pie-eating contest. Rap music cannot get us where we want to go. Politics is a machine owned and operated by a white-majority society that is filled with corruption. So where do we go from here?

Let's take a step closer to what is more truth than fiction: America is our home, and we helped build this country into a powerhouse nation, yet our pictures are on every Most Wanted poster, marking us as the enemy of America. Identity is what we need! At the moment, we are African Americans, black Americans, people of color, Negroes, and any other name that we wish to call ourselves, and we still don't have a home to call our own. How is that possible? After four hundred years of slave conditions and working every kind of thankless job that could be thrown at us, we are still fighting for our rights to be Americans. No other race of people who have come to this country had to jump through these racial hoops or go through this much hell.

Chapter 10

THE WAR ON DRUGS was probably the biggest law enforcement joke in the history of crime fighting. In the early 1980s, when crack cocaine became the most popular drug on the streets of America, no one took it seriously, or some people simply said that this was the only way that young black men could fight their way out of poverty. On the outset of drug dealings in the nation's inner cities, it was like a money-making bomb had exploded in the poorest neighborhoods and brought more money than these young black men and women had ever seen in three or four lifetimes. And make no mistake about it: cops had never seen this kind of money dealing before either. And immediately, there were more cops on the take than any time in history.

In 1984, Atlanta organized what was known as an anti-drug squad that became famously known as the "Red Dog Squad." The Red Dogs were made of twenty-five to thirty officers whose primary purpose in the department was to apprehend and lock up drug dealers on the streets of Atlanta. At least 99.9 percent of all drug dealings were being done on the street corners of every housing project in the city. In the beginning, the young sellers were rather easy to arrest because they were usually standing on street corners, waiting for buyers to drive by. The Red Dogs would roll up in unmarked vans or cars and make the arrests.

Needless to say, the money was rolling in so fast that whenever the officers would make five or ten drug busts, twenty minutes later, there would be twenty more dealers waiting to take the places of the ones who were arrested. However, the laws at that time were not written to address crack cocaine dealers, which meant that these young thugs paid low fines and were back on the streets by the time the arresting officers completed the paperwork.

Major problems arose for many cops when they made drug arrests inside of apartments where dealers were hiding their loot. If the cops made arrests inside of an apartment and the loot was for several thousand or a hundred thousand dollars, by the time the evidence arrived at the precinct, half of the cash was missing. Naturally, for many cops, this was a cash cow, and no one in the department could prove that there was more cash at the scene than what was turned in as evidence. And as time rolled on, cops began to get greedier and greedier, and the drug dealers could not be trusted if they complained that they had more money than what the cops reported as evidence.

Local cops were not the only crooked cops on the take; as the trade grew larger and larger, the Drug Enforcement Agency (DEA) began to get involved because they realized that for street corner drug dealers to be making so much money, someone outside of the inner cities had to bring the drugs in. More than likely, the suppliers were not your typical hustlers whose hands were quicker than their eyes. Now the plot was beginning to thicken! Who were responsible for trucks and airplanes filled with pure cocaine being shipped straight out of South America? It was obvious that the street corner dealers were only the guinea pigs who were expendable when cops such as the Red Dog Squad arrested them.

On the other hand, the DEA were a group of law enforcement officers who were in the business to make larger arrests, get rich quickly, and retire. In the late 1980s, a DEA officer, on average, collected several million dollars of his own within a five-year period. Then he would be transferred back to a desk job, and soon afterward, he or she would retire from the job.

To most cops, this whole idea of taking money from a bunch of criminals was a fair trade. On many raids, cops would collect several million dollars on a single bust. If they followed protocol, the money would be turned over to different agencies, and only God knows where the money would end up after that. Therefore, drug officers took whatever cash they would get away with and turn in an amount that would be believable to the courts.

So what do we say about the drug dealers who got caught with large sums of cash and the cops who stole it for themselves? There is nothing anyone can say about such a thing happening. In the late 1990s, drug dealers could not spend their money on new cars or buy homes like they had done in the beginning. Car dealers were required to report any amount over ten thousand dollars to the IRS, and banks were required to do the exact same thing. Therefore, drug dealers were placed in a position where the only way they could spend all the cash that they making were in strip clubs and buying old cars and making them new again, as well as financing the so-called "rap industry." And then there was the case of trying to laundry money.

The reason why this was a "cops take the money and run with it" kind of thing was that the drug dealers could not complain to the departments or to the courts without admitting that they were drug dealers themselves. However, some drug dealers did complain when they knew that they were going to get a life imprisonment under a new law of "one strike and you're gone for life." But no one in their right mind was going to take a criminal's word over a cop's word. And this kind of thinking did not always hold true for crooked cops.

In the Zone 3 precinct, which covered the southeast side of Atlanta, several Atlanta cops were convicted and sent to prison for taking drug dealers' money after the arrests were made. There were also several officers who were on drug dealers' payrolls for sounding the alarm whenever the Red Dogs made plans to raid certain areas in the Zone 3 neighborhoods. They were able to warn the street corner dealers by listening to the commands given by supervisors on the Red Dog Squad frequency to "Take 'em down!" On average, it would take at least fifteen minutes for the Red Dogs to get in position to make the raids, but by that time, the Zone 3 commander would have notified his officers to warn the drug dealers of the incoming raid.

On most occasions, by the time the Red Dogs Unit showed up on the scenes where such raids were to take place, all the dealers had ceased their operations and were acting like normal residents who lived in the area. This type of conduct in the Zone 3 precinct continued until several high-level drug dealers were arrested outside of Zone 3, and they dropped a dollar bill on the ones who were tipping the dope dealers off before the Red Dog officers could arrive on the scene. "The zone major and about seven of his men are the ringleaders of what was going on out there," one of the dope dealers told the Red Dog officers.

A trap was set for the cop-tipsters, and at least six cops were caught while being paid by drug dealers for information. But the major himself was not among the ones who were arrested. Somehow, he was told by someone to take the day off on the day of the arrests. The DEA was among the officers who made the arrests, and the six Zone 3 officers who were caught with their hands in the drug dealers' pockets received no less than five years in federal prison.

As the twenty-first century approached, the city of Atlanta saw a grand opportunity to get rid of the housing projects, which would also get rid of most of the welfare mothers and all the young drug dealers as well. Being pressured by a "white flight" moving back into the city, the then black mayor of Atlanta, Maynard Jackson, initiated an all-out effort to the bring 1996 Olympic Summer Games to the city. This could only mean one thing for the housing projects throughout the city of Atlanta: tear them all down and rebuild new high-rise housings for the rich and the young white and black working class, mostly of the gay persuasion, who would eventually move into the city after the Olympic Games were done.

This was Mayor Jackson's way of forcing the poor blacks and poor whites living inside the inner city of Atlanta out of town for good. But most importantly, he was eliminating all the problem areas that had been taken over for years by the crack cocaine sellers. The question is, however, "Did it work?" It worked like a champ! Of course, they told a few lies to get rid of the project dwellers. They were told by people from the mayor's office that they would be able to move back into the newer apartments when the Olympic Games were over. But when the games were over and done with, the rent rose to the sky, and the welfare recipients were forced to stay wherever they had moved to make way for the Olympic Games. But it was just another way of killing off two birds with one stone: drug dealers and the welfare recipients.

Needless to say, getting rid of the crack cocaine sellers on the streets of Atlanta worked simply because the dealers did not have anywhere else to hang out and sell their merchandise. The only thing the city of Atlanta did was shift its drug problems to the surrounding counties such as Dekalb County, Clayton County, Cobb County, and other parts of the area that make up Metro Atlanta. Currently, Atlanta is now suffering from the backlash of a problem that it assumed it had eliminated. Today, the city is racked with petty, senseless crimes that many of these young thugs are coming back into the city to do: rob, rape, and take from the wealthy people that have taken over the housings that were once the homes of so many low-income families.

Today, Atlanta is stunned by the turn of events because the city leaders never saw this coming. These young thugs are like roaches; two are eliminated today, but by tomorrow, three or four more will take the place of the ones in prison.

The war on drugs, as I mentioned earlier, was a joke in the beginning and still is today. Drugs today are very similar to the days of the Prohibition when alcohol was illegal in most of America. Law enforcement officers chased and arrested liquor makers for years with very little success. How do you stop people from doing what they really want to do? The same thing applies to any crime that has been committed. Cops cannot read the minds of people and make arrests. If the liquor-drinking market called for the makers of alcohol to make the stuff, cops and lawmakers can do very little to stop it. The Ten Commandments, as well as the laws of man, have made it illegal to commit murder, yet the homicide rate keeps rising every year.

The makers of illegal drugs are no more than a joke for the cops and the DEA who are battling drug dealers twenty-four hours a day and are trying to put a stop to drug dealings. But there are 129 drug-related deaths every single day in America. And there are people who are still trying to figure out a way to put a stop to drug crimes. If they haven't already, I can truly say that there is no legal way to stop drug dealing as long as there is a market for drug buyers. So how do we stop people from using drugs? We cannot! And that is a fact that seems to have escaped the minds of lawmakers and law enforcement officers.

The problem of doing drugs in America goes much deeper than most law enforcement officers as well as politicians are willing to admit. The number one reason is not so much about the drug dealers themselves, but it is all about the money on both sides of the fence. We already know that the drug suppliers and sellers are making a ton of cash. But we fail to realize that billions of dollars are spent each year on law enforcement officers who are baffled at the idea that they cannot make a dent in stopping the drug offenders. And here is the reason why: 18.4 billion dollars are spent each year on the war against drugs. Half of the 18.4 billion dollars go to the enforcement agencies that are not be able to make any progress in the battling the drug operation. And I ask, "How is it possible that nine billion dollars can be spent each and every year to fight the war on drugs, and yet there is zero progress?"

Therefore, if there is no progress being made in this enormous battle, why fight it? But the bigger question should be, "Who is footing the bill?" Who is paying the 18.4 billion dollars that are being spent on the war against drugs? The taxpayers are the ones who are paying the bill for a bunch of cops and politicians to get rich. But they are not being held accountable for the results that they are not bringing in.

Just think about this war on drugs for a moment; it has been thirty to forty years since we had first heard about the war on drugs, but drugs are still flowing in from Mexico and Columbia just as they were in the very beginning. The United States are paying billions to these South American countries to help in the fight, but they cannot stop the planes and the ships that are hauling the drugs into this country. And what is even worse is that there is no shortage of buyers for these drugs that are being shipped in. To make matters worse, inmates who are sitting behind bars in state and federal prisons are still controlling what is going on outside of their jail cells. And again, I ask, "How is this possible?" How is it possible that a felon convicted for drug dealing can still control his business from behind bars?

I know of such a case in Mexico where the biggest drug lord in the Mexican drug trade was still in command of his drug market while sitting behind bars. Naturally, we all know that to pull something like this off, guards and cops were on his payroll. And what is even worse is that the vast majority of his drugs being shipped out of Mexico were coming to America. The U.S. government is paying the Mexican government 1.4 billion dollars a year to help keep their drug suppliers from shipping drugs into this country, but not one ounce of heroin or cocaine has been stopped.

Therefore, it would seem that America is spending billions upon billions of dollars to fight a crime that is almost impossible to fight. And when we look at the amount of money that is being spent, we have to wonder, "Where is all that money going? Who is fooling who?!" Well, we can look at three different probable recipients: the politicians who make the drug laws with holes in them, the agencies that are given these funds to finance and buy guns and equipment for their officers to carry out these so-called drug raids, and the officers themselves who are appointed to enforce the laws that are filled with gaps and loopholes. Of course, do not let me fail to mention the judges who are appointed to carry out the sentences of the arrested drug criminals because they are the ones who keep the revolving jail doors turning. So where are we in the fight against drugs? We are right back where it all started.

We started it in the Vietnam War where soldiers learned the meaning of the black market and the effects that drugs had on human beings. Pres. Richard Nixon saw the effects that drug abuse had on the soldiers in Vietnam. And in 1971, the president tried to get Congress to help do something that would aid in the prevention of drug abuse. But apparently, Nixon's efforts did not work because many of these same soldiers returned home after the war with drug habits that they could not control. That was the beginning of the major problem of Americans becoming a part of the illegal drug culture.

Today, when we add up all the money that is funneled toward the so-called prevention of illegal drugs in this country, we are talking about a sum well over fifty-one billion dollars annually. In my world, that is a lot of money. However, it would not seem like such an enormous amount if I could see where there is progress being made. But after forty years of doing the same things over and over again with no one figuring out how to stop the flow of illegal drugs from entering this country, it is like throwing gasoline on fifty-one billion dollars and setting fire to them.

Of course, there is one statistic that I have to confess shows law enforcement officers are probably doing well, which could justify some of the money that is being spent toward curving the drug problem. Think about this: 8 percent of the American population is sitting behind bars all because of illegal drugs. That is a lot of human beings that could have been working on jobs, trying to make this a greater nation. But instead, they are all in jail, taking up a portion of the fifty-one billion dollars that is being spent annually. To me, that within itself is a crime.

This is my personal opinion on the war against drugs: the substance is a slave master, and all the sellers, pushers, dealers, and users are no more than slaves. And as the old saying goes, "Money is the root cause to all evildoings." Here, we have one of humanity's most evil deeds known to mankind, and man has not figured out a way to stop it. This is a product that is so harmful to the human body that it destroys the body as well as the mind. And yet people are helpless and hopeless when it comes to using it. It is a Satan-driven product that has placed blinders over the eyes of man, and he cannot see past the so-called "good feeling" of it.

Now we come to the most important question of all as far as the war on drugs is concerned: "What is the one reason why the fight against illegal drugs continues to go on and on?" The answer is quite simple: the demand for illegal drugs continues to go on and on. And now I will step back and ask another important question: "Why do human beings feel the need to use illegal drugs or drugs that will ultimately destroy their bodies?" It is because they need to feel a certain way that they cannot feel normally. In other words, drugs give people a false sense of reality that makes them feel as if they are on top the world or someone very important that they cannot be otherwise. Or I could simply say that drugs are a costly way for people to lie to themselves.

When I look at people from that particular aspect, it makes me wonder what that says about human nature. You mean to tell me that being alive is not enough of a natural high that would make most people jump for joy just to be able to see the sun shine? Mankind's ability to cope with life itself is constantly dropping to an all-time low. And as a result, he feels that the only solution to his problem is to turn to illegal drugs. There is something sadly wrong with the world of today, and I believe that Satan is the creator of all weak-minded individuals.

Once upon a time, I interviewed a person whom I came in contact with, and since I had never used cocaine myself, I was curious as to how it made him feel when he first tried it. "Cocaine is a very tricky drug," he started. "It has a way of getting you hooked from the very first time you try it. You see, that's the funny thing about cocaine. You're not expecting what you're about to get when you first try it." He paused and smiled from the thought of using it his first time. "Then you try it, and bam! You're completely blown away by the feeling you get."

I laughed at the way he was describing it. "It was that good, huh?" I asked.

"Man, let me tell you something! It was that good, and it was that great of a feeling! But that's the trick to using cocaine. That first high is like nothing that the human brain has ever experienced before. If there is a heaven, cocaine makes you feel like you've risen above the clouds to heaven, and suddenly, you've stepped off and left the whole world behind you."

"It was that powerful, huh?!" I asked because it seemed that he was having flashbacks to when he first tried the drugs or when I first experienced the Holy Spirit.

"Yeah, that's the way it makes you feel the very first time. But that's the trick to it. That's what gets people hooked on cocaine because they go back again and again, trying to find that very first feeling, but they can never get that first feeling ever again. Do you remember what it felt like the first time you really had sex? Well, it's kind of like that but probably better."

"Really?!" I asked, knowing what it felt like the first time I had sex. "So you're saying that all it takes is one time for cocaine users to get hooked, and no matter how many times they go back for that same feeling, they can never reach that first-time high ever again?"

"Never again can they accomplish that first level of high or that first feeling that they achieved. Like I said, you will never forget the first time you had some good sex and who it was you were with when you got some no matter how old you get. You will always remember that one person a hundred years from now."

Therefore, if drugs are similar to having sex, whether it is the first time or the last time, human beings are always going to need something to make them feel good. I suppose that is why prostitution is the oldest occupation in the world. And with that in mind, we will never eliminate illegal drugs from a free society. It is just like trying to eliminate the idea of women or men selling their bodies to anyone who is willing to pay for them.

So the world continues to turn . . . !

Chapter 11

MY THOUGHTS ON WHITE AMERICA are not fictional ideas that seem to have appeared out of nowhere and suddenly popped into my head. No, my thoughts are real and take me back to many years in my past. And when I think of how I became an American citizen from all the way deep down in the jungles of Africa, I suppose I owe a certain amount of thanks to the slave owners who brought my ancestors here as slaves. I realize that the purpose for bringing boatloads of black Africans here in cramped, overcrowded conditions was not what they had originally planned, that we would eventually become American citizens. But I have to wonder, "What were they planning to do with the millions of black people when all was said and done?" Were we supposed to remain on the farms, picking cotton and plowing the fields forever? If that was not their plan, then what was supposed to happen to us years later?

Maybe when it was all said and done, their plan was to kill all the African people like they did to many of our brothers and sisters of many years gone by. But then maybe this was not something that they had even considered once we had done all there was to be done. However, after the slaves were freed, the idea of "What shall we do now?" began to sink in. And after four hundred plus years have gone by, I imagine that white America is still trying to figure out what and where they went wrong in their so-called perfect plan for the Negroes of Africa after all their hard labor was completed.

Sometimes, it appears to me, knowing the struggle and the fight for survival that my ancestors had to endure just to make it from day to day, that we have not accomplished very much as African Americans. It would seem that since we were the backbone or the main reason for this country's becoming the strong nation that it is today, we would have received more credit than we have for being a part of American history. But instead, all we have is black history, which does very little in the grand scheme of things as far as giving black people full credit and recognition for our help in making America the greatest country in the world is concerned.

Black history doesn't mean much to anyone except black people. And even for some black people, they believe that they have outgrown such out-of-date nonsense, and they have reached the point of thinking like white America. "If it makes you feel good to talk about black history, go ahead." But in reality, black history does not make us more American in the eyes of white Americans. If anything, we only count for something when white people need the black vote to get elected to office. However, once they have been elected, they quickly forget the promises that they made to black people before the election ballots are counted, and this is referred to as "selected amnesia."

Going back to the days of slavery, I believe that white slave owners never gave much thought to the days when we would become free men and women. That was one of the primary reasons why they tried everything in their power to keep slaves from learning how to read. In their minds, an educated slave was a dangerous slave. They felt the same way that God felt when he commanded Adam and Eve not to eat from the Tree of Knowledge. But then Satan let the cat out of the bag; he told Eve, "Look, God is lying to you and Adam. He simply does not want you two to become as smart as he is." Slave owners tried to do the same thing to slaves. If slaves learned how to read, they would know for themselves that the things that white people were telling them were lies. They would know not to fall for the old slave owners' tricks that were being played on them. They would know what the road signs were saying when they tried to run away. There were many advantages to knowing how to read that slaves were not privy to.

Going back to the Tree of Knowledge, God knew from the very beginning that by planting the two trees in the Garden of Eden, he would test the obedience of his first two humans. If Adam and Eve obeyed his command not to eat the fruits of the two trees among many others, they would prove that they were obedient to his commands. And like slave owners, the white man did not want slaves to learn how to read for fear that black people would discover what he already knew. And they would become disloyal and run away. So what did the white man know that he did not want the people in bondage to know? He knew that if black people had the power of knowledge, they would think of themselves as equals. Education is the kind of power that cannot be erased from the minds of those who have it. And once they are educated, the eyes of the beholders are opened to a whole new perspective on life.

To be ignorant is to have a lack of knowledge, and a lack of knowledge is not to know of what is being done to the ones who are ignorant. To be knowledgeable is to desire more than one's present situation, which was slavery at the time. To be knowledgeable is to find a way to escape present conditions by any means necessary. And this was the one thing that the slave owners feared most. They said, "An educated slave is a dangerous slave!"

Now when I fast-forward from the slave conditions that occurred a few hundred years ago to today's race relationship between blacks and whites, if we look closely at the treatment that blacks are receiving from white America, we see that the mindsets of whites are slowly reversing back to those of slave owners. First and foremost, in 1970, the American government passed laws that would integrate all public-funded educational systems. Naturally, white people said that was what black people wanted due to the riots and demonstrations of the 1960s. Black America screamed "Racial Equality!" And white America honored their request by integrating all public-funded schools.

Black America was duped into thinking that white kids were getting better education in the public school system than black kids. It was just the opposite! The truth of the matter was black teachers were teaching black kids ten times better than white teachers today are teaching black kids or mixed classes. How is that possible? It is possible because black educators knew what black kids needed education-wise to succeed in the real world. Furthermost and primarily, black kids were taught the "golden rule" (Do unto others as you would have them to do unto you). Growing up in a black society and trying to make it in a white-controlled environment, knowing the "golden rule" is very important.

The second most important thing that was taught in black schools was the Ten Commandments. The Ten Commandments were the Holy Grail that black Americans conducted themselves by. The Ten Commandments are Biblical laws passed down from God to Moses to give to all mankind. And we as black Americans believe that God, above all else, controls the lives of mankind as well as the world we live in. This same belief helped many slaves escape from slavery to freedom. And some of us still rely on God's promises to make it through the hard times to a better way of life. Education today is just as important as it was back during the time of slavery. Why? Because white America still believes that some blacks are still living their lives in the past, which is attached to "slave mentality."

The transition from slaves to "freemen" has not attached itself to many black Americans as it has to many white Americans. Unfortunately for us, however, to a certain degree, some black Americans keep depending on white America to show them the way to the Promised Land. But the most pressing question is, "Where is the Promised Land?" For many years, the Promised Land was in the ghettos or the housing projects. Today, however, the Promised Land is a no-man's-land for black America. The projects and the ghettos are fading away quickly. The suburbs were never ours in the first place. So where are we in American society? We are in a land that has only three escape routes: sports, rap and hip-hop, and the drug trade. When we get past door number three, the room is totally dark, and the exits are far and few in between.

The American dream offers very little in ways of progress for black America, especially when it was the hard labor, mixed with blood, sweat, and tears of blacks, that helped build America. Today, it would seem that every other race and nationality has had more success in the American dream than the black people who actually helped make this a great nation in the first place. What can we say about a country that has actually done very little to upgrade its original workers to a standard above that of the "Johnny-come-latelies" who contributed absolutely nothing to the making of America? Think about this just for a moment: there are "Little Chinas" in America. There are "Little Vietnams" in America or whatever. But you will never see or hear about a "Little Africa" in America. Why is that? The last "Little Africa" was in Tulsa, Oklahoma, in 1921, in the Greenwood section where African Americans built their own section of town that was completely made for the black people living the dream. But lo and behold, the white people of Tulsa came up with a reason to destroy "Little Africa."

In my way of thinking, the same thing would occur today if African Americans could ever come together long enough to build their own neighborhoods to that of a wealth magnet for just black people. Just as in Tulsa, white people will find a way to destroy the wealth movement of black people. In our present state, black people may well earn millions of dollars by working in a white-owned business, but unfortunately, these millions of dollars earned by blacks remain or are spent in white businesses. For instance, black sports figures and entertainers earn millions of white dollars but then spend all of their millions in housing, clothing, and automobiles that are owned by white companies.

In Black Wall Street, a single dollar bill was spent twenty times in Greenwood before it traveled outside of the black neighborhood into the white community. If the same thing happened today, white businesses would go bankrupt waiting for a black dollar to be spent in their establishments. Therefore, it is clear as to why "Little Africa" was destroyed in 1921, for there were no dollars going out of Greenwood into downtown Tulsa. Today, black America spends a swopping 507 billion dollars annually with white businesses.

If I could visualize 507 billion dollars every year being spent to build a black city where the dollar bill would circulate ten to twenty times before being spent in white businesses, white America would change its tune in a single heartbeat. There would be no louder tune being sung by white folks than "Love thy neighbor!" I can only imagine how 507 billion dollars could change the landscape of America if black people decided to build their own factories, stores, schools, hospitals, and transit systems. How can we do this? Well, if black people were able to build Black Wall Street in Tulsa in the twentieth century, I am sure we can do the same thing today in the twenty-first century. But then I might want to consider how many black people have been brainwashed by the white power structure into believing that America belongs to the white man and that we are simply an unwanted people who just happened to have been brought here on slave ships. Therefore, we have no rights to think that we can own any piece of America . . .

My thoughts about white America run somewhere between hot and cold, meaning that I can never really love white Americans because white America has never really loved me or my people. Growing up in the segregated South, I remember the many racially motivated, hateful things that were done to black people there. Since then, no white person ever personally apologized to me or anyone I know for the treatment and torture that they were responsible for committing against black people. They more or less accepted the laws that were changed to protect black people from white brutality. And what I find more challenging for black people today is that when white people accepted the changing of the laws, the laws did not change their way of thinking. And make no mistake about it: if many whites could go back in time and change the lynching laws back to prior 1946, I firmly believe that they would.

There are no more cotton fields or farms where, once upon a time, blacks worked from sunup to sundown for only pennies a day. And if a time machine could take us back to the days of old, someone white would turn the hands of time back. And regardless of how far we believe that we have moved forward in America, we have not moved far enough in the ways of making the hardships of the past disappear. Many of us in this great land of America are still living in the same conditions that many black people lived in back in the 1950s and 1960s. To me, this is totally unacceptable. One primary example is Watts of Los Angeles, California. In 1965, a major riot occurred in Watts due to the shooting of a black youth by a California highway patrolman. The entire neighborhood was destroyed in the aftermath of a riot. And the lingering question today is, "Could the situation have been handled differently with less destruction?"

Violence occurred not only in Watts but also all across America because of an unjustified act by the police that created total chaos in the black communities. And here is the one unanswered question that not one black person can answer: "Why destroy our own neighborhoods because of an illegal act perpetrated by white cops?"

There is something wrong with that picture! It may appear that we are blaming ourselves for something that someone else did. A better question would be, "Why not burn and destroy white neighborhoods instead of our own?"

Think about this just for a moment. Before the destruction of and killings in Black Wall Street, a group of angry white men went to Greenwood and destroyed the homes and businesses of African Americans, not their own neighborhoods. Why didn't the white people of Tulsa burn and destroy their own neighborhoods? Because they knew if they had done such a thing to themselves, they would have to rebuild and start all over again. And here we are at the turn of half a century later; places such as Detroit, Watts, and many such inner cities that were destroyed in the mid-sixties due to race riots are still suffering from a half-century of ignorance.

I cannot blame white America for our own ignorance. But I blame white America for seizing an opportunity to make millions of dollars off the ruins of our own lack of respect for private property. The property damage in Watts was estimated to be about forty million dollars in 1965. And more importantly, the value of life in Watts did not improve at all. As a result of the damage and loss of lives in Watts, the drug dealers and gangbangers found a breeding ground for a drug trade that is still alive and well today. The question now becomes, "Is this what black America has become due to white America shutting down all the factories and labor jobs that would have benefitted many blacks?"

Why didn't white America rush in and rebuild Watts as well as many other riot-torn communities back in the 1960s? It would seem that there would have been an economic opportunity to rebuild what had been destroyed. But apparently, they did not see it that way; instead, they created what was known as the "white flight," where every white family who could afford to move packed up and moved to the suburbs. This sudden exit by the white middle class helped to increase poor black living conditions more than before. And gradually, certain sections of the inner cities across America became known as "ghettos."

Despite what I may think about white America, they did not intentionally or purposely play a hand in creating the ghetto; black people did that all by themselves. When the ghettos came about, there were many good paying jobs available that some black men and women took advantage of. The available jobs at that time were the ones that helped black people join the "blue collar" workforce and placed them in middle-class neighborhoods. Needless to say, the years between the '70s and the '90s were the best of times for African Americans. So what happened to the good times for black people in America? Along with Pres. Bill Clinton, the loss of middle-class jobs, and the hustling of crack cocaine on the sidewalks of the inner cities, the middle-class workforce vanished. However, we can still ask the question as to why President Clinton signed what is now known as NAFTA. Was it because he wanted to see the middle-class blacks lose everything they had worked for and gained to pull themselves up out of the ghetto? Not one so-called black leader ever asked President Clinton that question because many of them thought of Clinton as their "black president." But not once did Bill Clinton ever consider himself as a "black president." Why should he?! The man is a Southern redneck who became a Democratic president primarily because black people voted for him and nothing more.

Nevertheless, there was a time that men like Bill Clinton did not want blacks to have the right to vote. Why? For the same reason that we gained a half-black man to be president of the United States. In a million years, this should have never happened in America, but it did primarily because black people voted in record numbers.

Because I was born and raised in the South, I can spot a Southern cracker a mile away. They are the people who despise seeing a black man with a white woman. In fact, there was a time when black men could not even walk on the same street next to a white woman. There was a time when I would go with my father to a service station to get gasoline, and a group of white men were sitting and talking, and all we could hear was the word "nigger." And now, we call each other niggers. Why?! Is it because they did it, and we learned it from them?

The so-called N-word is just another way that white America taught us to hate each other. To white America, once upon a time, the N-word or nigger was the worst kind of name for a human being. They said, "The only good nigger is a dead nigger!" Now the question is, "Do they still feel that same way?" This is the one question that black people need to know and ask themselves. We talk about how cops are repeatedly killing black men; could it be because white cops still feel or think that "the only good nigger is a dead nigger"?! If that is the case, what can we do about it? The first thing we should do is stop calling each other "nigger."

Now the plot begins to thicken! White America brought black people to America as slaves, and I would like to thank them for that. But do I have to like them because they paid some black chief in Africa for all the so-called worthless natives in the jungle and hauled them over here to be their slaves?! I don't think so! My ancestors were unwilling slaves to a bunch of white people who were too lazy to do their own work. And who do we have to thank for the idea of slavery? The same white people who taught us about religion and Christianity. If we take a closer look at the Bible, it tells us about all of God's favorite men and women in Biblical times who owned slaves. But just because it is written in the Bible, does that make it right?

The bottom line to my thoughts on white America—and I am speaking from the bottom of my heart—is that there is no way that any black-faced African American should ever trust white people. It does not matter if they are a total redneck, cracker, or a suit-wearing businessman or woman. It does not matter if she is a white supermodel or a wrinkled-up, snuff-dipping old white housewife. I would not give a thin dime for anything that white America has to say or offer to me. Why? Because in my seventy plus years of living in America, I have yet to meet an honest, down-to-earth white person who was worth anything more than lies, cheating, and corruption. In other words, I would not trust white America any further than I can throw him or her. Therefore, white America is totally untrustworthy, and as far as I can tell, they are the disciples of Satan.

Chapter 12

WHAT HAPPENED TO THE REAL MEN?! My mother once told me, "Son, you may not understand what I'm talking about right now, but there will come a time when real men will become such a rarity in this world that when women see one coming their way, they will stand up and applaud with the joy of just seeing one." Wow! Women will stand up and applaud at the sight of a real man?! Of course, my mother was right, for I had no idea what she was talking about when she said "real men." I thought all men were real men at the time. Today, many years later, I clearly understand what she was referring to by her statement. And what is even worse is I don't think my mother could have envisioned what the men of today's world have turned out to be. But then maybe she had a vision of what the world of men would turn out to be.

Naturally, it would be totally unfair to my mother if I did not examine the meaning of a real man or what kind of man God really created when he scooped up a handful of dirt and molded it into a human being. I can even take it further by saying, "What kind of man did God expect him to become when he breathed into his nostrils and man became a living soul?"

When God created the first man, he called him Adam because he was created from dirt. But here is the part that really gets tricky:

God created man in his own image. If that is the case, it must be a fact that when we look upon the face of man, we are actually looking into the face of God. And if I understand the Bible correctly, God is the creator of all things, which includes the universe. By that, I can clearly see how much love, care, and patience God must have had when he decided to create the earth. Not only that, but if we pay close attention to our own bodies, we will quickly realize how much thought and work had gone into the creation of man. But despite all the work, love, care, and attention that God put into the creation of the human body, how could man go so wrong soon after he was created?!

The first thought that comes to my mind is woman. It was the woman who caused man to become unglued from God's original plans for man, and man has not been able to get back on track since then. It is my belief that God wanted man to be like himself, to be perfect in every way. Otherwise, why would God have created man in his own image? Yeah, God wanted man to be like himself in every way, but God had no idea that man would become the idiot that he has become. But for some unknown reasons, Adam listened to his woman Eve who had been tricked by a subject named Satan.

Now here is where it gets even trickier in the creation of man: why did Eve listen to Satan in the first place? She must have known that God had an adversary. How is it that she did not know about the fallen angel whom God had kicked out of heaven? Did God omit telling them about Satan intentionally? Well, if she did not know that Satan was lurking around in the Garden of Eden, it must have been because God trusted them. But if God told them not eat from the tree that was in the middle of the garden, he must have told them to be aware of Satan. There is no doubt in my mind that God was aware of Satan's presence in the garden.

Naturally, I can blame Satan for what has become of the man in the beginning. But as time passed, man has had more than enough time to gain knowledge and wisdom to get himself as well as his woman back on the course that God originally set for them to travel. But instead, man has grown further and further away from the plans of God, and he has written his own ideas and game plan for living. Man today has dealt with Satan enough to know what is being offered, and he should know the end results of dealing with Satan. There is no hidden agenda about what Satan will do to and for man. The question is, of course, why does man cater to Satan?

Obviously, the problem lies in man's belief system; he does not believe that Satan has any effect on his lifestyle. There is a logical scenario for not believing that Satan is alive and well; if man does not believe that Satan can teach him to do evil, then he does not believe that God can save him. And that is where the problems begin with nonbelievers. But there is a bigger problem with nonbelievers; if they do not believe in a creator, how do they account for their own existence? As some creative minds have suggested, the world suddenly appeared approximately a few million years ago without one single logical explanation. There is a reason for everything that happens under the sun in the sky. Human beings may not know the reasons for their existence, but they understand that every living soul must one day depart from the earth and resume his or her position in the ground. How do they explain that?!

So what happens to the real men, the ones whom God created to be leaders of their families and to become the dominant figures on the earth? The answers are probably too many to count, but I can safely say that man has fallen from God's grace the same way the rebellious angels fell from heaven when God kicked them out. The question is, however, how did man fall so hard from God's grace, and why did he fall? Outside of the influence of Satan, he began thinking for himself as the Evil One suggested would happen when Adam and Eve ate the fruit.

The problem that I see with the creation of man is that if God had wanted him to be perfect, as the "image of God" would have suggested, why did he give man the ability to think for himself? Thinking for oneself did not necessarily mean that God wanted man to think outside of the box, which he ultimately began to do. Okay, if God did not want man to think outside of the box, what did God want him to do?! God wanted man to be the head of his family, which means he was to take charge of everything that was pertaining to the wellbeing of his family. That also means that man was to work and provide food, shelter, and clothing for every member of his family. Man was designed to be the rock or the shoulder for every member of the family to lean on and to cry on. Whenever the family is in need of something other than a mother's love, the man is the one whom they should be able to depend on for all things.

For many years after man was created, he knew his place in the world, which was raising his family, despite the fact that Eve tried to turn Adam into a weakling. But as time continued to pass, man became weaker and weaker by the day until he is now considered to be no more than a lapdog for every woman who looks his way. Why? It all started with sex and more sex. Throughout the writings of the Bible, man after man became weaker in the eyes of God primarily because of sex. Why sex? It is because God created the idea of having sex as the only source of reproduction that was put in place with a natural feeling that is unmatched by anything else in the world. And because of this beautiful natural feeling between men and women, man felt as if sex was a gift from God to help make the world continue.

Sex was made to be a wonderful feeling by God between men and women because this was God's way of making sure that the earth was continuously being multiplied with babies that would grow into the next generation. Plus, this was also God's way of making sure that the human race would continue as time continued to pass. This idea was put into place, pertaining to every creature that God created. But lo and behold, only man's way of thinking outside of the box caused him to take sex to a whole new level of pleasure rather than being God's way of replenishing the earth.

Sex between man and woman was the original plan of God for the two falling in love and producing a family. Today, of course, sex is everything but falling in love with one another for the purpose of raising a family. Sex is no more than a tool for men and women to get whatever monetary or material favors that they can agree upon. Women used men to get monetary favors to trade for sexual encounters. Men are doing the exact same thing with the exception that men are mostly the ones who are doing the buying of sexual favors. Oftentimes, unwanted children are the results of these sexual encounters between men and women. And then there are times when having children is preplanned by women to trap the men and gain monetary favors or child support. Either way, these sexual encounters outside of marriage were not part of God's original plan for having sex.

Therefore, if we take sex out of the equation between men and women, what do we have left? According to the Bible, sex was not put into play until after the first sin when Adam and Eve disobeyed God's command not to eat the fruit from the tree. That was when God placed a curse on the two people, which caused the woman to have labor pains during birth and the man to work hard to make a decent living for his family. And because sex became such an exciting punishment that God had placed in their lives, it also became one of the greatest sins of all time for men and women.

If we travel all the way back to the beginning of time, we will learn that sex has been the single biggest downfall for all men. When God destroyed the world the first time, it was because of all the sexual sins that were being committed by man. And despite all the thousands of years that man has existed on this planet, he has yet to learn that sex is the real root of all his evildoings. Some people, of course, believe that the love of money is the reason for all of man's evildoings. No, it is sex! Sex is the only reason why man believes that he needs money. It has been proven through man's existence that if there were no women for men to impress or to buy sex from with their money, they would not have a reason for having money.

There is little doubt in my mind that my mother was absolutely correct when she declared that real men today are few and far between. There was a time when there were certain things that real men would not stoop to. There were certain acts of sexual activities that real men held themselves to a higher standard against. More importantly, real men did not disrespect women or their children simply because women were created to be men's helpmates. Without women or children, there would be no future for anyone. Men have obviously forgotten the fact that women have one primary responsibility in the world, and that is to give birth to their children. Men, on the other hand, likewise have a single responsibility, and that is to make sure that they are the seed barrier for women to bear children. Other than those two primary responsibilities of men and women, their purpose on earth is limited or even eliminated.

When the Bible talks about the "last days" and how men will become lovers of themselves, it is not necessarily referring to men loving themselves as individuals; it is referring to men who become lovers of other men. We often like to refer to this as the "gay lifestyle" or homosexuality. But regardless of what we call it or label it, the Bible condemns it as being a sin. Needless to say, I am not here to condemn the lifestyle of gay people or judge whether they are right or wrong. Only they will have to answer to the Creator for their actions here on Earth. Judging other people is never the right thing for mankind to do, for I believe that no man on this earth is so righteous until he can stand in judgment of other people's sins.

However, what I am saying is if the sole purpose for the creation of man and woman is reproduction, which means we are to replenish the earth with children, what then is the purpose of the gay lifestyle? The short version is that there is no purpose! The long version is, however, there are all kinds of people in the world who all have the freedom to choose their own lifestyles. They have the freedom of choice that God gave to every living human being. Therefore, whatever happens in the afterlife or "Judgment Day," it is every man for himself.

Again, it is obvious that real men are no longer a part of God's equation. The vast majority of men's sexual morality began to die along with them when Jesus died on the cross for the forgiveness of every man's sin. Today, in many cases or situations, it is difficult to determine the men from the women. Women are presently in charge of households and businesses, as well as politics and churches. Men, on the other hand, have taken a back seat primarily because women are now displaying strength, courage, and discipline to their Creator. God created man to be the head of the household and the family. The man was placed in charge of the entire planet by God to be the dominant factor of all other creatures.

When I think about what the Bible has to say about the "last days" of the world, I am forced to believe that based on what the apostle Paul wrote, he was able to see far into the future. And all of what he wrote in 2 Timothy was due to the fall of real men. He wrote the following:

> *In the last days, there will be many troubles because men will become lovers of themselves, love money, brag, and be proud. They will say evil things against others and will not obey their parents or be thankful or be the kind of men that God wants. They will not*

love others, they will refuse to forgive, and they will gossip and will not control themselves.

They will be cruel; they will hate what is good. They will turn against their friends and will do foolish things without thinking. They will be conceited and will love pleasure instead of loving God and will act as if they are serving God but will not have his power. It is very wise to stay away from these people. Some of them will go into homes and gain control of silly women who are full of sin and are led by many evil desires. These women are always learning new teachings, but they are never able to understand the truth fully.

The writing above is what man has become, a shell of the man that God created in the beginning. Man has forgotten everything that he was created to be. He does not raise his children anymore; women have taken over every duty that man was created to perform. Man does not respect and love his wife as being a part of his own body, which God created from his own rib. Children are supposed to draw strength from their fathers who were created to be heads of their families and households. Fathers were supposed to be role models for their children to look up and believe in. The Bible was given to man to read and teach his children the right way to live. But man is far from being the teacher.

The Bible is the only book in the world for the man to use to teach the correct path in which his children should travel. But the man in today's world cannot teach that which he does not know. This, of course, means that his children are forced to learn whatever is out there in a world that is filled with evil.

What about the mothers in situations such as this? The woman was not necessarily created to train the children on how to become men and women; that is the father's job. Women were created to be homemakers, to make sure that the children are well nourished and have good home training. Women were created to be the extensions of men. That is why God called the woman a man's helpmate. What exactly is a woman's role at home? Her role is to provide whatever the man cannot provide at home, which is preparing meals and making sure that the children are properly dressed whenever they leave home for school or outings. Mothers and fathers are a team when it comes to raising children. The fathers have their roles to fulfill as well as the mother, and they are to work as a unit. Together, they are there to make sure their children receive the best of training that they can give for their entrance into a world that is yet to come. Whatever children fail to learn at home, they will learn in the streets.

The role of the woman has changed today simply because the man has fallen down on his job as the head of the family. Women are now working and taking the lead roles in many households only because men have relinquished their responsibilities as to what used to be known as the weaker sex: the women. Men are no longer the so-called "breadwinners" in the families; bringing home the bacon has now become the women's responsibility.

By no means was this a situation that God had planned for men. By no means did God want for his precious "man image" to become such a disappointment. By no means did God want men to simply be sperm donors for women to have their children and then do a disappearing act like a puff of smoke in a windstorm. This is totally blasphemy at best in the eyes of God. Why? It is because men were not created to be sperm donors and then walk away from their children.

What is happening to the children of men today? The children are being half-raised by their mothers without their fathers. Children are looking for their father's love anywhere they can find it, which is nowhere to be found. More than likely, the children will often turn to gangs and street crimes because there is no one at home to teach them the right way to live. As much as mothers would love to raise young boys and girls by themselves, it is virtually impossible for a mother to properly raise a son without the input of a father. Why? Because mothers do not have a clue as to what it takes to be a man or a father. This is a secret that God implanted into man during the creation period. Inevitably, man has now become so weak that he does not know why God created him and his secret of being a man.

What is the secret of man? Man was created to be a leader, a father, a husband, and a warrior. He was created to be the guidepost for all the members of his family. He is the second-string quarterback at home and the first-string quarterback outside the home. He is the protector of all family members. He stands watch over his daughters, and he makes sure that his sons know how to treat and respect all women. The fathers make the rules of the house, and they make sure that the rules are followed to the letter unless otherwise stated. The fathers are constantly working with the mothers on everything that they do because the mothers are sometimes changing the rules for the children.

There are three "key factors" to make most families work together like a smooth-running, well-oiled machine. Firstly, the mothers are the key-masters; they are the only ones who hold the keys to the family's wellbeing. Secondly, the fathers are the gatekeepers; they are the only ones who stand watch over the mother and the family to make sure that they are safe and that their basic needs are met. Thirdly, the children are the keys; they are the ones who have the ability to lock or unlock their families.

Only when all three key factors are working together will we see a beautiful family, the kind of family that God envisioned when he created Adam and Eve. But none of this will ever take place until man takes his rightful place as the head of his family. The children will continue to go astray as "runaway sheep" until the parents become the key-masters and the gatekeepers. One factor of the family cannot function properly without the other two. It takes all three to make the world go around and around; fathers, mothers, and children go together just like God had planned them to.

Chapter 13

THE B-I-B-L-E — It has been said time and time again that BIBLE means "Basic Instructions Before Leaving Earth." Obviously, we can easily say that is exactly what the Bible means to all who take the time to read the book. Or one can say it is a way of controlling the masses, especially the ones who believe that the Bible is a direct quote from God, written by men of long ago. But to believe that the Bible is the Word of God, we must first believe that God exists and that he actually spoke to the men who made claims that God did in fact give them the information that they wrote in the Bible.

The fact of the matter is that the Bible was written by many men over a period of many years. In fact, according to my Biblical dictionary, the Bible is a collection of books recognized and used by the Christian Church as an inspired record of God's revelation of himself and of his will to mankind, which is pretty much as what I have said already, that the men who wrote the Bible believed that they were given messages by God, which they were compelled to keep written records of. But then the first question that comes to my mind is, "Was it really God who talked to these men and told them what to write down as his words?" Or could it have been the right brain talking to the left brain, and could they have begun a conversation with themselves about right and wrong, which caused them to believe that they were actually talking to a "higher power" or God?

The origin of the Bible was written in Hebrew, the language that was spoken by the Israelites in Canaan. The ancient Hebrew alphabets had no written vowels, which were later invented by the Jewish Masoretic scholars around the sixth century. Although the Bible was written over a period of approximately 1,400 years from the time of Moses to the end of the first century AD, its text has come to us in a remarkable state of preservation. In other words, the writing looked real. However, it was nevertheless not the same text as that of what the original writers had written down. So the next question becomes, "What happened to the original text that was written by the men who believed that their message was indeed the Word of God?"

It is very difficult to say what happened to the original text, but my guess would be that a vast majority of the writing was done by hand on some sort of cloth designed as paper. In the beginning, there was no such thing as a printing machine to actually print the Bible, which means as time passed, the material was lost or simply faded to the point of being unreadable.

What I find so amazing about the Bible and its writers is that in the beginning, the Bible consisted of many different books written over a long period of time by a variety of writers, most of whom did not know each other. All of this means it has been an organic unity that can only be explained by assuming that all these writers were inspired by God and the Holy Spirit. But regardless of what anyone may assume about the Bible or its writers, the message of the book is very clear: it is for the "redemption of mankind." And this is why it is called the Basic Instructions Before Leaving Earth. It is the only instruction booklet available to mankind.

The one thing that we must all understand very clearly is that the Bible is a book that was written by men who believed that they were inspired by God to tell other men what they must do to make it into the kingdom of God when they die. And I am forced to believe that the men who wrote the Bible had to be inspired by someone who was much greater than they were and much more intelligent than they were. I can say that because mankind has an inborn evil inside of him that has been around since the beginning. There is no doubt in my mind that this evil nature came from someone other than God.

If the Bible is correct, it states that God is a spirit of love, not evil. And I doubt very seriously that God can be all love and all hate at the same time. What would be the point in being evil and good all wrapped up in one spirit?

Needless to say, there are many things in the Bible that are very doubtful or debatable. And these are the same viewpoints that the so-called atheists or nonbelievers try to base their arguments on. First of all, the Bible tells us that in the beginning, God said, *"Let us make human beings in our own image and likeness."* Suddenly, the first question that comes to mind is, "Who was he talking to when he said, *'Let us make human beings in our own likeness'*?" And of course, we have to assume that God was talking to his angels, who were already there.

Secondly, we learn that God made the Garden of Eden for Adam and Eve, and he planted fruit trees in the garden, but there were two trees that the two humans were forbidden to touch. They were the Tree of Knowledge and the Tree of Life. *The Lord commanded them, "You may eat the fruit from any tree in the garden except from the one which gives knowledge of good and evil, or you will die!"* Of course, the nonbelievers would pounce on this one by arguing, "Why would he put a fruit in the garden where he placed his humans and then tell them not to eat from it? That is like saying that I am going to give someone a million dollars, but I do not want them to spend it." It is an argument that can be made by humans, but if they are not God, they will never know why God does things without much explanation. Of course, this is a failure that we can easily blame on the writers of the Bible. Over the hundreds of years that many men wrote the Scriptures, there were many things left out, or they simply failed to explain why they wrote what they did. This, of course, means that we cannot necessarily point the finger at God, for he was not the one who put the pen to paper.

Before the English-speaking world could read the Bible, a man named John Wycliffe, born in Yorkshire in the year 1320, was the first to entertain the revolutionary idea to make the Bible available in English during the fourteenth century. Before then, the Bible was not available for the common people to read, whereas only monks and nuns were able to read only the Latin version of the Bible. In other words, if it had not been for people such as John Wycliffe who wanted all people to be able to read the Bible, we would still be living in the Dark Ages as far as knowing the Word of God is concerned.

Naturally, this was a period of time when America was yet to be discovered, which meant the Bible was still in the hands of the Eastern Empire, the Greek, and Western Europe. By the year 1500, most of the countries in Europe had scattered copies of the Wycliffe manuscript of the Bible in a language that had become obsolete. England was now ready for the new translation of the Bible in English from the original language. But before that happened, in the year 1494, William Tyndale was the next great figure in the history of the English-speaking world who was able to make it possible to read the Bible in English.

By now, William Tyndale was in possession of the first printing machine and produced the first copies of the New Testament. After that, he began working to bring out the Old Testament. However, that was not the end of the Bible story. Tyndale ran into many difficulties in trying to get the first copies of the Bible out to the public. His primary foe was the bishop of London, who eventually forced Tyndale to flee London with his all scraps of loose paper that he hoped one day to translate into an English Bible. Tyndale finally settled in Cologne, where he also was able to locate a printing machine. And in 1525, he finally printed three thousand copies of the first Bible in English, which included the first ever copies of the New Testament.

I am not really sure, but maybe this is why so many people find it hard to understand or believe some of the passages in the Bible. To get the Bible out to the vast majority of the English-speaking world, William Tyndale had to run for his life from the every people who should have been supporting his efforts. But no, they had a different idea of the Bible and what it would mean to the people who would eventually read it. It would be difficult to say whether Tyndale actually printed all the facts in his Bible the way these messages were interpreted by the men who actually talked to God. We will never know. And obviously, this is why there are so many gaps in the Old Testament that will leave most people asking, "Why did God do this?" or "Why did he not do that?"

A prime example of what I just said is this: there were only four human beings on the planet after Adam and Eve gave birth to Cain and Abel. And for unknown reasons, Cain killed his brother Abel because he assumed that God favored Abel over him. Later, the Lord showed up and asked Cain, *"Where is your brother Abel?"* And Cain, being a smartass, said to God, *"I don't know where my brother is. Am I supposed to be my brother's keeper, or is it my job to take care of my brother?!"* This, of course, showed how much God loved his humans. If it had been me, I would have slapped fire from Cain's crazy ass. But it does not stop there; it gets even weirder. Then God went on to say to Cain, *"What have you done? Your brother's blood is crying out from ground. And now you will be cursed in your work with the ground where your brother's blood fell and where your hands killed him. You will work the ground, but it will not grow good crops for you anymore, and you will wander around the earth."*

Then Cain had the audacity to say to God, *"This punishment is more than I can stand! Today, you have forced me to stop working the ground, and now I must hide from you. I must also wander around the earth, and anyone who meets me can kill me."* Okay, who is anyone? There were only four people on Earth, and one was dead, so who was it that Cain was afraid was going to kill him? This is one clear example of how William Tyndale did not have a clear understanding of what he was writing in the Bible. It does not matter how we try to explain the other people Cain were referring to because in the beginning the Bible, it does not mention any other people who had been created other than Adam and Eve. So does this mean that Tyndale fabricated this part of the story, or was he simply unable to identify the other people whom God had created?

Nevertheless, this story gets even better. So the Lord said to Cain, *"No! If anyone kills you, I will punish that person seven times more."* Then the Lord put a mark on Cain, warning anyone who meets him not to kill him. Again, there was no indication that God had suddenly created a bunch of other people at that time except Adam and Eve who gave birth to Cain and Abel. So why did God have to put a mark on Cain to keep other people from killing him?

That is still not the end of the story. So Cain went away from the Lord and lived in the land of Nod, which was just east of Eden. There, he had sexual relationship with his wife, and she became pregnant and gave birth to Enoch. When I first read this story in the Bible, I searched out several ministers and asked each one of them, "If God created Adam and Eve, and they only had two children, Cain and Abel, that would have made only four people on Earth at the time.

Now tell me, who was it that Cain got married to and had a child with?" Not one of these so-called preachers could tell me who the woman was without admitting that it had to have been his sister. But the Bible does not mention Adam and Eve having a daughter who could have been the mother of Cain's child. And the question now becomes, "Why?"

It is obvious that the writers of the Bible omitted the fact that Cain and Abel were fighting over their sister and not because God favored Abel over Cain. So why were they deliberately trying to hide that fact of the Bible if we are to believe that it contain the Word of God? Common sense should automatically spell out to us that the only way that Adam and Eve could multiply or fill the earth with other people was that there had to be many acts of incest. It was impossible for the earth to grow in population without brothers and sisters having sex.

Obviously, God knew that there was no way around incest if man and woman were to obey his commands. But why did the writers of the Bible intentionally omit these facts of the story? Did they not think that the readers were not going to notice that many parts of the story were missing or the things that were written just didn't add up? They did in fact make those assumptions simply because most Bible readers will ignore these facts out of fear that they will disrespect God by asking questions.

However, let us assume for a moment that God gave all of us a body without a brain; we can walk, talk, and make babies, but we cannot think for ourselves. Of course, as unlikely as that may or may not sound, there are many in the world today who are walking around on this planet, talking, and having babies but are totally mindless. For many of these same people, the Bible became their living God, which is no more than a pillar to lean on when times are bad. And due to that same reason of having something to lean on, other people who called themselves men and women of God discovered a gold mine in the ignorant and the mindless.

This is by no means a fault of God; it is, however, a fault of man who, in many ways, did not print the exact words of God because over a period of time, he misplaced his own notes of what God actually said, or he simply forgot the message that God gave him. And yes, the Bible is a basic rule for man to live by until he departs the earth. The

Bible was not and is still not God himself who has the living power to save souls. Man must save his own soul by living his life according to the basic principles of the Bible. As I have often said on many levels, if man can live his life according to the Ten Commandments, the rest of the Bible is meaningless. Ninety-nine percent of the Bible is based on Biblical history or historical facts of men and women who lived before us and who believed in the power of God.

The good news concerning the Bible is if we take away all the sixty-six books of the Bible and leave just the Ten Commandments, man could still live a righteous life with God. When we read the Bible, we are reading about the lives of Adam and Eve, Abraham, Isaac, Jacob, and Moses, as well as Jesus in the New Testament. And we will soon realize that all these men were talked about in stories of their lives. But if we look closely, they all were in agreement with the Ten Commandments that God gave to Moses in the Old Testament. Therefore, if we go back to the simple fact that the Bible is no more than "basic instructions" that we should follow "before leaving Earth," we will probably be in good shape as far as God taking a liking to us is concerned.

When it comes to God giving mankind instructions as to what he wanted to be written down in the Bible for the rest of us to live our lives by, why is it that God doesn't find it necessary to have men of this modern world following the suit of their ancestors? Does the Bible cover all that needs to be said in today's world and that was recorded thousands of years ago? Why is it that man has not tried to add scriptures to what has already been said in the Bible from these modern times? Could it be that God has not found anyone who is qualified enough to add his or her name to what have already been written in the Bible? Of course, these are questions that may or may not need answering due to the fact that the Bible covers everything that man can possibly get involved in.

But then on the other hand, man has misused the Bible for his own monetary gains so much, it would not make sense to add to the one book that has the power to destroy souls or to deliver souls to God. The Bible has also been the primary source of evildoers in and out of the church. The one primary example is the Catholic Church, which, in my mind, is the worst religious organization in the entire world. There are evildoers across the board in the Catholic Church, from sex abusers of young boys to murderers of women many years ago, claiming that they were witches. To me, the Catholic Church is a statement of power, which means some of the most powerful people in the world belong to the Catholic Church. The Catholic Church has been a staple of power since the days of the Roman Empire. Today, when the Pope speaks, everybody listens. When the Pope walks, it is as if God is walking and talking to the people personally. But does the Pope have any more power or connection to God than anyone else? I think not!

What makes people like the Pope so special? Is it because he has God's ear or because he can get God's attention when no one else can? I am sure that God has handpicked people to do what he cannot do, and the Bible talks about these people from the Old Testament to the New Testament. And there is no difference in how God communicates with people today. However, except for Moses who may have laid eyes on God when he accepted the Ten Commandments, no other man or human being has ever seen the face of God and lived to tell anyone about it. In other words, whoever says that they have seen God is either lying or insane. God does not reveal himself to any living persons regardless of how godly he or she might be, including the Pope.

So what does the fact we cannot see God say about human beings? It says that the only proof that we have that God exists is by the words printed in the Bible. If the Bible did not tell us that we were men and women, we would not have a clue as to who we are. The only source of information we have to prove that we exist is in the Bible. There is no scientific proof that the world we live in exists except from what we read in the Bible. Man has spent thousands of years trying to prove that the Bible is wrong as far as creation is concerned, but he has failed on every attempt. There is no proof or explanation as to how the world or the universe became what it is today except by the way of a creator, whom we now call God. But if it was not for the Bible telling us these things, we would have no other way of knowing.

Many years ago, in the 1800s, Charles Darwin tried desperately to prove that man evolved from an ape into what he looks like today. However, his theory sounded good to a good many people because if he could somehow prove his theory, that would automatically eliminate the possibility of God's creation. But there was one small problem with Darwin's theory: he could not find the origin of the ape. In other words, if man evolved from the likes of an ape, who created the ape? As I have often said many times, Darwin's theory is the same as explaining which came first, the chicken or the egg. For there to be a chicken, there has to be an egg. But for there to be an egg, a chicken has to lay the egg, which means to solve this riddle, one must know what or where the egg came from. Therefore, scientists or any other group of smart human beings has yet to solve the chicken and the egg riddle.

The Bible is the only written document that gives mankind half of a chance of knowing who we are and how we have come to be what we are. Without the Bible, we would be like a bunch of chickens running around the earth with our heads cut off, not knowing our asses from holes in the ground. Of course, even with a Bible in every hand, there are still many people today who fit the description of not knowing their asses from holes in the ground.

Without a doubt, the Bible is the only book in the entire universe that gives mankind a chance to be civilized or act like human beings. Otherwise, we would all just be cave dwellers or simple savages. And if we pay close attention to the world of today, when people stop reading the Bible in their homes or disallow the Bible from being a part of the public educational system, our children will slowly revert back to the days of cave dwellers and plain old savages.

The Bible is a tool that is very much needed in every home, school, jail cell and government office. The Bible is the only instructional booklet that will help maintain order in an uncivilized society. God knew exactly what the world needed a million years ago. And today, it is time for mankind to get to know what God already knew, or we will destroy ourselves. But evidence of the human race turning back the hands of time is clear today.

In spite of me knowing why some people find it difficult to read, understand, or even believe what the Bible is telling them, it is nevertheless the only book that can save mankind. This much, I know, and no one living or dead can dispute what the Bible is saying. Sure, there are some Scriptures that seem far-fetched or too good to be true, but there is not one word in the Bible that anyone can prove is a lie. We all may disagree with some of the things written, but they are not lies. The fact of the matter is we can either believe what the

Bible says and live our lives accordingly and maybe have a shot at seeing what heaven is like or take our chances on Judgment Day and go straight to hell. In other words, the choice is strictly ours to make. To read the Bible or not to read the Bible: that is the question!

The Bible clearly states that going to hell is an option! We do not have to end up in some deep, bottomless, fire-filled pit with a bunch of demon assholes. We can end up walking around heaven all day on streets of gold and glass. Now whether these things are true or false, we as living human beings will never know until we die. But what if they are true?! Are we so big, bad, and educated enough to say, "To hell with the Bible. I'll take my chances by ignoring what the Bible says, and I'll do my own thing"?! Okay, you do just that, and we will see who ends up in hell. But then some people may like the idea of going to hell. It makes them seem bigger than life and bad as hell. After all, God gave every man, woman, and child the right to choose his or her own place to spend eternity. Therefore, what comes after death is strictly ours to decide.

Chapter 14

ATLANTA: THE GAY CAPITAL OF AMERICA — Having lived and worked in the city of Atlanta most of my adult life, I can honestly say without an "I beg your pardon" that the city of Atlanta is the "Gay Capital of America." Why Atlanta?! I remember when gay people were "sitting on the dock of the Bay" in California, which was the number one city for them to live in. Not anymore! Atlanta has gained that number one spot. And again, I ask, "Why Atlanta?!" The idea of Atlanta becoming a gay city started way back when Maynard H. Jackson was the mayor of Atlanta, and every mayor after Maynard Jackson has personally welcomed every gay person in America to come to Atlanta for what started out as the Gay Pride Weekend.

Every other city in America has been slow to embrace the gay society, much less having a bunch of homosexuals marching down the middle of the city on floats, trucks, motorcycles, and cars, doing their thing to attract as much attention as possible to their gay lifestyle. But the question remains, "Why did Maynard Jackson, the city's first black mayor, so eagerly welcome gay people from all over the country to Atlanta?" It was not known whether Maynard was homosexual himself or not, but he did, however, start a movement that everyone who lived in Atlanta knew about. And most people who lived in Atlanta could not swear whether Maynard was gay or straight.

However, this chapter is not about Atlanta being the gay capital of America but more about the people who encourage the city leaders to make Atlanta the city of gay pride. So one might ask, "What is the big deal about being gay in the gayest city in America?" Well, the big deal became a bigger deal when there was a murder attached to some of the high-profile members of the gay community.

Being the cop that I was, I had a very nasty habit of trying to get to know everything about everybody who ever lived and died in Atlanta. And more importantly, I got to know who was doing what, and who these people were was at the top of my list of knowing things. "Sex in the City" should have been the main title of Atlanta instead of "The City Too Busy to Hate." Atlanta's cops and politicians were more like animals in heat. There were many cops and politicians whom I knew had sex on their brain all the time, on or off duty. As I said before, the first warning that I received when I joined the force was, "There are three things that will get you fired from the police department, and I call them the three Bs. They are booze, bribes, and broads." In other words, cops in Atlanta have always had a bad reputation for taking bribes, drinking a lot of booze, and screwing around with a whole lot of women on duty.

But let me get back to the story of a particular secret society of gay men and women. Jackson was the first black mayor elected in Atlanta in 1973, which made him the first African American to be elected mayor of any major Southern city. In spite of being the brilliant politician that he was, he also knew of a deep, dark secret that only a few people knew about. He had firsthand knowledge of many people within his administration who were gay. In fact, there were two separate elaborate, secret sex organizations within the city government where the men and women were engaging in their own separate sex parties. But as most situations where men and women are violating the laws of God, some things are almost automatically going to get out of hand and go awfully wrong. And that is exactly what happened in my next case.

One early evening in the mid-seventies, the wife of a well-known politician and a second woman who was a teacher in the public school system got into a heated argument over a third woman whom they both were sexually involved with. The murder occurred on the south side of the city at a well-known attorney's home who worked for the state. The victim was the wife of this well-known attorney. The Atlanta police was called to the attorney's home to investigate the brutal murder where the third woman had been stabbed fifty-six times and castrated. A close friend of mine was the lead investigator who was trying to solve the unthinkable crime and later voluntarily gave me the scoop on the case. In a private conversation with me, he described how he intentionally arrested the wrong man for a murder that he did not commit.

"Why would you do a thing like that?" I asked, knowing that there were political ramifications behind his actions, which came directly from the mayor at that time.

"I didn't have any choice after I realized my investigation was pointing its finger at the politician's wife and another woman who was only known as Mrs. B. They were both at the home of victim on the evening of the murder. There was a really big fight among all three women. The politician's wife apparently left the scene and returned later, only to find the body of the woman who had been brutally murdered," he explained as I listened very carefully.

"So there was no doubt in your mind that this Mrs. B killed the third woman? However, the politician's wife knew who the killer was because all three women were involved in a three-way lesbian brawl earlier, right?" I asked, but I already knew what his answer was going to be.

"Yes! But before I could go any further with the investigation, the politician showed up on the scene and began to inquire about what had happened. Based upon my initial finding, I did not mention that his wife was a suspect or a primary witness to what had happened. At the crime scene, there were two different blood types near the body that led outside the house. This could only mean one thing. The perpetrator was wounded as well."

"So what did the politician say, or what was his excuse for being there?" I asked.

"Well, he said that he knew the victim and her husband well. They were very good friends. And he was concerned and wanted to see if there was anything that he could do."

"So who was the husband?" I asked.

"The husband was a big-time attorney, and he was on the governor's short list for being the next state court judge."

"So you assumed that this was going to be a case that you had to get right because there were a lot of people watching you to make sure that you didn't point the finger at the wrong person or, in this case, the right person, who was the politician's wife?"

"Now you're getting the picture!" he said with a quick smile. "Not only did I assume, but I also knew exactly what was on his mind. But there was nothing that I could do until I knew whose blood was on the scene besides the victim's," the detective explained.

"Were you thinking that the blood could have been that of the politician's wife?" I asked curiously. "Or did you know for certain that it was not hers?"

"At that time, I had no idea whose blood it was, but I was hoping that it was not hers because I knew if the wife was my prime suspect, I was going to have to deal with the politician first. And that was going to mean that I was going to have to do some serious covering up."

"Why would you cover up anything if the wife was guilty of murder?" I asked in a very serious tone of voice. "After all, murder is a crime where you can't just wash away the evidence if it's pointing toward a particular person."

"And you're correct, up to a certain point. But you never had to deal with a case such as this one, especially when the wife of the most powerful politician in the city was involved. Not to mention that he was a close friend of my boss, the mayor," the detective responded to me, just as serious. "However, as it turned out, the politician's wife was not my prime suspect based on the blood found at the scene. The crime lab reported the blood at the scene was that of the woman we called Mrs. B."

Now things were beginning to make sense as far as who murdered the attorney's wife was concerned. "So I am guessing you went to Mrs. B's house to arrest her for murder?" I asked.

"Yes, but that was just the beginning of how things would later turn out," he responded with a strange look. "On my arrival to Mrs. B's house with an arrest warrant for murder, she immediately called the politician and ordered him to come to the jail for a private meeting."

"Really now?!" I snapped surprisingly. "What was that all about? But let me guess, she wanted to tell the politician that his wife was involved with the attorney's wife as well, right?!"

"That's what she had in mind, but that was not all she wanted to say. She wanted to say a few other things before being charged with murder. When the politician arrived, I could tell by the look on her face and the anger in her voice that this was going to be a heated conversation."

"And when he arrived, what happened? Did she slap his face?" I asked with a grin.

"At first, she didn't want me to hear what she had to say, but she quickly changed her mind. She wanted me to be a witness to what she had to say to the politician. So I stood back on the wall while she and the politician sat down face to face and she began to tell him, '*If I go to prison for this murder, you, your wife, the attorney, the mayor, the police commissioner, and all the rest of your homosexual friends are going to be exposed to the world.*' Suddenly, my eyes bucked, and I moved in a little closer to hear clearly what else she had to say."

Suddenly, the detective had really gotten my attention. "What did she mean by 'all his homosexual friends'?!" I asked.

"Okay, she went on to say to the politician, '*You think we didn't know about you and your gay weekly parties that you and about seven or eight other men were having at the hotel?! In fact, I have pictures of you and others coming out of the hotel on several different occasions. I'm warning you! You better find a way to make this murder charge go away. Or I will ruin you and all the rest of your friends in your little gay parade.*' That's when I knew she had him by the balls, and she was squeezing them tighter and tighter by the second."

"Wow! And she also put you on the spot because you knew that the politician was about to turn to you for answers," I said, knowing that she wanted the detective as her witness. This was her way of making the murder charge disappear. "But how is it that you can change the outcome of the blood found on the scene to implicate someone else?" I asked. "And by the way, did she injure herself during the commotion of the crime?"

"When I arrived at her home with the murder warrant, there was no doubt that she committed the murder because she had cut her own hand while slicing and dicing the other woman. Anyway, when the politician and I talked privately away from her, he said, '*I don't care how you do it or who you get to blame for this murder. I cannot allow this woman to go public with all that she knows about me and a lot of other powerful people in this city. If she has pictures of us as she says she does, it will expose a lot of important people.*' I was stunned by his willingness to become a part of this crime by telling me to cover it up."

I laughed at what he said because I could almost guess what was coming next. "But cover it up is what you did, right?" I asked. "So how did you manage to do that?"

"Well, the first thing I did was find the perfect suspect, one who could not talk his way out of being a suspect. I needed someone that I could frame as having the same blood type that would match the blood at the crime scene."

"Wait, wait!" I cut him off. "Where was the attorney during all of this? I am sure he had something to say about what had happened with his wife's killer, right?"

"Oh yeah, he was around, all right! Remember when Mrs. B mentioned the attorney as being one of the men at the hotel during those gay parties? Okay, he was also one of the politicians who would have been ruined by what this woman knew."

"How was he involved other than being gay?" I asked.

"Like I said, he was slated to be named the next state court judge by the governor. If his name had suddenly appeared on the front page of the local newspaper as being gay, as well as his murdered wife, his chances of being chosen would drop to zero."

"Now let me get this straight," I stopped him again. "Okay, on one side of the room, you have a bunch of lesbians who are the wives of a bunch of men who are gay as well. Now within each little group, they all are doing each other sexually. The one exception is this Mrs. B who knew that one day, she might end up in a situation where she would have to use her leverage to expose all these well-to-do businessmen and politicians. Therefore, she gathered up enough evidence that would bring down the mayor as well as a lot of other people. And now she was using this evidence to get out of a murder that she committed. Am I right?"

"That's pretty much what happened," the detective said with a serious expression.

"But that's not the end of the story, is it, Detective?!" I asked him point-blank.

"No, it's not!" he said, still with a serious expression. "For the next several weeks, we searched high and low for the perfect suspect, one whom I could easily pin the crime on and someone I could convince the DA and a grand jury about. Finally, I found my suspect! He was a demented young man who had been in and out of jail, and he lived just three houses down from the victim. Not only that, but he had the same blood type as that which was found at the crime scene."

"Wow! Now that was a lucky break!" I said, thinking that this was a stroke of genius. "Were you able to convince a grand jury that you had arrested the right man for the murder?"

"They were totally convinced that we had the right man who committed the murder," he said with a slight smile. "In fact, they were almost convinced just by the insanity plea."

"Okay, listen to this . . ." I said. "I realize that you were only trying to save the reputation of the politician and his wife, as well as many other high-profile men and women in this city, not to mention your own job. But now that you look back, knowing that an insane, innocent man is sitting in jail for a murder that he didn't commit, do you feel that you are just as guilty as the woman who actually murdered the victim?"

"Why do you think I am telling you all of this?!" he snapped. "I know that one day, you're going to sit down and write about all of the mess and the corruption that has gone on for many years in this city. And yes, I am guilty for staging a fake murder scene for a jury in a court of law. But sometimes, there are situations, regardless of how wrong they are, when we just can't always do the right thing simply because it is the right thing to do. Consequences come as a result!"

"Okay, I clearly understand consequences, although I may disagree with you. So what happened as a result of what you did for the politician?" I was sure there was a high reward given.

"Well, the attorney went on to be named the state court judge. The politician was elected to a third term. He was even successful in helping bring the 1996 Olympic Games to the city, something that no one had ever dreamed would take place in this city. As for me, well, I went on to be promoted, as well as winning a pending lawsuit for a hundred thousand dollars. In other words, everybody who was connected to that case came out of it looking better than before, including Mrs. B. She went back to her job of teaching at school. And of course, the politician and his wife ended their marriage in a divorce, which I knew would probably happen anyway."

I laughed softly, thinking that the mentally challenged young man had gotten a serious raw deal just because he was not mentally capable to defend himself. I did not have to ask if he was represented by a court-appointed attorney because I was sure that he was, which was not in his best interest. But I wanted to know the outcome of the trial. "What happened to the young man? Did the judge sentence him to a mental institution, or did he end up in prison?"

"He was sentenced to a mental institution, which means he will probably be in there for the rest of his life," the detective answered. "And the reason I say that is because he was born into the world mentally challenged. But he was not violent, and his family saw no reason to have him committed to a mental institution. That is, until the murder occurred."

"Which you have willingly admitted he did not commit," I said sharply.

"Yes, and I'll probably go to hell for what I did," he said as he ended the interview.

As I began to wrap up my interview, it became very obvious to me that Atlanta had become a gay city primarily because of the late mayor Maynard Jackson, who had rolled out the red carpet to all gay people across America. And they came running to the city like flies to honey. Today, Atlanta is a great city to a lot of people. But for them to take advantage of the many opportunities that Atlanta has to offer, they must know how to make the right connections with the movers and shakers, who are more than likely in the gay community. In the following chapter, I will give you a brief summary of what makes Atlanta tick like a clock. It is an intriguing eye-opening experience that very few people other than myself has little knowledge of and that makes the city what it is today.

Chapter 15

A LITTLE KNOWN TRUTH ABOUT ATLANTA: Today, the city of Atlanta is the most progressive city in America. Once upon a time, Atlanta was known as "The City Too Busy to Hate." It was a title given to the city simply because while many other cities across America in the 1960s were going through rough times with race riots, demonstrations, and the destruction of businesses in black neighborhoods, Atlanta was steadily moving forward peacefully. This was not to say that Atlanta did not have its share of problems as is in a racially divided America, but the city found other ways to solve its racial problems.

The story of Atlanta is almost as old as America itself. In December 1843, the town was incorporated as Marthasville, a name chosen in honor of the sixteen-year-old daughter of then governor Wilson Lumpkin and Martha Lumpkin. But in 1845, the town folks decided that Marthasville was not a suitable name for a booming town with obvious possibilities in the future. They wanted a name that had the right poetic sound, and in early 1846, Atlanta became the name that we all know today.

In 1864, during the Civil War that brought General William T. Sherman and his Union army to Atlanta, they were in pursuit of General Robert E. Lee and his army of Confederate soldiers. In the midst of the war, one of the biggest battles occurred in the middle of downtown Atlanta, where General Sherman decided to commit large-scale arson in the autumn of that year. Sherman ordered his troops to burn every building to the ground with the exception of churches. It is my guess that he may have been a religious man who believed that God would have punished him for burning down the houses of worship.

The following year in 1865, the Civil War came to an end when General Lee and his troops were surrounded at Appomattox. And of course, the people of Atlanta wasted little time in getting started with what was known as the Reconstruction Period. The Union soldiers stood watch over the city, making sure that the lovers of the Old South did not raise their ugly heads again. By 1868, General George G. Meade and his troops withdrew from the city, and the period of direct military rule in Atlanta came to an end. Needless to say, as Atlanta continued to grow in size as reconstruction was at full speed, the population of the city grew as well. The resurgence of Atlanta brought about many construction jobs for all those who wanted to work.

In spite of all the great success that Atlanta was having, it was not without its racial problems. In 1906, Atlanta suffered from what was known as the first "race riot." The riot occurred due to the fact that black people were arrested 56 percent more than any other race in the city. Blacks in Atlanta felt that the police were targeting them more than anyone else, and they wanted it to stop. The police figured that regardless of any crime that was committed in the city, nine out of ten times, someone black was the guilty party. The race riot was due to the treatment that had been brought on by the Atlanta Police Department a few years earlier.

It all began in 1902 in a predominately black suburb of Atlanta known as Pittsburgh. Pittsburgh was not as heavily populated compared to other black communities in the city. Pittsburgh was comprised of rickety houses, barns, chicken coops, pig pens, and other rural-type buildings. This incident went down in Atlanta's history as the Pittsburgh Riot. It began with one angry young black man named Will Richardson who was sick and tired of Atlanta's cops racially brutalizing black men in the area. Richardson, of course, had been sentenced to a few years on the chain gang by one of Atlanta's white cops, and he was out to get revenge. Samuel A. Kerlin, a former Atlanta police who was now a county officer, was responsible for Richardson going to prison. He was out for a stroll one evening near the Pittsburgh neighborhood. He was suddenly approached by Richardson and four of his companions or friends.

Kerlin knew Richardson on sight, and when he saw him and the other men approaching, he immediately suspected that this was not going to be friendly chitchat. Kerlin turned and began running, with Richardson and his four companions following close behind. Not far down the street, the men caught up with Kerlin, and they began to beat him by punching him. One of the men suddenly lunged at Kerlin with a knife as Richardson fired several shots, intentionally missing him each time.

Eventually, a pair of soldiers along with two other county police officers who were passing by came to Kerlin's rescue and chased off the suspects, who then ran back into the Pittsburgh neighborhood to a general store on the corner of Amy Street and McDaniel Street. There in the store, Will Richardson took refuge to put up a fight unlike any battle that the Atlanta police had ever seen before. The question was, "Had Will Richardson preplanned this attack to draw the Atlanta police out into an ambush?" No one knew exactly what was going on at the time except they had one angry black man on the loose in a neighborhood that cops had problems with before. The county cops gave chase to where Richardson and his companions were held up.

At that particular point and time, the county police were unsure if all the men were armed inside or not, therefore they approached the building very carefully. Obviously, they would have been better advised if they had not approached the store at all. From a carefully concealed position inside the store, Will Richardson watched the two county cops as they approached the building. And with a high-powered rifle with a scope attachment, he aimed and fired once. The bullet tore through the first county officer's neck, killing him instantly. When the second county officer realized what he was up against, he turned and ran to a safe place for cover.

That one shot that killed his partner convinced the county officer to call for help before he made any such attempt again to get the shooter out of the store. It took a few hours for the Atlanta police to arrive and surround the building to prevent any attempt to escape by Will Richardson or his friends. Little did they know, however, Will Richardson had no intention of trying to escape. He was doing just as he had planned, waiting for an opportunity to fire again.

Before the city police arrived on the scene, Police Chief Ball had ignored the call for help by the county officer since Pittsburgh at that time was just outside the city limits. And as far as Chief Ball was concerned, the situation did not seem serious enough to involve the Atlanta police. So what if they had a dead officer?! By the predawn hours, a large group of white bystanders had gathered in the vicinity of the shooting, and it appeared that things might get out of hand or that an innocent bystander might get killed as well. Therefore, by early dawn, Chief Ball had dispatched a squad of men to the scene to join their counterparts from the county. Just as dawn arrived, Will Richardson, with his high-powered rifle, spoke once again as Officer Hugh Osburn, who was cautiously peering out toward the store from behind cover, fell dead with a bullet to the head. Tension now began grow as the second officer had been shot dead by Will Richardson, and the second death sent the entire detachment of officers present into a frenzy. Suddenly, they all opened fire on the store, which totally destroyed the outer structure of the building, but it had little effect on Will Richardson.

Apparently, the barrage of gunfire from the police was enough for Henry King, one of Richardson's companions, to decide that he had had enough. He opened the door of the store and ran out, surrendering himself to the police. Naturally, he was questioned extensively about the man named Will Richardson. Of course, he told the cops that Richardson had forced him and the others to enter the store against their will and that he informed them that Richardson was both a very desperate man as well as an excellent shooter. "He plans to kill as many of you cops as he possibly can before y'all get him!" Henry told the police.

Based upon the information that Henry King had given to the police, it was apparent that Will Richardson was armed with a high-powered rifle and that he was a sharpshooter. This, of course, meant that he could hit anything that he aimed for. At that moment, the police knew that it would be suicide to try and rush the building, and that was when someone in the group suggested burning him out by setting fire to the store. But who would be brave enough to get close enough to set the fire? They all looked at Henry King as being the one to set the fire. "So what if he kills that nigger? He won't be a great loss to us," someone in the police group said.

Henry King was finally convinced to set fire to the store after being told that he would be killed anyway if he did not. Henry King set the store on fire while the police fired at the building to keep Richardson's head down and to keep him from firing on them. King did, however, manage to set the fire, but Richardson was able to fire his weapon once again and killing another police officer as well as his old friend, Henry King.

Soon after the store was set on fire, the entire block of houses caught fire as well in Pittsburgh. The burning houses quickly brought out a large crowd of black and white people on both sides of Georgia Avenue and McDaniel Street. When most of the fires went out, especially the one in the store where Richardson had been held up was put out by the fire department, the police began to search the building for bodies, but nowhere did they find Will Richardson.

On the southeast section of Atlanta, race riots and violent crimes continued through the years, making Atlanta the "Murder Capital" of America. Killing cops on the Atlanta streets became about as routine as killing deer in the forest. The only men who were willing to join the Atlanta Police Department were members of the Ku Klux Klan. To them, becoming a cop in Atlanta gave them a legal right to go "nigger hunting" or "nigger chasing." And that is exactly what they did for many years afterward.

After the end of World War II, things began to change for the better for the black communities in Atlanta when several high-profile black ministers and educators came together to try and rid the city of the terrible image that it had gained over the years. However, before the end of the war, 50 percent of all Atlanta and Fulton County police officers were involved in "profit-sharing" with bootleggers. And the only thing that brought a little respectability to the Atlanta Police Department was the hiring of eight black police officers in 1948.

Naturally, this was not an act that would go over well with the mostly KKK department. But it was the only thing that Police Chief Herbert Jenkins could do to bring any kind of order to the still-raging chaos on the southeast side of the city. After many years, including the incident when Will Richardson killed several white police officers, the Pittsburg community was still a powder keg that would explode every time a white cop showed his face in the area.

The high-powered ministers, educators, and businessmen urged Mayor Hartsfield to hire black police officers if he wanted Atlanta to emerge as the next great city of the South. The mayor heeded their advice and hired the best eight black men whom he could find in Atlanta. But there were stipulations to the hiring, of course. All eight men had to be college-educated or have at least two years of college or military backgrounds. Naturally, this was a stipulation that was not required for their white counterparts, for many white officers did not even have high school diplomas. But if that was what it was going to take get black officers on the force, so be it!

From that point in time for blacks in Atlanta, things began to change dramatically. Black power began to raise its head in a place where blacks began to discriminate against each other. Powerful black people began to do powerful things in Atlanta to make the city one of the most dynamic cities in America for black people. It all began to unfold noticeably in the early 1960s when historically black colleges such Spelman College decided to educate black women. If black applicants were a darker skin pigmentation, they were the least likely to be accepted into that school. This was accomplished by having any female who wanted to attend Spelman College send in a black-and-white photo to accompany the application.

Along with Spelman College, Atlanta quickly became a dark-skin-versus-light-skin city among African Americans, whereas light-skinned blacks lived on the west side or the "West Hunter Street Community." The West Hunter Street Community included all the historically black colleges, such as Morehouse College, Spelman College, Clarke College, and Morris Brown College, all of which were privately funded by rich, powerful white people and well-to-do blacks who made their homes on the west side of Atlanta.

The power-players of Atlanta lived on the west side, and the mostly poor blacks lived on the south side, in places such as Pittsburgh, Summerhill, and Mechanicville, which were all considered as the poorer side of town. Hunter Street was the main thoroughfare that ran from downtown Atlanta westward, connecting with Gordon Road that ended in Fulton County. On the west side of town was the location known for all the civil rights movements and demonstrations, including that of Martin Luther King Jr., who was born on the east side of the city. All of this meant that for anyone who wanted to become a major player in the city of Atlanta, Hunter Street was the place to find power brokers and players.

Atlanta is the only major black city in America when it comes to being a part of a certain clique or special group of Negroes. If anyone comes to Atlanta and does not know someone who is a part of a so-called establishment clique, he or she will find it very difficult to fit into a smooth groove that is worth their efforts as far as rubbing elbows with who's who is concerned. Again, Atlanta is a racially divided city among black people themselves—the rich blacks versus the poor blacks.

During the 1980s and the 1990s, when Atlanta was widely known as "Chocolate City" or the "Black Mecca," many African Americans flocked to Atlanta, believing that there was "Black Gold" in these here streets. But they soon found themselves standing on the outside looking in, trying to figure out how to get on the inside with the "movers and shakers" of Atlanta. There have been many outsiders who have come to Atlanta to make it big and did not know whose shoulders they had to rub to make it. It was a must-know whose asses they must kiss or who they must sleep with to make it in Atlanta. Otherwise, they would become as so many have already become, just another black face in Atlanta with no idea how they were going to make it. Until recent years, Atlanta has been known as "The Black Man's Paradise." But as of today, not so much! It is now known as "The Gay People's Paradise."

Speaking more on the racially divided blacks in Atlanta, the history of the city has clearly shown or indicated that dark-skinned blacks do not fare well in this city. Until recent years, all the African American mayors of Atlanta have been light-skinned. There has been only one who was dark-skinned. I remember it was a darker-skinned man who ran for mayor against Maynard Jackson, and the voters, in no uncertain terms, let him know that in spite of all his qualification, the city was not ready for a dark-skinned mayor. Today, the mayor just happens to be dark-skinned. However, he would not be mayor under the old light-skinned-versus-dark-skinned rules. The city today is ruled by the Gay Rights Commission, and they supported this dark-skinned mayor simply because he caters to their wishes and demands.

To further illustrate how Atlanta became this dynamic city that it is today, once upon a time, in a downtown location, there was the first known black mega-church: the First Congregational Church located on the corner of Courtland and Houston Streets. The members neither allowed dark-skinned people to attend their services nor did they allow any members of their congregation to marry into a dark-skinned family. The church is the second-oldest African American congressional church in the United States that was often visited by some of Atlanta's elite blacks, such as Alonzo Herndon and Andrew Young, just to name a few. Anyone else who was on the dark side of skin color was not welcomed at the First Congregational Church.

Again, I would gladly argue that this was the exact same attitude and treatment that black people received from the white race. So why would a lighter-skinned African American treat the darker-skinned African American the same way? It was done that way because lighter-skinned black people believed within their own minds that they were better than darker-skinned black people. Atlanta led the nation into this kind of attitude among black people. Why Atlanta? No one really knows the answer except that Atlanta was the first city in the South where blacks began to emerge out of the darkness and into the light as far as obtaining wealth was concerned. And the wealthiest African Americans in the South were living in Atlanta.

Today, many of those same elite light-skinned African Americans have either died out or have gotten too old to matter anymore. The old heads dying out is what brought about a change in the First Congregational Church that led to the younger generation to marry into the darker side of black Americans. In fact, the old church is nowhere near living up to the standard that it once held. Maybe it is the same reason why there was a generational shift among the families and members of the church.

The church was not the only organization that discriminated against the darker black people in Atlanta. In 1921, Citizens Trust Bank was first opened in downtown Atlanta on Auburn Avenue by a wealthy black man who looked white named Heman Perry. And for many years, bank tellers were hired based on the color of their skin and their beauty. Not one of Citizens Trust Bank's branches, as they grew into several around the city, would hire a dark-skinned or unattractive woman as a teller. "They had to be beautiful and high yellow!" someone once said.

Again, I will say that there is no other city in America that is quite like Atlanta when it comes to skin color among black people. Light-skinned African Americans have always risen to the top of being the wealthiest blacks in Atlanta. Why? It is because they were the mixed-race offspring of many wealthy slave owners in Georgia who ended up in Atlanta after the Civil War. And like many whites, light-skinned blacks had a tendency to live among themselves, and they only catered to other light-skinned blacks in an all-light-skinned community such as the West Hunter Street community.

This is why when outsiders come to Atlanta looking for a pot of gold in "Black Mecca," they often do not find what they are looking for. It is because they are looking in all the wrong places. And anyone who knows the score of what is going on in Atlanta will not inform them of such a lifestyle. And as I have said many times before, if a person is not a part of a certain clique or group that knows how to rub shoulders with the elite group of people, they will not make it to the "Big House" in Atlanta. Who live in the Big House? They are the movers and shakers of Atlanta who know what it takes to rub elbows with the right people. Believe it or not, those are the true nuts and bolts of Atlanta.

Chapter 16

THE SECRET OF SUCCESSUL PEOPLE — In this world, everybody who wants to make a dollar knows something that you do not know, and it becomes a secret. But why is it a secret, and if it is secret, how did they gain possession of it?! No, becoming successful in life is not a secret, and if one man can make a million dollars doing something, two, three, and even four men can become millionaires by doing the exact same thing. However, it is a secret to those who do not know what to do to become successful in life. But wait! The first question we should ask is, "What should we as human beings consider successful?" It must be the money because wealth is the first thing that comes to most people's minds when we talk about being successful.

Needless to say, material things, which include all the things that man can buy with money, are not the true meaning of being successful. A truly successful person is one who has lived long enough to have done all the right things to raise a family properly. After all, what other purpose do we have as human beings for occupying the earth? The one thing that most human beings miss in their quest for living is that regardless of their accomplishments, not one item and not one red penny can be taken with them when they die. Therefore, material goods and money will not prevent anyone from their departure from Earth. But there is a satisfying feeling for those who are left behind that everything possible was done to make a lasting effect and memory of those who have gone on.

One might ask, however, "How do we as human beings find the secret to being the best of what God created us to be?" Again, I will say there is no secret to being a successful human being. But if there is such a secret, it is hidden within the scriptures of the Bible. And to fulfill the mission that God intended for mankind, we must become obedient creatures. Needless to say, man has forced himself to believe that obedience is a by-product of that which has been dismissed as a part of God's demands on mankind. Therefore, he assumes that it is not necessary for human beings to be obedient to God or to himself.

One of the biggest misconceptions of mankind is the coming and dying of Jesus Christ. In the Old Testament, Moses went up on the mountaintop to have a little chat with God himself. And during that conversation, God gave Moses the Ten Commandments to take back to his people. The Ten Commandments are no more than the ten laws of God to help mankind survive and not destroy each other. However, little did God know that by the time Moses walked back down Mount Sinai from his forty-day stay with God, many of his people had made their own god of a golden calf. This was another example of just how ungrateful and stupid the very people whom God had sent Moses through hell and back to rescue from slavery were.

I must ask, "What were they thinking?!" The answer is they were not thinking. The same thing applies to people of today. People have made their own gods out of everything on Earth except the God who created them. And they actually believe that they can be successful by ignoring the Creator and placing their faith in things and objects that were made by man. It is totally insane. Being obedient to the laws that God gave to Moses is the only key to being a successful human being. And to think that Jesus came to replace the laws of Moses is wishful thinking— or I can say it is downright stupid. This is the text that Jesus explained to some of the people who had the same idea as some people who are living today:

> *Don't think that I have come to destroy the laws of Moses or the teaching of the prophets. I have not come to destroy them but to bring about what they said. I tell you the truth: nothing will disappear from the law until the heaven and the earth have all*

disappeared. Not even the smallest letter or the smallest part of the letter will be lost until everything has happened. Whoever refuses to obey any command and teaches other people not to obey that command will be the least important in the kingdom of heaven. But whoever obeys the commands and teaches other people to obey them will be great in the kingdom of heaven. I tell you that if you are no more obedient than the teachers of the law and the Pharisees, you will never enter the kingdom of heaven.

Here we are, two thousand years after Jesus explained the purpose and the reason for obeying the law, but we still have yet to adhere to anything that he said. Mankind, including the teachers of the Scriptures, would have us believe that as long as Jesus died for our rights to pray and ask God for forgiveness, nothing that we do is wrong. And the reason why is they claim, "Because Jesus died on the cross for your sins, and there is no sin too great that we cannot be forgiven for." That is a lie! If the Commandment says, "Thou shalt not kill," and Jesus said, "Nothing will be taken away from the laws of Moses until both the heavens and the earth shall pass away," how do we explain disobeying the Commandments and expect to be forgiven for them? There is no way this is going to happen because as far as we know, Earth is still in place, and we can only assume that heaven is still where it is supposed to be.

I am here to say that this is no more than wishful thinking at its best or simply twisting the Scriptures around and hoping that God will not see what we are doing. But that would be a lie as well because according to the Scriptures, God is omnipresent. He is in all places at the same time, which allows him to see everything that we are doing. He is also omniscient, which allows him to be aware of everything anyone is doing anywhere on the face of the earth. In other words, we cannot speak, do, or hide anything from God. He knows all the little tricks that we might try to pull on him. Of course, this is not to say that if we commit adultery, God will overlook our sin because we prayed for forgiveness when we got back home to our wives or husbands. That is a lie as well! It is a lie because we are not smart enough to hit it once and then leave it alone. We went back again and again and committed the same sin over and over again. Human beings are, by nature, creatures of habit. If we think that we have gotten away with something once, we are prone to do it again and again. How is God going to forgive us for committing the same sin over and over again?! God may be good, but I seriously doubt that he is that good.

To be successful, there is a price that must always be paid. Nothing in life that is worth anything can be had for free. Of course, there is a good price, and then there is a bad price to be paid for our successes. "GP" and "BP" are the same as good and evil. God is good, and Satan is evil; it is up to us to choose whom we want to pay the price to for our successes. For anyone who has already made it to the top of or is still climbing the ladder of success, there is an old saying that goes, "Be careful of the people you step on or mistreat on your way up that ladder of success because you will meet those same people on your way back down that ladder."

The ladder of success is like a two-edged sword; it will cut you both ways. And sometimes, when we plan to cut someone else, we can also end up cutting ourselves in the process. Therefore, it is wise to always take the road to obedience to make it to the home of success. There is nothing secret, mysterious, or tricky about being successful. However, one must learn what success means to him or her. Some people have a tendency to believe that money is the key to solving all their problems. Others believe good health is the key to a successful life. And if we really think about success, both people are right. However, without good health, all the money in the world does not seem so important anymore.

Nevertheless, or regardless of what we might think is the key to success, none of what we think is as important as being obedient to God. Make no mistake about it; whatever God says to us by way of the Holy Spirit or through the words we read in the Bible, it is in our best interest to obey his Word. Now I am probably like most people who try to take God seriously, and I try to obey everything that I believe he has put in place for me to obey. But there was a time when I remember that I was totally confused, and I did not quite understand what God really wanted from me or wanted me to do. To be honest, I thought sending Jesus Christ into the world to give us a way to be forgiven for all our sins was a bad idea.

Okay, why did I believe that Jesus Christ was a bad idea?! First of all, the Bible tells us that Moses brought down the Ten Commandments from Mount Sinai for mankind to obey. Then Jesus was born to tell us that he brought good news, which was that it was okay to commit a sin as long as we go through him and ask God for forgiveness. Okay, this where the Lord and I disagreed. I said, "Okay, Lord, you need to make up your mind as to what you want us to do! First, you say it's not okay to commit a sin. Now with the help of Jesus, you're saying that it is okay if we ask forgiveness. But you are still saying that it's okay. Come on, Lord, give me a break!"

That was when God made me pull over to the side of busy Peachtree Street and stop. Then he snapped at me, "First of all, who do you think you're talking to?!"

I had the nerve to look around as if someone was sitting there in the car with me. Slowly, I glanced upward as if I was looking God in the face. "Lord, I didn't mean it the way it sounded. All I'm saying is I've got several women out here in these streets, and I love each one of them. Now if I go by your rules, I can only have one. But if I go by my rules, I can have all of them at the same time. All I have to do is ask in Jesus's name to be forgiven, right?!"

"Okay, I have dealt with men like you before," God said in a forceful voice. "They all prayed to me when they were climbing that ladder of success, but as soon as they arrived, they turned their backs on me as if they didn't need me anymore. You obviously want to do the exact same thing. Therefore, my advice to you is if you want to stay in my good grace, put me first in your thoughts and prayers, and you can continue to live the life of a millionaire."

"Okay, is this you talking, Lord, or is it the Holy Spirit?" I asked, not really knowing why I was asking such a dumb question.

"What difference does it make as long as you are getting the Word of the Lord?!" the voice snapped at me once again.

"I just asked, Lord! I thought it would be nice to know who I'm talking to."

The spirit of the Lord suddenly left me, and from that day forward, I knew what I had to do if I wanted to stay on God's good side. Naturally, staying on God's good side takes more than me simply saying I will do that. No, God is not so keen on lip service because he knows better than anyone that people can make their mouths say anything until they get what they want. And then they go right back to doing whatever they were doing before. That was the one thing that I learned as far as Jesus coming into the world as our savior was concerned. Yes, it is true that he brought us a way to escape the torment of hell's fires for our sins. But mankind has determined that hell is no more than myth or a scare tactic to keep human beings on their best behavior. Therefore, the birth of Jesus, as some religions teach, did not happen.

To be successful in this life, we first must realize who controls our destinies. It is obvious that some people believe that they are in control of their own lives. And of course, they do up to a certain point simply because God gave us all "free will." But who do we think gave us life in the first place? We certainly did not make ourselves, and if we did, who made the first human beings? Somehow, someone started the process of birth. This means that we as human beings have no other choice but to believe that someone or some greater power made them. Therefore, whatever that greater power may be, it can obviously pick and choose what we will be or not be. That alone has forced me to give whomever it is we call God the credit for choosing me to be alive. Because if he or whoever the Creator might be has the power to create, he also has the power to destroy. Therefore, my success lies in the hands of the Creator.

The one thing that should rattle the brain of every human being is that if God has the power to create the human body, he also has the power to make the same human being successful if he so chooses to. But without being obedient to the one who made all of us exactly who we are, flesh-and-blood human beings, we do not have a chance at becoming successful. However, I am sure there are people in the world who have tried to become all that they might become by their own efforts or by avoiding God in their travel to success. We have seen many people such as entertainers, sports figures, ministers, and even inventors who have been doubtful that God exists. But on their road to disaster, they quickly saw the errors of their ways and began to call on God to come to their rescue. Obviously, in the vast majority of the cases where these situations have occurred, calling on God has a greater possibility of falling on deaf ears.

In the grand scheme of reality, who can blame God for not listening to what we have to say after this situation?! Some people will place God in the back room after he has cleared the way for them to make it to the top of the ladder of success. And when they get there, they pretend that God doesn't exist. "No, I don't believe in God," they all claimed. It is amazing to me how often we see that successful people are some of most foolish people in the world. Only a fool will believe that some of the world's greatest wealth just fell in their direction simply because they were in the right place at the right time. Nothing on planet Earth just happens by chance. The weather is a prime example of something not happening by chance. Why are there four seasons in every year? Why are the trees and the grass green in the summertime, and why do they both die in the wintertime? We may not know the answer to these questions of nature, but we do know one thing for sure: none of these things were made possible by chance.

Again, I will guarantee that for anyone who wishes or dreams of becoming successful in anything that their hearts desire, the first thing they must do is believe that it is possible. And after that, anything is possible when they pray on it. And the question is, "Who do they think they are praying to?!" In most cases of prayer, if people have good sense or know what is good for them, they do not necessarily pray to Satan. They believe that they are praying to God to make it possible for their dreams of success to come true.

Yet again, I can guarantee you that there are no hidden secrets in praying to God when we want to become successful in life. In other words, if we want to become successful, all we need to do is read his words in the Bible and abide by them. The promises from God for success are already written in the Bible, and all it takes for everyone and anyone to become successful is to simply read the Bible and then apply that belief to the promises that are already laid out for us in the book.

Once upon a time, there was a man who lived in my hometown of Monticello. His name was Jim Jefferies, and he started out as a bootlegger then turned into a drug dealer. And according to many people around my small country town, Jim Jefferies was the epitome of success. In other words, he had everything that a man could every want in life. He had a big house out on a big plot of land, several expensive automobiles, and even an airplane to haul in his drugs from South America. But according to the Word of God, this may have been success at its worst. And to prove my point, the DEA, along with local authorities, eventually moved in for the bust, a move that sent him as an old man and members of his family to prison for life.

To even think that this type of lifestyle is being obedient to God is the greatest act of stupidity in the history of mankind. Needless to say, there are many people in this world who believe that criminal acts that make them huge sums of money make them successful. There are no guarantees in life when we go against the Commandments of God. Only the act of obedience is the right way and the only way to become successful in life when we go with God.

The more money some people have, the more they want, and this is called greed. Bernie Madoff is a prime example of how greed can transform a human being into a money-hungry monster. This man of greed came up with a brilliant scheme that is better known as the "Ponzi Scheme," which was no more than convincing other people with money to invest their life savings into a rip-off hedge fund. Needless to say, if these people—over four thousand of them—who thought Madoff's scheme was such a good idea had not been so greedy and had left their money in bank savings accounts and settled for less interest, they would not have been defrauded penniless. But no, they were looking for a huge payday based on a lie that Madoff was telling them.

Okay, as a result of a giant-sized lie, Madoff collected over fifty billion dollars and tried to spend every dime on himself and some of his greedy family members and friends. Now the question becomes, "What kind of monster can become so greedy to think that he could ever get away with stealing fifty billion dollars?!" But then I believe that things had gotten so far out of hand that he knew he would never get away with it. He had come to a point of no return, and he knew that he would spend the rest of his natural life in prison for his crime. So should the gray fox Bernard Madoff take all the blame for what he did, or should those four thousand stupid rich investors who were trying to earn even more money share the blame? In my opinion, everyone who fell for Madoff's Ponzi Scheme deserved exactly what they got in return.

It is a known fact that if people learn to follow Biblical principles as far as money is concerned, they would not be so eager to jump at the first get-rich scheme that comes along. And if people would also learn to spend only the money that they have and not the money they are expecting to have next week or next month, they would be more financially stable. In the New Testament, Jesus drew an interesting parallel between the way people handle their money and the way they handle the spiritual things in their lives. He said, "The way you handle your money is the best outside reflection of your true inner values." In other words, you can tell more about a person's spiritual life by looking at his or her checkbook or bank account than anything else. People can fake anything that other people want to hear, and let's face it: many people are geniuses at faking their true attitudes, but the way they handle their finances is usually a dead giveaway as to what is really going on in their money world.

As I have said before, being successful starts with being obedient to God. Once we have mastered the total appreciation of who God really is and what he can do for us, half the battle is won. The only thing that is left is to make plans as to how we are intending to become the financially successful people that we have always dream of being and then do them. We will never have to worry about how we are going to achieve success, for all we have to do is take God at his word, and we will eventually find a way to work things out ourselves.

Chapter 17

THE TIME IS NEARER, and the signs are clearer. When I think that we are running out of time as far as existing here on Earth is concerned, I am actually thinking of Armageddon. So what exactly does the term Armageddon mean to me and life itself or life as we know it? It means the end of all life and everything as we know it to be today. Or I could simply say it will be the end of the world as we know it. There is a great battle that is going on in the world today between good people and evil people. As much as I hate to say it, it seems to me that the bad people are winning this battle. And if I were sitting where God is sitting right now, I would thoroughly be pissed off to the highest level.

Naturally, there are people who will argue with this point of view and say, "There have always been evil and good people in the world." And they would be absolutely right. But the problem is there is no end in sight of what evil men are doing today. And what is even worse is there is no one in the world today who has the ability or the capability to bring this choke hold to an end. Everything that Jesus Christ brought with him as the "Good News" has been totally forgotten or were never known in the first place, which makes Jesus coming and dying an absolute waste.

In the Old Testament, God did not give us a second chance to get it right. He would send down a firestorm from heaven and kill everyone when they did wrong. But after bringing the Great Flood and killing everything in sight except the ones that Noah was able to put into the ark with him, he told Noah that he would never do that kind of thing again. Okay, so God made Noah a promise to never destroy the earth again, but now as we look at the way things have turned out due to his promise, what choice does God have? He has no other choice but to destroy the world once again, maybe not by a great flood, but something drastic and devastating to the point of making people believe that he is still alive and that he is pissed off.

The problem is the same as it was back in the days of the Old Testament when people lost faith in God simply because they could not see him. But if they read their Bibles, it tells them that only one man has seen God up close and lived to tell about it, and that was Moses. No one else will ever see God and live to tell about it. In other words, people do not believe in anyone or anything that they cannot touch with their hands or see with their eyes. That is why so many people think that God is a myth or some made-up boogeyman by someone who wanted to instill fear into the masses for control purposes.

Today, there are more than seventy-five different religions in the world, which all are serving different kinds of gods. No one religion can accuse the other religion as being a false religion simply because no one knows who God really is. They want to know why he is hiding and what the "big secret" is. The only evidence that God exists is the planet itself and the people who live on it. Life is one big secret; no one knows why they exist and where they go when they die. In other words, this whole idea of life is one gigantic mystery. Therefore, people are confused and frustrated with the way the world is going. They are afraid that man is going to destroy Earth and everything on it. So where does that leave man? It leaves him wondering and waiting for Jesus to return. But that is the big question: "Will Jesus ever come back?"

However, there just might be a bigger question on the return of Jesus: "When he does return, how is he going to judge and forgive people of their sins at the same time?" We must keep in mind that the only reason Jesus came into the world in the first place was to give mankind a way out of his sins. And the only way we can be forgiven is that we must go through Jesus to get to the Father and ask him to forgive us. Therefore, if that is the case, why is Jesus coming back when he has already provided us a way to the kingdom of God? It is mankind who has turned his back on Jesus, and man is saying to Jesus, "Screw all your loving kindness and your only way to the kingdom of God! I'll do things my way! Now take that back to the Father!"

Now do you see why God is so angry with mankind?! Do you finally understand why God has to do something terrible quickly to man to make him understand that this is not a "man's world" regardless of what James Brown once said in a beautiful song? This world belongs to the one who created it. Now as far as I can determine, it was not created by the hands of mankind. And because man did not create this world, he has no say-so in what God does to it. The only way man can save the world and himself is that he must change his sinful ways. But as we have already witnessed, man is not about to change his ways from sin. Why is this? It is because it is much easier for man to commit sins against God than it is to obey his commands.

We have already heard and read for ourselves about the "last days," which we are living in today. Apparently, the writers of the Bible knew a long time ago that this time would come. Everything that the Bible predicted would happen in the last days is happening today. And based upon what I am seeing, the last days are upon us. The third chapter of the book of Timothy tells us exactly what the last days are going to look like.

> *Remember this! In the last days, there will be many troubles because people will love themselves, love money, brag, and be proud. They will say evil things against others and will not obey their parents or be thankful or be the kind people God wants. They will not love others, they will refuse to forgive, they will gossip, and they will not control themselves. They will be cruel, they will hate what is good, they will turn against their friends, and they will do foolish things without thinking. They will be conceited and will love pleasure instead of God, and they will act as if they are serving God, but they will not have his power. At all costs, stay away from these kinds of people because they will go into the homes and take control of silly women who are full of sin and are led by many evil*

> *desires. These women are always learning something new, but they are never able to understand the truth.*

The last days were written to describe the ways and methods of men and women when that time gets here. And what do we see today? We see in real time everything actually happening that is written in the book of Timothy. But of course, most people will never read that part the Bible, and most preachers and ministers will never speak on that particular subject. Why? It is because no one wants to hear about how weak and sinful mankind has become or how much worse he will get before the end, especially if was written several thousand years ago.

Needless to say, in my opinion, Timothy did not take it as far as he should have in describing the last days. When he wrote that the people will be lovers of themselves, he was not just speaking of loving one's self in admiration; he was actually talking about men loving men and women loving women sexually. This, of course, redefines the entire process of God's creation in terms of men's and women's relationships. This also redefines the reproduction process that was put in place to continue the generations for the future. But of course, we know now that this will never happen when two people of the same sex become lovers.

The question then becomes, "Has mankind become so sinful and evil in his ways that he actually believes that he can undo and redefine everything that God has already put in place for the betterment of the human race?" This is obviously man's belief, and from the writing in Timothy, these things that are taking place in today's world, such as diseases and disasters, are unlike anything we have ever witnessed before. Man has obviously taken his beliefs much too far for God's satisfaction. So with that in mind, will Jesus really come back as he may have said that he would? Or will he allow God to send a firestorm to Earth that will destroy every living animal, plant, and, of course, every human being?

Some people might say that this will never happen simply because God is a loving creator, and he would not dare to do such a horrible thing to the people he loves so dearly. Really?! Are we so naive to think that God is so in love with a world full of sinful people that he will not dare wipe us from the face of the earth? Maybe we should wake up and smell what we are cooking, which is no more than a lie! How stupid do we have to be to think God will not destroy the world and everything in it?! Okay, maybe I am being too dramatic about this! But how much effort would it take for the Creator of all things to destroy everything that he has made and start all over again? You say God would not do that. Why wouldn't he? He did it before! And I am sure that there were people whom God loved very much. They were just like we are today. They were people who turned against God and everything that he stood for. They disobeyed God's laws and rewrote their own rules on how mankind should live his life.

Therefore, God is sending us a clear, undeniable message other than the ones that are written in the Bible. We are now seeing people of all ages dying from all kinds of diseases that are totally unknown to man until they are staring him in the face. There is one disaster after another, killing people by record numbers. Things are happening to man today that he has never seen or suspected would have occurred in the past. In spite of all that is taking place, many people have yet to realize that these things are not happening just by some strange coincidence. They are being caused by God's anger with the people who all are sitting around, doing everything except the things that God wants them to do, which is obey his commands.

The churches are supposed to be a safe haven where people can go and be protected from the evil that men are doing. But instead, man has turned the church into a juke joint where they are all hoping to find a pot of gold at the end of the pulpit. As I have said so often, the only reason why preachers mention God's name is because it makes them sound as if they are doing it for God, but it is a lie! They carry the Bible to legitimize the things that they are doing.

Again, time is running out, and the end of the world is getting closer. It does not take a genius or one who has been anointed by God to see the handwriting on the wall. Everywhere we look, we see the signs of God's destruction all over the world. This is no more than God getting our attention before it is too late. However, the more God sends us signs of what is yet to come, the more man ignores them. We are fighting wars in every part of the world. We cannot live in peace for fighting wars no one understands are being fought. We are killing an enemy of the people who looks just like us for reasons unknown. The soldiers are fighting and dying to protect who from what? They do not have a clue! They are fighting for a nation that has forgotten how to bring about a peaceful solution to unwanted wars.

The Bible is filled with things to come that are actually happening now before our every eyes, and we still refuse to believe. And God is sitting on his throne, asking himself, "What is it going to take to make my people realize this is not a joke?" All across the globe, people are dying in record numbers for no apparent reason by terrorist groups and anyone else who has the strength to pull the trigger of a gun or enough brains to make a bomb. Every city, town, and jump-off station in America is being overtaken by thugs who have no sense of direction, and the only thing that they know is violence. America today is more afraid of its own people than it is of some outside groups who call themselves terrorists. The terrorists are living next door to all of us, and they are our neighborhood children.

Furthermore, we often wonder why we are having so many police shootings in America recently. The police are doing what they get paid to do, killing the terrorists! It does not matter to the police whether these young thugs are homegrown or foreigners. A terrorist is a terrorist, and all a terrorist wants to do is to kill and/or be killed. In other words, God is using our own ignorance against us. We were created to love and care for one another and take good care of the planet, but we are doing just the opposite. We are destroying the planet with violence.

People all over the world are holding prayer meetings, trying to pray all the evildoers into oblivion. Well, I have got some bad news for all the worshippers who believe that God is going drop down to Earth, wave his magic wand, and make everything that is happening today suddenly come to a standstill. First of all, to all the brilliant theologians out there, this is not going to happen! They should already know that God sent Jesus into the world to give every man, woman, and child everything that we need to solve every imaginable problem that we have. And here is the reason why God will never solve the problems that we created: God said if we stop looking for divine interventions and solve our own problems, we would have a better world.

Moses had the same problem when God recruited him to rescue his people from Egypt. Every time God gave him instructions as how to do it and when he should do it, Moses would ask God for more instructions. God finally grew tired of Moses asking a hundred questions on how to accomplish a simple mission. So God eventually told Moses, "Look, I have told you what to do, and I have given you everything you're going to need to get the job done. So why are you still standing around, asking me what you should do next?" The same thing applies to the people of today. God has given the people of today's world one simple instruction: "Obey my commands!" His instructions are written in whatever Bible we choose to read. And if there is a Bible that tells you to commit evil acts against humanity, you are reading the wrong Bible.

All the problems of the world today are man-made and not the problems of God. But if we are having problems that are coming from God, it is only because God is trying to get our attention. And once God gets our full attention and we begin to obey his laws, then the problems will eventually go away. In other words, if we are having a problem with God, it is because God is having a problem with us. If we learn to get ourselves to "act right," by all means, God will act right by us. Needless to say, he is waiting on us to grow a brain big enough to do two simple things right: love God with our heart, mind, and soul; and love our neighbor or our fellow man as we would love ourselves. Now I ask you, "How simple is that?!"

Despite how simple those two things seem to be, they are the most complicated and difficult things in the world for people to do. And we wonder why God does not answer our prayers. Why should God show his love to mankind when mankind does not even love himself? God has already determined that this whole idea of creation has been a total waste of his time. Adam and Eve failed the very first test that was given to them, and we have been failing God since that day. This is by no means a reason why God should be celebrating the creation of man. The only reason why man will call on God is when he wants something or thinks he is about to die or is in trouble. Otherwise, man has absolutely no use for God. Why is this true? It is true because God is too perfect. He is too absolute, and he is a spiritual being that no one knows or understand. The only thing people know or understand about God is what they read in the Bible.

Moreover, we expect only good things to come from God, but we never give anything back to God. Sure, we are told by every minister in the world that if we give 10 to 20 percent of what we earn to the church, God is happy with that. That is a lie! The only thing the ministers do with the money that we give to the churches is buy big houses, clothes, and expensive automobiles. Of course, that may or may not apply to all churches, but the point is simple: we can give the church every dollar that we have in the world, and it is still neither going make God love us any more nor get us a free pass into the gates of heaven. That's never going to happen. As I have already explained, the only thing that matters with God is our obedience to him. Anything other than that does not stand a chance.

The signs are very clear that the world cannot stand much longer, going in the direction that it is going. Every time I watch the evening news, I am more convinced that we are headed to a climax that we have seen before.

When I watch cities such as Chicago, Los Angeles, and Atlanta, as well as many other major cities around the country, give reports on homicides that are being committed, it seems like every minute of every day and night, I realize that it is time for God to step in and do something. I do not think at this point that mankind is capable of turning this crisis that has overwhelmed him around. Man has run out of ways to fix his own problems. But the bigger question is, "How will God fix our mess without destroying the whole world?" Based on the fact that he has not destroyed us before, God is waiting for mankind to fix his own mess. So in the meantime, where does that leave us?

The only way that man can survive his own destruction is that he must reach back and begin to reeducate himself and educate the young people who will be leading the world in the future. Of course, in America, educating young people must start at home. That is where the problem lies. Young people who are having babies are not educated enough to teach their children how to live in world without chaos or how to live in a world without creating chaos.

Although I make a point that this is a world that God created, the teachings of God primarily comes from many different religions in the world. And some of those religions teach violence. Therein lies the problem of every nation on Earth that has a different religion. And every religion has its own definition of who and what God is. Naturally, some of those religions teach that killing people in other countries or even in their own country is going to solve the problems of the world. None of this is true! But how does anyone tell someone else who lives in another nation that their religion is wrong? Of course, the question that comes to my mind is, "If every nation who has its own religion and its people worship a different mythical god instead of the God who created heaven and earth, why have a god at all?"

In good conscience, I would be remiss to leave out the religion of worshipping no god at all. I will talk more later about the secular world, which plainly puts me into the world of "atheists," who believe that they are responsible for their own existence. They are the people who live by the code that there is no such creature as a deity or a mythical creature that created the universe and all that we see and know about. But I would argue with that ideology and ask one most important question: "How can a human being live and breathe air twenty-four hours a day and not have a clue where it comes from or how or who or what makes it all possible?" So far, there is not a person alive who can explain how the world came into existence without sounding like a blooming idiot.

Chapter 18

THE TWENTY-FIRST-CENTURY RACE RELATIONS IN AMERICA — Since the 1970s, black people have pretended that the race relationship between black and white folks in America is in their rearview mirrors, and white folks are finally coming around to accepting them as their equals. It is obviously one of the biggest lies that black people have ever told themselves. There is nothing in the minds and attitudes of white America to indicate that they have accepted blacks as their equal. And black people are simply stupid if they think or believe otherwise. The racist flags or Confederate flags are flying higher now than ever before. And the only thing that keeps white people from having an all-out racial confrontation with blacks is because there are many cowards in America. That includes black and white people alike who will only attack each other when no one is looking.

Why is there still a problem with race relation in the twenty-first century? I would like to think or imagine that people of all races would have developed enough brain power to realize that this world does not belongs to white people or black people or any other race or color. This is a world that was created by God or some other much higher power than mankind. No particular race or color owns the earth, for the planet was here when we all got here, and it will be here when we all leave. The only good thing about having a racist individual is that if we live long enough, we will eventually see him or her die like every other asshole in the world. There is nothing good that can come from being a racist! And we would think that a racist person would know that by now.

The question is and always has been, "Why is it that some people never learn that the earth does not belong to them?" Well, let's say that they actually have enough intelligence to know that, but they refuse to accept the fact that other races of people, especially black people, are just as important or are just like every other race or nationality in the world who had no other choice but to live on this earth-rock together. And what is more important about living together is we cannot escape each other, which means there is no other place to go except right here on Earth.

Just to show you how stupid some people are, there have been some people who have tried to figure out how they could travel from Earth to another planet and set some kind of colony there. So far, this idea has fallen way short of becoming a reality by ten million years. There is no way that human beings can survive on another planet that was created by the same God or higher power that created the earth just for mankind. It is not possible because no other planet that we know about was created to become habitable by mankind. That is why God is one giant spirit, and we are no more than pebbles on a sandy beach. God could simply step on every human being on planet Earth and smash us into the dust particles that we actually are.

Since we are no more than the dirt that came from the earth—and back to the earth we will all return—it often makes me wonder how one color of dirt can have the audacity to think of itself as superior over another shade of dirt! Human beings are nothing but lumps of dirt with rocks for brains, and there are some who actually think they are intelligent creatures. How is it possible that a lump of clay or dirt can think about anything other than returning to the ground from which it came? And what is even worse than that is that dirt is dirt, regardless of the colors God painted on the outside. As amusing as it may sound, after thousands of years have passed, mankind is probably the only creature on planet Earth who is still trying to figure out who he is, what he is, and why he exists. All other creatures simply accept life as it was given to them.

I would like to think that for five hundred years, black and white Americans should have found a way to work out their differences. So why has no one found a solution to this five-hundred-year struggle? It is because white Americans seem to think that black Americans are inferior human beings and that they do not have the ability to become intellectuals compatible to themselves? And I have asked this question many times because history tells me that there was a time when white slave owners would rather see a black man dead than know that he could read. However, the reason why they felt that it was necessary to establish an "affirmative action" program was because blacks were inferior or unqualified to enter the job market or the white school system without laws.

Needless to say, affirmative action was not completely the white man's initiative. It was an action that black people highly approved of as well. Why? Because black people felt that affirmative action was a quicker or surer way to gain access to better employment and higher education. Today, of course, these programs have all but vanished from the American way of life for allowing blacks equal access.

Admittedly, affirmative action was a program that never should have happened. The reason is because it was just another way for white America to say that they gave black people a chance to make it into all-white schools and job positions when many were much less qualified. Today is a prime example of what they have been saying all along. Young black men, especially those who are lacking college degrees, are an even greater disaster as far as employment is concerned. With or without a degree, young black men finding work in America are at the minimum rate, to say the least. What does that mean? It means that jobs for young black men without any formal training or schooling are as scarce as hen teeth. And it is even worse than if the young men have criminal backgrounds, which will automatically eliminate them.

So where are we in America as far as race relations are concerned? As I said before, we were under a false impression that we have somehow arrived in a world of equal opportunities until Barack Obama was sworn in as the forty-fourth commander in chief of these United States. Then all hell broke loose, and the demons of hell were running through America like young black people had never witnessed before. Barack Obama brought out the racial demons in white people that even they thought were locked up for good. Suddenly, white people realized that the America that they had built for themselves was slipping into the hands of black people. And no way in Satan's hell were they going to allow that to happen in a white-majority America.

White America has allowed too many things to take place to reverse the old racist trend, such as African American athletes who have taken over the sports world. Primarily in basketball and football, these young men are making billions of dollars for team owners and merchandise companies. Then there is the hip-hop culture that is raking in billions of dollars, making music for a predominantly white listening audience. All of these young entertainers are given a free pass to white women, and this is an indication to the sports players and music makers that they are have arrived in the "White World." Needless to say, the reality of African Americans arriving in the white world is no more than a smoke screen. If it were not for their money-making abilities, which produce mega wealth for the white owners of these big-time money-making franchises, this would not even be a conversation.

The number one attention-getter that we are now seeing in the twenty-first century is the fact that white cops are still killing young black men just as they did in the past. The only thing that has changed and brought this situation to the attention of black people is the fact that everyone in today's world has a camera phone to take pictures of such incidents. These incidents occur more frequently with each passing year: "White cops kill black man!" In every city across America, identical stories are being told and recorded. There was a slogan that was being heard and read on the Internet, on the radio, in magazines, and on television: "Black Lives Matter!" But there is a more pressing question that should be asked by the people who believe that black lives matter: "Who are they trying to convince that black lives matter? The police, white America, or themselves?"

This question was asked for one simple reason: "How do black people convince anyone else that black lives matter when they do not even matter to black people?" Because if black lives mattered to black people, black people would not be murdering hundreds of other black people each and every day of the week all across America. It may be a hard pill to swallow for some black people, but until black people come to the reality of accepting the fact that they are their own worst enemy, not one thing is going to change. Change can only come when people are willing to work and make the best effort possible to change their own situations.

To believe that white people or the police are going to change black people's way of life is a dream that is not coming true. No one can make a change in other people's lives except the other people themselves. White people are comfortable with the way things are going in America, and they demonstrate it every day by not accepting black people as their equals. Why?! Because of their own belief system: "Once a slave, always a slave." Yeah, it is true that some black people may slip through the cracks and end up in the White House such as Obama. But in the final analysis, even as president, Obama found himself in a stalemate that he would have never dreamed of before becoming president. But none of what President Obama went through or had to endure trying to fulfill his obligations as commander in chief was the making of black people. This was all manufactured by a white-majority Congress or white people. And let's not forget that Obama was elected president in the twenty-first century.

Therefore, for those people who believe that time has brought about a change in attitude among those who hated black people the most, you may want to look around to see who has your back when racial situations unfold. Even in the 1960s, during marches and demonstrations, there were many white sympathizers who marched along with blacks to help make their voices heard. And to think fifty years later, we still have a number of white sympathizers who are still trying to help get the message across to only-God-knows-who to make things right. Fifty years later, black people are still marching in the streets and shouting to someone other than those in charge to stop the assault on young black men and women. But who is in charge? Are they listening? Are the police listening? No! Are the mayors of American cities listening? Only until the crowds disperse. Are white people in the comfort of their homes listening? Why should they? "We do not have a dog in this fight!" they are saying to themselves or to each other.

This is why I will say to anyone who is reading this right now, "If you expect a different result from the one you got fifty years ago, it is obvious that you are going to have change the way you do things." Singing "We Shall Overcome!" is not going to help you in today's world. You need a new method to get an old message across. Marching and shouting is old and outdated.

The question I must bring to the forefront is this: "Why didn't the 1960s hell-raising bring about the change that was being sought after?" Naturally, there are several reasons, but the one reason that stands out the most is because white people killed off the black leaders who were leading the charge. The number two reason is because black people did not pick up the baton and carry it on to the finish line. Once the brave black leaders were killed off, the so-called second-in-command leaders turned and ran like scared rabbits. And of course, they later tried to capitalize financially off the names of the fallen leaders.

The second most-asked question that comes to my mind is this one: "After all the marching, singing, and shouting are over and done with, what comes next?!" Here is where the problem lies. The number one fight that black America has with white America is racism, period! But how do black people get past the racism issue?! What has to happen to make white America understand that black America is just as important in this land of the free as they are? Two things have to occur first and foremost! Black America has to be able to make a statement in the voting booths. Get rid of all the white trash and replace them with people who are going to put their interests in first place. Secondly, black America has to take the five hundred billion dollars that are being spent in white businesses and build businesses of their own. We all know that when money talks, bullshit will walk out the door.

Needless to say, the only way the two necessary steps above can take place is for black people to be willing to take a step back in history and take a page out of the Black Wall Street success story. The reason I point to Black Wall Street is because as long as black America is depending on white America to be their only source of power and success in America, they will continue to struggle economically as well as politically. In addition to the list of things that black America must do to regain respectability in America, black people must begin to look at each other as their only way of survival. If we go back in history again when black people depended on each other to make it in America, they were much a stronger people, and they achieved much more in togetherness than they are doing today in a separate black America.

In the days of past America, and if we look at the Willie Lynch story, White America has always used the "divide and conquer" method to keep black America separated and dependent on the white American's way of life. Black America can never be white, and they will never be accepted as white regardless of how light-skinned their offspring are. This is the way America became America. And as long as there are whites in America, their mindset and their culture will never change. The one factor that many black Americans do not get is that many black people grew up wanting to be white or wanting to be like white people simply because they believed that white people had something more beautiful than what they had, which was white skin.

Moreover, these same black people never once thought about how many pale white people wanted the skin color that black people had. And in later years, they even wanted to look like black people with big lips. Black people have always wanted to do what white people do! A good example is tattoos! There was a time when a black person would have never considered getting a tattoo. To black Americans, tattoos were taboo because it was not becoming to black skin. In other words, getting a tattoo is simply "acting white." And who in their right mind wanted to act white after all the hell black people have gone through at the hands of white people since coming to America as slaves?!

The twenty-first century has not done much to improve the education of black people as to how not to allow white America to take advantage of or misuse them. Here is a prime example of how white America is using big money to misuse or trick black people. The NBA is crowded with young black players who are paid millions of dollars each and every year. The NFL is loaded with black players who are making millions of dollars every year. And last but not least, the hip-hop world is making millions of dollars every year. Now when we add all of these millions of dollars that are earned by black people up, we could easily topple several billions of dollars that go straight back into white businesses and establishments. Why is this true?! It is true because no one in the black communities have anything worthwhile to offer these black stars in ways of spending these millions of dollars that they have earned.

This, of course, can only mean one thing for the black people who are super wealthy: they spend their money on the things that they desire, which can only come from white America. Those things are cars, houses, jewelry, clothing, and sneakers, which all are sold by white America. As for the music industry, like I have mentioned before, this is a black market that is sold to a predominately white buying audience.

Therefore, instead of black America building its own stores, factories, and means of distribution, they rely on white Americans to do the job for them. This method of operation will never help black people get jobs and build their own communities and stores and factories. The amount of money being earned by black Americans should give them the power to build their own neighborhoods. Instead, some black neighborhoods in America look worse than some places in Third World countries. Why?! It is because many black people have lost their identity when they began to look at the way white America is living and convince themselves that "White is right!" Is it really? But black people will never know as long as they continue to allow white America to dictate their ways of living.

Over the years, white Americans have been rebuilding a wall between themselves and the rest of the American people. Behind that wall—if we are ever lucky enough to look behind that wall—we will find something that is called "white privilege." White privilege is found in a group of white people who we might say may consider themselves above the law. What does "above the law" really mean? It means that when laws were written and then rewritten again in the law books, they were actually written for the people who were prone to violate them. In the vast majority of criminal courtrooms across the nation, we will never see a lot of white Americans. The majority of criminal cases that are tried in this country are against black Americans. Why the disparity? It is because most white people consider themselves above committing armed robbery, car theft, drive-by shootings, and other petty, low-life crimes. Only "white trash" and blacks commit such crimes.

Gangs are formed in poor black neighborhoods or in the neighborhoods of Asians and Hispanics. It is very unusual to hear someone speak of gangs in white neighborhoods. And the question immediately comes to mind as to why. White people remind their kids that gangs are for the minority groups in America who have no parental guidance in their homes. And in the twenty-first century, in high schools as well as colleges, white kids will often make friends with black kids to try and understand firsthand some of the things that have been passed down to them from their parents, grandparents, or even older people in their families concerning black Americans. Some tales are not true at all while others may be as they were told. And white kids want to know if they are true.

The twenty-first-century American people have a lot to learn as far as knowing how to be just "one nation under God" is concerned. Admittedly, this only applies to white Americans. Black Americans have to learn a lot as to how to apply themselves as intelligent human beings and try not to be like white people. Black Americans need to know for themselves just who they are and where they came from to call themselves black Americans. Black people did not just suddenly show up on the shores of America while white people gladly welcomed them into this country. They were brought here as slaves, to work themselves half to death to help make this nation what it is today. Ultimately, black people have a legitimate right to be here. They are here to stay despite some folks who might have us believe otherwise.

Therefore, it is only right that black Americans treat others and expect to be treated by others as if this is a land of one race, but they must know the difference. It is time for black people to take a history lesson from past generations and from other races who are making this land their land. Blacks must build their own communities and businesses to shop and buy from blacks who have total control. But despite the color of their skin, white people only recognize one color, and that is the color of money! When black people take their money away from white businesses, there will be changes in attitudes as well as racial relations. Nothing talks louder than the dollar bill! However, are black people willing to let their money do the talking?

Chapter 19

THE GOD OF CHAOS — It is obvious that the world is filled with chaos. All we have to do is listen to the news feeds, watch television, or read local newspapers, and we will know that the world seems to be on a collision course with the pits of hell. But here is the one question that I am asking myself: "If God is the creator of all things and if he is the God of love who gave his only begotten son to save all the sinners in this world, why is he allowing mankind to destroy all that he has put together?!"

Before I make an attempt to get into the answer, let me give you a definition of "chaos." According to *Webster's Dictionary*, the word chaos means a state of confusion. Let's say the world was in a confused, unorganized state of existing before the creation of any distinct forms. In other words, the world today is pretty much like it was before God decided to create a universe of organized planets along with Earth in which he later created living creatures to inhabit the planet.

Then Webster went on to say that chaos also means an inherent unpredictability in the behavior of a natural system (as in the atmosphere or a beating heart), all of which I might remind you are the exact things that are happening right here on Earth today in the twenty-first century. So with these things happening in total disarray today, some of us might be wondering why God is allowing these things to happen. Does he not care about all the confusion and all the craziness that is occurring in the world that he so patiently and carefully created with his own two hands or spoken words? When God looks out across the universe and sees all the violence that is occurring on planet Earth, what is he thinking? What does he think his next course of action will be? Should he destroy the world again or simply allow his people to continue doing what they are doing? These questions must be very complex for God to answer because people are his first love, probably more so than the angels who are camped all around his kingdom.

So what is the problem?! The problem, as we already know, is obviously Satan. There is no other answer that needs to be talked about except Satan who is the sole reason why the world is in such chaos. Satan is the god of chaos, which he began to cause for God in the very beginning, even before God created the first human beings. Satan knows better than anyone how to rub God the wrong way, and he does it constantly, every minute of every day. However, Satan could not do the terrible things that he is doing without God's permission. And more importantly, Satan could not do what he is doing without mankind's permission. In other words, we, along with God, have given Satan carte blanche to do whatever he wants to do to, and he caused as much havoc as he possibly could on Earth.

The secret to man's weakness was discovered in the very beginning, according to the book of Genesis in the Bible, with the creation Adam and Eve. However, the question has always stumped man's intelligence as to how did man and woman became so weak if they were created to be the best that God had to offer. Did the most powerful God in the universe know that he was putting together a couple weaklings when he created those two? Yes, he did! But God also assumed that if he told the two knuckleheads to do a certain thing or not to do certain things, they would have enough obedient brain matter to obey what he said. But lo and behold! Adam and Eve did not have the sense that God had given to any of the animals that he also created, and they were too dumb to come in out of the rain.

Who is Satan, and why does he torment God in the ways that he does?! Because he knows better than anyone why God allows him to run free; his job is to make people choose their own eternal destiny when they die, which will eventually be heaven or hell. However, that determination came much later after God had destroyed the earth a few hundred years after creating it. Obviously, the problem started with the first two human beings or the two knuckleheads who chose to listen to a two-legged walking and talking snake instead of doing what God had told them not to do.

We have all obviously heard and read the story of Adam and Eve and how they were the ones who committed the first sin. But we never really understood why they were so easily convinced to disregard God's previous command of what not to do. Satan popped up out of nowhere and convinced Eve to eat some fruit that God has already told her not to eat. Was she that hungry, or did God make a terrible miscalculation by assuming that Adam needed a helpmate? Not only that, but why did Satan not approach Adam and instead went to where Eve was? Was he afraid that Adam was much wiser than Eve and probably would have told Satan to back off?

There are too many questions about Satan that I do not know how to answer, like why he did all the things that he did and is still doing. But what I do know is that according to the Bible, God created Satan just like he created the first human beings. And I know that God gave Satan ultimate powers to do things that other angels could not do. He was beautiful, and he was talented, more so than any other angel in God's kingdom. So much so that Lucifer, as he was known in the beginning, began to tell himself that he was as powerful as his creator. How does anyone become so stuck on stupid that he begins to believe that he is more powerful than the one who made him?! Well, Lucifer did just that! And now that he has remained stuck on stupid, he was allowed to bring his stupidity to Earth and spread it all over the world to millions of walking and talking stupid human beings.

Today, Satan is on the move! He realizes that his time on Earth is winding down to zero days, and his intention is to steal as many souls as he possibly can before his time expires. Everything evil that is happening today all over the world is because of Satan. Satan is moving fast today to steal the very souls that God loved so much until he gave his only begotten son Jesus and allowed him to die for those same souls. However, God will not interfere with Satan because he gave human beings "free will" and his Word of how to save them in the Bible, and all mankind has to do is read the book.

Needless to say, Satan has found new ways to sway the minds of human beings away from the Bible by simply making them believe that the Bible is filled with lies and that God doesn't really exist. As I stated before, many men wrote the scriptures in the Bible based on their own beliefs, as well as the scriptures that were passed down by the writers before them. However, previous writers do not necessarily mean that the Bible is less true. It does not mean that the men in Biblical times did not walk and talk with God. God is just as real as Satan is real. There is no denying that Satan is real, and he is working his evil tricks all over the world. All you need to do is look around at the world today, and Satan is written on everything that is happening.

The men and women who are members of ISIS are no more than Satan's advocates who believe that they can control the rest of the world by murdering innocent people. Young thugs and gangs members in America are members of Satan's vast organization of evil and corrupted individuals. To recruit members today is no different than it was for Satan in the beginning, when he recruited a third of the heavenly body of angels to overthrow God's kingdom. It is said that every secret organization started with the Illuminati, which is believed to be the ringleader behind all the other corrupted organizations in the world. These organizations are responsible for all corruption. I highly disagree! Satan is responsible for every evil thing that is going on in the world. The Illuminati is made of no more than human beings who are followers of Satan.

Satan has been the leader of every evil occurrence in the world since the beginning, when he organized a bunch of angels to follow him in his effort to take God's kingdom away from him. Unfortunately for Satan, his takeover bid did not work as he had planned, and as a result, God kicked him and all of his rebel angels out of heaven. But that was not the end of the story; Satan was given a free run of the earth to do what he will until God sees fit to send him to hell along with all of his followers. Of course, his followers also include the angels who were with him in the beginning. And every human being on Earth who has done evil deeds will end up in hell because of Satan's influence on them.

When God gave every human being free will (to do as one sees fit for himself), mankind had a choice to do the right thing, which is always on God's side of the fence, or the wrong thing, which is always on the side of Satan. Either way, the choices are always left to human beings to make for themselves. The world is evil because of free will.

At times, it seems that Satan has the upper hand on God simply because man has not learned from the mistake that Adam and Eve made. Man has gotten even weaker than the humans that God created in the beginning. No one, not the disciples of God or even God himself, has been able to understand why it is so easy for Satan to recruit human beings to do evil, the one thing that makes God very angry. It is difficult for God to understand because if human beings have faith in him, they can have and do the same things that Satan is offering. The only difference is, of course, Satan has a hidden agenda attached to his promises. The person must commit to doing something wrong or evil for Satan to keep his promises. And what people are failing to realize is when they turn to Satan for anything, most of them can never return to God for salvation. They become enemies of God, along with Satan.

Naturally, there are many people on the planet who say that Satan is only a myth that was brought about by the Christian faith to scare people into doing right or getting into the Word of God. Satan is no myth! He is a spirit just as God is a spirit! No man has ever seen God and lived to tell anyone what he or she saw. The same thing applies to Satan. No man or woman has seen Satan, but every time we think of doing something wrong or evil, we are being influenced by Satan. Satan's thoughts are our thoughts, whereas our thoughts are not God's thoughts. What is the difference? The difference lies in Satan's ability to influence us right here on Earth in our everyday association with other people. Every minute of every day, someone is in need of something or feels the urge to do something that Satan has control of. It could be sex, money, drugs, or the need to rob, steal, harm, or kill another human being. All of these things, Satan will strongly influence mankind to do. And in most cases, a vast majority of people are too weak to say no to the urges that are being influenced by Satan.

There is, of course, a bigger question that we should ask: "Why does Satan do the things that he is doing?" Or better yet, what does he get out of being an adversary of God? Well, as I have already discussed, Satan is highly pissed off with God for kicking him and his rebellious group of angels out of heaven in the beginning of the world. You see, Satan has always had this great idea that despite the fact that God created him and all the angels, somehow, God made the terrible mistake of creating him as the supreme angel of all the angels who ever existed. Whether it was a mistake or intentional, Satan is a problem that we must all face.

Perhaps Satan's thinking is not as farfetched as it may seem, for he was God's special kind of angel. God also gave Lucifer the kind of powers that he gave to no other angel, and of course, this convinced Satan that his powers were greater than those of God. Therefore, the idea of taking over God's kingdom became Satan's obsession. However, since his great plan failed and God sent him to the world of human beings, everything that Satan does to try and steal the souls of people is no more than his way of getting revenge against God.

Human beings are no more than guinea pigs who are trapped in the crosshairs of Satan's powerful gun. And in reality, the people on Earth do not mean anything to Satan except the fact that he uses them as pawns, with the hope that God will surrender to his demands. But Satan's demands are totally unrealistic to God because initially, Satan had already received his sentence to hell for one thousand years from God. After the thousand years have been served, he will return for one season for a full repentance or an admission of guilt. And if Satan does not repent to God for the wrongs that he has done, he will return to hell forever and ever. But as we all know, Satan will never repent for his wrongdoings to God.

Satan is the god of chaos, plain and simple. In other words, whatever Satan is doing to mankind, he is enjoying it to the fullest. And he has no intention of giving up his mission of getting back at God regardless of the punishment that he is going to receive in the end.

This war between God and Satan originally had nothing to do with mankind. That is, until Satan discovered man's weakness and realized how much God loved his creation of mankind. Suddenly, the idea flashed in his brain like a light bulb coming on for the first time: go to Eve and convince her that everything that God had commanded of her and Adam not to do was nothing but a lie. He was so convincing that Eve believed Satan in spite of his serpentine appearance. And as a result, human beings whom God created in his own image had committed what is known as the "First Sin."

As some of us might have already figured out for ourselves, the war that is going on between God and Satan is a spiritual war that no man can fight. The only thing mankind can do is try to avoid being tricked by Satan, which is something that he has mastered doing. We have to realize that Satan has been lying to people since the very beginning, and by now, he is very good at what he does. "It is a war between good and evil," as many believers know it to be. Despite the fact Satan has no chance of winning this war, God has allowed him to win many battles. And if mankind's faith was stronger in God, Satan would have less chance of winning any battles. As I have already said, God could care less about Satan, for he has already been sentenced to hell. But it is man who concerns God, for we all still have a chance if we learn to do as Jesus did: tell Satan to move aside because there is only one master that we will serve.

It is without a doubt that Satan has a huge following, and there is one major problem with many of his followers: they do not have the slightest clue as to why they are actually following the devil. But why do they follow Satan?! Because Satan disguises himself as anyone he so chooses, including God. We often believe that we are praying to God when we are actually praying to the devil. And Satan loves those who think that they have a special connection with God and that it is God who is answering their prayers. How does this work? Most people who believe in God will also believe that God will answer all their prayers. But what they fail to realize is that Satan is always on their prayer request line too, and he is listening to the requests that are meant for God. And Satan has the power to grant their requests just as God does.

So what happens when Satan answers our prayers? He speaks to us with his own demands. He puts it our minds that we must do something evil or against the will of God before he will grant our requests. Most people will follow the advice of Satan, not realizing that they are doing something wrong in the eyes of God and that they have been tricked by Satan into doing it. And by the time these same people realize that they have been duped by the devil, they are much too deep in trouble with the laws of man as well as the laws of God.

If and when man learns that he has been tricked by the devil, he will begin to pray to God, asking for forgiveness. Sometimes, forgiveness is with God but only if man is sincere and repents for the sins that he has already committed. The problem, however, comes in when people fail to recognize who or what caused them to sin in the first place. Very often, when people fail to understand who is really behind their actions, they become repeat offenders. God nevertheless is not too fond of repeat offenders simply because he does not believe that the Commandments should be broken over and over again. But what does Satan care about people breaking God's Commandments?! Not one thing. For him, the more people he can convince to offend God, the better he feels about what he is doing.

The one thing that people must always understand about Satan is that he is mad at God and he will misuse, mistreat, trick, kill, and destroy people's lives all over the world just to let God know that he will do anything in his powers to make mankind's lives as much a part of his hell as he possibly can. But the one thing that Satan knows is the fact that he cannot compete head-to-head with God (no one can, for that matter). So instead of Satan going into combat directly with God, he takes out his anger on the people of God, which he figures is just as good.

There is only one way for people to understand and know how to fight their battles against Satan, and it is to simply stay away from him and ignore his temptations. Satan can be beaten, and if we do that, life can be as sweet on Earth as it is in heaven. But we cannot entertain the temptations of the devil and be obedient to God's Word at the same time. We cannot serve two masters and expect to love and honor both at the same time. We will fall in love with one and eventually hate the other one. In other words, we cannot have our cake and eat it too. To receive God's promises, we have to give up the devil's temptations.

The question is, however, how difficult is it not to entertain the temptations of Satan? God gave every human being an escape clause in his or her DNA, which means we all have the ability to escape or to avoid whatever Satan is offering or whatever trick he is trying. But how will we know if it is the devil that we are dealing with?! The good thing about Satan is he does not hide his intentions. He will let us know up front that his gifts always contain wrongdoings or evil. And it is up to us to decide if we are willing to follow his lead or not.

The next question becomes, "How strong is Satan's influences?" They are much stronger than most human beings' willpower to fight them off. That is why we all must keep our distance from the things that we know Satan controls. Satan's number one mind control substance is sex. His number two control substance is money. Numbers one and two are always the key factors to everything evil that involves most human beings. The reason why is a no-brainer! Most people believe that they cannot live a good life without sex, and most people do not believe that they can live a decent life without money, both of which are controlled by Satan.

Sex and money are the two biggest contributors to human chaos in the world. Anyone who controls sex controls the money! Anyone who controls money controls the sex! It does not matter which order they fall into, as long as they both go hand in hand. Therefore, do expect the devil to give up his control over sex and money for the love of God, for that will only happen when God decides to bring the entire world to a drastic end.

The bottom line for human beings is very thin, almost too thin for mankind to stand on. This, of course, means that Satan will continue to cause chaos throughout the world simply because he knows the two things that make life worth living for the vast majority of human beings. The proof is all around us, and every human being is infected with the disease that he or she cannot live without sex and money. And as long as Satan knows what people will do anything for, whether it is to die for or kill for, he will always be the god of chaos.

Chapter 20

IF THE WALLS COULD TALK — I have always thought to myself within the four walls I call home, if my walls could talk, what would they say about me and the things I have done over the past thirty years?! Personally, there have been some things that I have done behind closed doors that I would never dare allow to become public. But if my home's walls could come alive and tell all of my deep dark secrets, what would the conversation sound like? And I am more than sure that the same thing could apply for most people in the world.

Behind closed doors, we all have very nasty habits that we would prefer not to show the world outside our homes. That is the primarily reason for the old saying, "You'll never know a person until you've lived with them." That is a saying that is so true that it is frightening to even think about it. But here is the problem with that whole scenario of keeping our private lives a secret: there is, however, someone who is always watching and listening to what we do or say within the privacy of our own homes. That someone is God! Or better yet, that someone or something is the Holy Spirit, which happens to be a gift from Jesus Christ himself.

Needless to say, the Holy Spirit is a gift from God that most people are totally unfamiliar with, the reason being that the Holy Spirit doesn't necessarily talk out loud, but it always speaking softly to our minds, telling us what is right and what is wrong for us to do or say. But of course, we have a tendency to ignore the HS because we automatically assume that it no more than a thought that is running through our minds. I am here to tell you that the HS is more than just a thought running through our minds, for it is the Comforter that Jesus left behind when he rose from the dead and went back to heaven. The Comforter is a spirit buried deep within us that carries on a conversation with us about almost everything that we do and say. And the best thing about the Comforter is it warns us when we are blindly about to step off a curb into the flow of traffic during a green light.

What do you supposed would happen to those same people if the Holy Spirit was not there with them? And then, I also wonder, "How did people survive the horrors of life back in the days before the birth of Jesus?" But then I remember those were the days when God actually spoke to people directly. And because God has given us a replacement speaker for his actual voice, people now assume that God is dead. No, God is not dead! He simply has another way of communicating with us.

Now when we talk about whether the walls can talk or not, the walls can talk, and they are better known as the Holy Spirit. And if we are wondering whether the HS will ever reveal our innermost secrets or not, yes, it will! Why do we think God gave us the Holy Spirit if it was not going to record our every movement and speech?! We should know by now that God is much smarter than we will ever hope to be. The HS is like a "black box" that is placed on every aircraft to track planes' locations and the things that are said should there be a crash. Where do we think the idea of the black box came from if not from the Holy Spirit? Now it all begins to make sense.

We automatically assume that in the privacy of our own homes, hotel suites, or other secluded locations away from other people's eyes or ears, we are in a safe territory where no one will ever know what we did or said and with whom we did it. Oh, but we are so wrong! And just think, God has eyes and ears everywhere, and whatever he knows about us, everyone else will eventually know sooner or later. Now this does not mean that God is a blabbermouth or someone who goes around telling our business to everyone else. But when we do something wrong or evil, God has a way of making us tell on ourselves.

We automatically assume that our conscience will eventually get the best of us. Naturally, our conscience is just another word for the Holy Spirit that lives inside most human beings. But regardless of what we may call our inner spirit, it all comes from the Holy Spirit, which Jesus said would be with us until he comes again. And we have to believe that if the HS is the Comforter that was left behind by Jesus, it would make perfectly good sense for the Comforter to have us admit our wrongdoings whenever it becomes necessary. We have heard of violent criminals who often admit their wrongs to other people because their conscience will often get the best of them. They cannot keep it a secret any longer; they have to tell someone.

Obviously, there are those who might say that they have not been touched by the HS, and they might be correct in their way of thinking. Not every human has the luxury of being in the present of the Holy Spirit. Not every human being can testify to the fact that they have been touched or their bodies have been taken over by the HS. But there is one thing that I know for sure: when someone is struck by the HS, it may be difficult to know exactly what it is that keep telling them the right and the wrong way to live their lives in the beginning, but eventually, they will discover what it is. And when they finally understand what is behind the reason why they are changing their lives, it will become an awesome experience and awareness.

If the walls could talk! There is nothing that we can say or do that the walls are not telling everyone else. There is an old saying: "What we do in the dark will eventually come to the light so everyone can see." Here is the way that phenomenon piece of mythical saying works: regardless of what we may be thinking or hiding from the eyes and ears of other people, somehow, in some way, something mysterious will happen that will bring it all out in the open for all to see. Some people call these things a stroke of bad luck, or we make the horrible mistake of telling the wrong people, who will follow up by telling someone else.

To make the mystery soar even higher, there is no such thing as the "perfect crime." Why?! This is true because as long as a human being is the perpetrator of said crimes, there can never be a perfect crime. Human beings are never perfect regardless of how cautious or how particular to details they try to be. There is always a flaw in the details. That is why when cop or investigator arrives at a crime scene, he or she searches the area for clues. There is always something that the perpetrator or perps are going to leave behind that will become just enough of a clue to lead the investigators to the person or persons responsible. This, of course, means that the walls are always talking, and those talking walls will get the criminals caught for their crimes every time.

There are people who think they have committed the perfect crime or have "gotten away clean!" They always think that if they can get away one time, they can repeat what they did the first time and get away again. This is always a serious mistake! I remember once upon a time, there was a bank-robbing crew who managed to rob several armored trucks as the guards were delivering bags of cash to the banks. These thieves were able to pull off at least four heists at local Atlanta banks and were able to get away clean each time. But "Murphy's Law" always seems to catch up with the wrongdoers in the nick of time. What does Murphy's Law say? It says, "If anything can go wrong, it will go wrong every time."

Murphy's Law is a mysterious phenomenon that no one can explain, but it is all too real just the same. Some people might say, "Accidents happens!" But in Murphy's Law, there is no accident. This is a mysterious situation put in place by God that will cause mankind to pay for his sins before death. And only God knows what his punishment will be before and after death.

The armored car heists were perfectly timed, and each time, the bandits took advantage of the guards when they were making their delivery to different banks. In all the heists, there were approximately five million dollars taken. And naturally, these four middle-aged men wanted to make good use of the money that they were stealing. After laying low for a short period of time, they began to buy fancy cars and nice homes for themselves. The only problem for one of the robbers was that he moved into a very upscale neighborhood where mostly millionaires lived. After a few months had gone by, these same nosy millionaire neighbors began to wonder what kind of business their unknown neighbor was in.

The old phrase of being "thicker than thieves" began to pay off when all four robbers would meet up at this one location in the millionaire neighborhood. Naturally, the nosy neighbors assumed that these four men were common drug dealers. So they invited the local narc squad to investigate the situation. After some serious investigation, the drug squad found no evidence of drugs being sold or transported in or out of the location. But the thieves were still being watched for the squad to see exactly what was going on among these four well-dressed men and the fancy cars they were driving, but they found no legal business attached to them. Who were they?!

Finally, the day came when the money was running low, and the men needed to make another illegal withdrawal from the local armored car company. By then, the FBI was on the lookout for four men who had made their getaway with large sums of cash who fitted the description of these four men. Murphy's Law was about to go into play when the three men hit their next armored truck at a West End bank, leaving one man behind as the driver of the getaway car. The robbery went down as planned; the three men had taken three large bags of money and ran to the getaway car but did not realize that the getaway car had a punctured right front tire. The robbery call went out to all police units in the area, who also alerted the FBI. With their getaway vehicle running limp on one wheel, this made their escape very noticeable as well as difficult to make a fast getaway.

With a police helicopter flying above and police cars swarming the area, the robbery suspects were not difficult to spot, traveling at a high rate of speed west on Interstate 20 with a flat tire. Soon, the robbery suspects were captured with the bags of money in the trunk of the car, and the Feds were able to pin all the previous heists on these same four men.

The moral of this story is that the walls talked plenty and told the millionaire neighbors that something strange was going on with their new homeowner. Murphy's Law came into play when, for some unknown reason, the right front tire on the getaway vehicle went flat, which eventually led to the capture of the four men. If it had not been for the tire going flat when it did at the scene of the crime, they would have made a clean getaway once again. If it weren't for the walls talking to one of the robber's neighbors and Murphy's Law doing exactly what it is supposed to do, the robbers would have gotten away again.

There are many stories that have gone untold for many years by people who have done evil things in their lives and thought that they had escaped the grand old saying, "If the walls could talk." But in the end before the death of these people, something magical always happens that brings out the truth like a dirty rag with clues written all over it. No one to this day or since the beginning of time has been able to figure out or understand how and why these truths eventually reveal themselves. Naturally, I would assume that this was all a part of God's plan to make sure that no man could ever feel comfortable and believe that he has gotten away with a crime or an evil deed.

It is amazing how noticeable a human being can become when he or she has done something wrong and when they are watched very closely. They are constantly looking over their shoulders as if they think something or someone is trying to sneak up on them. And if we will notice carefully, when situations like these occur, the person or persons who are guilty of such crimes will eventually admit their guilt without anyone even asking for it. Again, we automatically assume that the person's conscience has played a major role in their surrender.

Having a conscience can be a very dangerous place for some people to be in. They do not know why the urge to feel guilty about the things they have done exists, but it is there, living inside them day and night. And there is nothing they can do that will make the urge disappear. Some people will turn to drugs, alcohol, or other addictive substances to try to make the guilt go away. But there is nothing that they can do to make a conscience forget what has happened. It is always hanging around, just waiting for a chance to make the people expose themselves.

I grew up in a small town where everyone knew about everybody else's personal business or affairs. I remember there was this particular well-known couple who had a male friend who visited their home on a daily basis. This male friend was thought by many other people to have been the husband's best friend. But apparently, the best friend had more on his mind than just being a good friend to the husband. And as time passed, when the husband would leave home going to work, the friend would always pay a visit to the stay-at-home wife. And what made matters worse was that the friend would be at the couple's home most of the day, every day.

It was amazing to me how the husband never suspected his friend of having an affair with his wife, especially since everyone else in the neighborhood knew of the affair. But as fate would have it, the wife became pregnant with the best friend's baby, which was assumed to be the husband's. Lo and behold, the husband was told many years before, when he was a teen involved in a motorcycle accident, that he would never have kids. And suddenly, he remembered what the doctor had told him, but he had never told his wife what the doctor said.

When the wife told her husband that they were having a baby, he simply went along with it until his condition was confirmed by another doctor. But he loved his wife even though he knew she was telling him a lie. And he decided to go along with the pregnancy, hoping that God had blessed them with a baby. However, in the back of his mind, his conscience was constantly nagging and telling him, "Don't be a fool! You know this is not your baby! What's going to happen when the baby comes into this world looking just like your best friend?! How are you going to explain your baby having the spitting image of the man who calls himself your best friend?! Face the truth now or forever live a lie!"

Finally, the day came when the husband was believed to have been at work, but he had decided not to go to work that day and returned home. In the meantime, however, the friend, who figured that the coast was clear as always, showed up like clockwork to be with the woman who was now pregnant by him instead of her husband. The husband, who was observing from afar, watched his so-called friend arrive at a time when the husband was thought to have been busy on the job. He waited a short while before making his grand entrance, but the feeling of not wanting to find what he positively knew he would find made him nervous. "Should I just pretend that I never saw this, go back to work, and forget about it?" he asked himself several times. He was afraid that if he caught them having sex, he would be become so outraged that he would pull the gun that was in his waistband and kill them both.

Like I said earlier, having a conscience is a very dangerous place to be in sometimes. "Okay, you know what you are going to see, and you know this is going to make you outraged to the point that you might lose your composure and end up in prison for the rest of your life for murder. But you also have to think about the unborn baby. Yeah, I know that it's not your baby, but it is still a baby just the same," his conscience was telling him.

"Okay, so what should I do?" he asked his conscience. "Tell me, should I just turn around and pretend that this is not happening?! I mean, that's my house that my wife and my so-called best friend are having sex in, and you want me to just close my eyes to what's going on?! Come on, conscience, how am I supposed to do what you're asking me to do, huh?!"

"Okay, here's what you do," his conscience said finally. "Leave your gun in the car because you are the last person they expect to see. The fear they are going to have just by seeing you will make them tell you everything from the beginning to the end. Your wife will admit that the baby she's carrying is your best friend's. He will have such a guilty conscience that he just might commit suicide. This is a situation where both parties know that they are wrong, and only by the grace of God will they still be alive this time tomorrow."

The husband decided to do as his conscience told him to do by leaving his weapon in the car. But he also knew that his best friend carried a gun sometimes, and it was possible that he would be armed and become frightened enough to shoot him. Nevertheless, this was a chance he was willing to take since his conscience had told him what to do.

Having a conscience is sometimes a very dangerous place to be in. The husband quietly entered his home, making sure that he was undetected by any sounds as he approached the bedroom where he was sure that his wife and his friend would be together. As he approached the bedroom door, he could hear soft moans and a lot of whispering coming from the two people inside. Slowly he opened the door while they were making passionate love like he had never witnessed before, coming from his wife. As he stood there, gazing down at the two naked bodies glued together as it seemed, it took him several moments for a sound to come out of his mouth. Finally, he uttered, "So this is what I get from my wife and the best man at my wedding?!"

Suddenly, everything seemed frozen in time; bodies stopped moving, and the moaning and the whispering came to a soundless halt. Both of the lovers' eyes were focused on the figure who now stood in the doorway of the bedroom. Being this surprised was way beyond their comprehension; they were startled to a point of no return. "This is not what it looks like!" the best friend finally said in a stuttering manner. "This just happened. . . . I mean, we were—"

"We were just what?! This is not what it looks like?! But what am I looking at?! I am looking at you and my wife having sex in my house!" the husband shouted at the top of his voice. "And then you have the nerve to come into my home, lay in my bed, and screw my wife, and you're going to sit there and tell me that this just happened?!"

The man immediately climbed out of bed while the wife was still too frightened to speak. "Look, if you just let me put on my clothes and get out of your house, you'll never see my face again," the man said because he was afraid that the husband was going to pull out a gun at any second. "I don't want to die over somebody else's wife! Just let me get my clothes, and I'm gone!"

"You're gone. . . . Where are you going?!" the husband shouted as he felt more in control of the situation now. He glanced at his wife, who was now sobbing with the sheet pulled up over her naked body. "No, no, you ain't going nowhere until I say you can go. And when you do go, you're taking her with you. After all, that is your baby she's carrying, am I right?! It better be yours, because it sure as hell ain't mine!"

The man suddenly looked at the wife and then back at the husband. He wanted to pretend that he did not know she was pregnant. "Wait! You say she's pregnant?! I mean, I didn't know she was pregnant! She never told me that she was pregnant!" As he tried to sound as if he was an innocent man, he began to sob like an infant.

The husband pointed to the wife, keeping one hand behind his back, and said, "Before I kill the both of you, you get your damn clothes on, and both of you get out of my house! And I mean right now! And you, my dear, you'll hear from my attorney real soon!"

Finally, the wife spoke, "Baby, don't put me out, I want to stay with you. He doesn't mean anything to me. He betrayed you, not me. I love you! Please, baby, don't put me out! Don't divorce me, please!" She began to cry and beg for mercy.

The husband remembered the image of the two making love when he walked into the bedroom. She had never made love to him the way she had to his friend. This was an unforgiveable moment, and he would never forget the image of her and his best friend. "I'm sorry, baby, but you and this worthless piece of shit get out of my house right now!"

The moral of this story is quite simple: the husband listened to his conscience, and he delivered the message that his conscience told him to deliver, which allowed him to walk away from what could have been a deadly encounter. From his vantage point, he was able to savage the little dignity that was left in his life and live another day to tell me his story.

In the finale of this story, it is a safe bet to always listen to your conscience, although it may land you in a very dangerous place. But if you listen to your conscience very carefully, it will get you out of the worst of terrible situations. And just in case you did not hear them, the walls were talking the entire time. Amen!

Chapter 21

WE ARE THE CREATORS of our own heaven and hell. The things that we do or don't do in this life are the initiators of our own heaven and hell right here on Earth. We do not necessarily have to wait until we die and be judged by God for us to live in hell for eternity. We can actually create as much hell for ourselves as we desire in the few short years that we have here on Earth. Needless to say, most people have a problem with believing or trying to understand the statement above. Why? It is because some idiot has convinced them that there is a heaven waiting just for them when they eventually take that eternal dirt nap.

If we fully understand exactly how God put all of this together, we will eventually see clearly that death is not the final step of our existence here on Earth. There is more to life and death than just merely being born, living a few years, doing all that we can to make it big while we are alive, and then suddenly dying and leaving everything that we have sweat blood and tears for for someone else to enjoy. Think about that for a moment! We come into this world for a purpose, but no one seems to know what that purpose really is. We who believe in God and in the birth of Jesus Christ believe that we are here to serve God. But the question is, "How are we supposed to serve God?!" Do we serve him by treating our fellow man right? Or do we serve God by attending church regularly and paying our fair share in tithes? Or is there some other way that we do not know about yet?

Here is what we know for sure: God is a mysterious spiritual being that no living mortal has ever laid eyes on. And according to the Bible, no one has ever laid eyes on him and lived to tell the rest of the world about it. But then we have to ask ourselves, "Why is it that God is so secretive?" Why does God not want mankind to see him? Is it because God knows that man has a way of exploiting everything that he puts his hands on? For example, let's take some pastors and ministers who claim to have gotten their calling straight from God but are exploiting their calling by defrauding their congregations and claiming that their blessings will only come by way of the amount of money in tithes and offerings that they are paying in church.

They say, "You're cheating God if you fail to give your fair share." Are you really? But a much better question comes to mind: "Who is it that is really cheating God or lying about their calling from God?" We know God is not lying to us simply because we neither know God nor have ever seen him. Again, here is what we know for sure: man can make and has always made his mouth say anything about everything. There is no limitation to what a man can say with his own mouth. Freedom of speech has guaranteed man's right to say pretty much anything he wants to say. Therefore, when he tells a lie about what God has told him, no one on Earth can rightfully say that the man is lying. Why? Because he knows, and we also know, that we cannot truthfully say who and what God has said to anyone.

Moreover, the statement above is the trick of the trade for most ministers and preachers. No one can deny or say for certain who has or has not been called by God to preach his Word. However, I remember once upon a time, there was a coworker of mine who would always come to work claiming that he had talked to God before coming to work. So one day, I asked my coworker, "Does God really talk back to you in a one-on-one conversation?"

"He talks to me every morning before I leave home!" he replied to me.

"Is it really God, or is it that inner voice that we sometimes call the Holy Spirit that only you can feel and hear?" I continued to quiz him, although this question was a little more complicated.

"No way, my brother, I actually talk to God every single day!" He confirmed his conversation with God.

"Okay, you say it's God's voice that you hear. . . . Can you describe what God's voice sounds like? I mean, tell me exactly what God sounds like because I have never actually heard God's voice. I have prayed to God, and I believe that he answers my prayers simply because what I pray for actually happens. The Bible says when I pray, have faith, and believe that what I am praying for is going to happen, it will happen. But I have never actually heard God's voice. And even if I did, how would I know that it is God?! I mean, it could be Satan's voice. After all, Satan does have the power to communicate with us as well as God."

"Are you saying that I am lying about God?!" he snapped at me angrily.

"No! I am not calling you a liar. The only thing I am asking is that if you heard God's voice talking to you—and you did say that he talks to you every morning— what does he sound like when you and he are having these direct conversations? I would just like to know." I was very serious with him about my question.

Instead of following up on my question, he simply walked away, mumbling and cursing to himself as if I had really said something awful about his mother. The problem was, of course, I knew when I asked him the question that he could not accurately describe God's voice without coming off sounding like a jerk. This is not to say that God did not actually have conversations with my coworker; it only means God does not want people running around making false claims that they cannot substantiate, especially about him. In most cases, that is why Jesus left behind the HS: to help us to understand what is expected of from God. Therefore, God does not need to speak to us directly. The Holy Spirit that is inside most of us gives directions and guidance when there is a need for it without having to say anything directly to us.

The problem with having the Holy Spirit inside of us, of course, is that most people cannot distinguish it from other voices that are speaking in their heads. And the one thing that those same people are failing to realize or even comprehend is some of the voices that they hear are coming directly from Satan, who has as much influence over our actions as the Holy Spirit.

Therefore, what do any of the things I just mentioned have to do with mankind creating his own heaven or hell? It has everything to do with what we do with the lives we live or the things we do not do with our lives. Evil thoughts are never good for the lives of human beings primarily because evil thoughts have a tendency to encourage us to do evil things. Needless to say, evil thoughts are the foundation for creating our own hell. Not one thing good has ever come from or been created or even built from the minds of evil thinkers. The minds of evil people have always been to destroy and kill innocent people.

When speaking of evil people, there is always one group of people who will immediately come to mind; they are people who are involved in terrorist activities. But the question is, "What is a 'terrorist'?" A terrorist is a human being who lives to implant fear and terror in the minds of other people. The only thing that a terrorist can think about is to kill innocent people who pose no threat to anyone. Innocent people are completely unarmed and unaware of what is about to happen to them. Therefore, what is the purpose of killing innocent people who mean the terrorists no harm at all? In four words, "Because they are evil!" Where did it come from? According to the Bible, Satan was the originator of evil who planned to steal God's kingdom.

There are no scriptures that were ever written that tell us that God created mankind to be evil. And the very next question would most likely be, "If God did not create mankind to be evil, did he allow it to continue even after he realized that Satan is the real culprit behind it?" Okay, God saw that all he had created in the beginning was good, including man. But soon after God created the woman to be man's companion, along came Satan whom God already knew was corrupted and evil. But he allowed Satan to implant his evil thoughts and corrupted ways into the minds and hearts of mankind, God's precious little human souls.

Then the question becomes, "Why on earth would God allow such a thing to happen to the very human beings whom he loved so dearly?!" He could have stopped Satan in his tracks just as he had kicked Satan and his followers out of heaven. But no! God actually allowed Satan to do his evil deeds on human beings. However, that was not the end of the story; God had already given mankind the "freedom of choice," which meant Eve and Adam were allowed to make a clear choice without interference as who they would believe, Satan or God. Naturally, we all know the choice that the two human beings made. They chose to listen to Satan rather than believe and obey the command that God had previously given them. And because they did not listen to what God had told them, they assassinated their own chance to live forever.

Today, mankind is no different than the very first two human beings that God created. Man has defied and is still defying, with every breath in his body, every opportunity that God put before him to make things right for himself. But obviously, the few people in the world who still absolutely believe that there is a creator of this world and who also believe that heaven and hell only come after death are wrong! And the truth is we can all create our own heaven and hell right here on Earth before we die. The hell or heaven that we create on Earth before we die will also determine whether we go to heaven or hell after we die.

Admittedly, that might sound like some sort of metaphor or wishful thinking that came straight out a fantasy novel. No, it is not! If we would give some serious thought or consideration as to how truthful the Bible might actually be, we would see that it gives us all the clues that we need to know about heaven and hell long before we die. You do not have to believe me! Take it straight from the Bible. These are the words of God; the choice of belief is yours.

> *Look, I will make new heavens and a new Earth, and people will not remember the past or think about those things. My people will be happy forever because of the things I will make. I will make a Jerusalem that is full of joy, and I will make her people a delight. Then I will rejoice over Jerusalem and be delighted with my people. There will never again be heard in that city the sounds of crying and sadness. There will never be a baby from that city who lives only a few days. And there will never be an older person who doesn't have a long life. A person who lives a hundred years will be called young, and a person who dies before he is a hundred will be thought of as a sinner.*
>
> *In that city, those who build houses will live there. Those who plant vineyards will get to eat their grapes. No more will one person build a house and someone else live there. One person will not plant a garden and someone else will eat its fruit. My people*

> *will live a long time, as trees live long. My chosen people will live there and enjoy the things they make. They will never again work for nothing. They will never again give birth to children who die young. All my people will be blessed by the Lord. They and their children will be blessed. I will provide for their needs before they ask, and I will help them while they are still asking for help. Wolves and lambs will eat together in peace. Lions will eat hay like oxen, and a snake on the ground will not hurt anyone. They will not hurt or destroy each other on all of my holy mountains.*

Naturally, some Bible-thumpers will assume that the message simply means or refers to what is to come after death. But if you read the message carefully, it does not mention anything about "after death." God is simply talking about a "new world" that he is going to build for his people. And all of this is going to happen while his people are still alive and kicking. If you will also notice, the message says nothing about heaven and hell for the good and the bad people; it is only referring to the people whom God is calling "his people."

Now of course, the major question suddenly becomes, "How does anyone who is alive today become part of 'God's People'?" We have to assume that to become God's people, we must turn our lives around from living the lifestyles that is pleasing to us into one that is pleasing in the eyes of God. In other words, this is not about us committing sinful acts then praying to God and asking for his forgiveness as a last result. This is all about getting our acts together now and keeping it together throughout our lifetime. God's people do not forget who they are and indulge themselves in sinful acts simply because it is in their nature to do so. God's people will never forget from the time they rise in the morning until they retire at the end of the day as whom they are serving. The first Commandment says it all: *We must serve God with all our minds, with all our hearts, and with all our souls.* Obviously, if we can do his will without deviating from the first and foremost Commandment, we will become a part of God's people.

In God's new world, there is no such thing as people being evil-minded or developing corrupted behaviors. In the "new world," the only thing God's people have to do is continuously thank him for being the magnificent Creator of all things. It is a wonderful feeling to know that such a place will exist eventually. We cannot write off this message as a joke or, as I said earlier, "wishful thinking" because it is written in the Bible. And if we wish to call the Bible a lie, then we may as well call our entire existence a lie, for we simply cannot exist without it.

The whole idea of believing in God is we have to believe that he has a plan for the people who take his words seriously and obey them. I do not believe that God went through all the trouble of creating an entire universe and the human race just to dismiss them all one day as if they had never existed. To me, that would be a total wasted effort of all the time and energy that was put into his entire act of creation. No, I believe that God will eventually take the best and the brightest of the human race and give them a place where they can work together in a harmonious fashion. If that is not his plan, what would be the purpose of him wanting mankind to believe that he even exists? That would make no sense. Therefore, it seems perfectly feasible to me that God wants to create a new heaven and a new Earth. Heaven is for himself and all of his angels who are now working under his total control. The "new Earth" is, of course, for us humans.

Heaven is a very special place for the people who have already died and made it into the angelic society. This is a society of angels whom God has already handpicked to go throughout the earth, telling his people how good it is going to be in the new world. Naturally, there are going to be those who will have doubts or simply do not believe in such a promise. But for those people, they will probably die and go to hell or continue to live in the old world where it will eventually catch fire and burn to ashes along with everyone who is still alive.

Now you might be asking yourself, "How is it that I know these things?" The answer is quite simple: all we have to do is look around us and see all the destruction that mankind is causing to this old world. God never said that he would come in and remake this world; he emphatically said that he would create a "new" heaven and Earth, which means he would start from nothing again and create an entire new world. And I am forced to believe that he is not creating a new world to put the same old evil people today in. There has to be a new way of thinking, a new way of acting, and a new way for people to worship the Creator of the new heaven and the new earth.

One more message of proof of what God is planning to do goes like this:

> *Heaven is my throne, and the earth is my footstool. So do you think you can build a house for me?! Do I need a place to rest? My hands made all things. All things are here because I made them. These are the people I am pleased with, those who are not proud and stubborn and who fear my words. But those people who kill bulls as a sacrifice to me are like those who kill people. Those who kill sheep as a sacrifice are like those who break the necks of dogs. Those who give me grain offerings are like those who offer me the blood of pigs. Those who burn incense are like those who worship idols. These people choose their own ways, not mine, and they love the terrible things they do. So I will choose their punishments, and I will punish them with the very things that they fear the most.*
>
> *I will make a new heaven and a new Earth, which will last forever. In the same way, your names and your children's names will always be with me. All people will come to worship me every Sabbath and every new moon. They will go and see the dead bodies of the people who have sinned against me. The worms that eat them will never die, and the fires that burn them will never stop, and everyone will hate to see those bodies.*

Now, those are the words of God and no one else. If the God who spoke those words is the same God who created heaven and Earth, it is imperative that we believe that he meant every word that was written. In other words, we are living in our heaven and hell right now, right here on Earth. Therefore, if we plan to pack up all our belongings and move into the new earth, we had best get started while we still have the opportunity. Amen!

Chapter 22

GOD HAS ALREADY PROMISED US 120 YEARS OF LIFE. In the beginning of the world, according to the Bible, men and women lived to be hundreds of years of age, something that is totally unthinkable in our world today. But then we have to ask ourselves, "Who was it who caused our years of living on Earth to be cut down to a fraction of what they were in the beginning?! Who was it?!" Well, besides Adam and Eve, who were the originators of sin, I have to blame the entire human race, who became very evil as a result of what Satan had done to the first of human creation.

Let's go back and look at the number of years that human beings were living on Earth before they became evil in the sight of God. Adam, for instance, lived to be eight hundred years old before he died despite the fact that he helped initiate the first sin along with Eve. But I noticed one thing about the son of Adam and Eve; after Cain killed Abel, there was no mention of how long Cain lived in the land of Nod. However, the Bible does mention the age of Seth, who was the next born son after Cain killed his brother Abel. Seth lived a total of 912 years before he died.

Obviously, due to the fact there is no mention of how long Cain lived, his life was probably cut short due to his sinful act of murder. Nevertheless, many men lived to be hundreds of years old on

Earth before they died. But because of the evil nature of mankind, God decided to cut man's life expectancy down to the bare-bone minimum. The Scriptures tell us the following:

> *The number of people on Earth began to grow, and daughters were born to them. When the sons of God saw how beautiful these girls were, they married any whom they wanted to.*

It was clear that this was an act that God highly disapproved of because these sons of God were thought to have been fallen angels who had descended to Earth as a result of the rebellious act of following Satan. And God said as a result of this, "My Spirit will not remain in human beings forever because they are flesh. They will now live only for 120 years."

These sons of God were described by some writers as giants, but there is no history that has been recorded as to where these giants came from. They were called "Nephilim," and according to the Scriptures:

> *The Nephilim were on Earth in those days and also later. And that was when the sons of God had sexual relations with the daughters of human beings. These women gave birth to children who became famous and were the mighty warriors of long ago.*

Okay, here were a bunch of people known as giants who apparently were already on Earth before God created Adam and Eve. And because they had sexual relationships with human beings, God became very unhappy with them and cut the lives of human beings short. However, whatever became of the Nephilim? Where did they come from, and more importantly, where did they go? And one other point I may add is that even after the "Great Flood" when God destroyed everyone on Earth with the exception of Noah and his family, the Nephilim showed up on Earth again. And the question that immediately comes to my mind once again is, "Where did these larger-than-life people come from if everyone was killed except Noah and his family? How did they survive the Great Flood?!"

So here we are in the twenty-first century, many years since the beginning of time, where we are looking at a life expectancy of less than seventy-five years for the vast majority of people on Earth. And it is all because of a race of giant people that no longer exist, as far as we know. And what makes this situation even stranger than fiction is that they were known as the "sons of God." If they were not fallen angels, then who were these beings? And more importantly, if they were not fallen angels, how did they survive the Great Flood? As far as we know, the only human beings who survived were Noah and his family. But after the flood was over, the sons of God were back in business again.

When I think seriously about why God severely cut our lives short on Earth, he knew that the fallen angels had infected the human race with evil, and there was no way that he could allow human beings to live hundreds of years with their evil ways. The Scriptures may not refer to the sons of God as fallen angels, but I will! And because I am convinced that they were the fallen angels who rebelled against God along with Satan, what better way to strike back at God than to infect human beings with evil simply by having sexual relations with all the human women? This was a direct hit on God's people, and we have yet to recover.

Okay, here is what the Bible does not tell us: the "sons of God" were Satan's followers who saw beautiful human women willing to have sex with these giant creatures simply because they were giant creatures. But the Bible did in fact point out that the children of these giants became famous and were mighty warriors. Again, this was a direct blow on God, aimed by Satan, while human beings were the main targets.

The question now is, "Are these sons of God still around today and still marrying human beings for the purpose of having sex to create a race of evil children who will eventually become great leaders and warriors?" My answer is certainly; they are still around! If the greatest flood of all time did not kill them, how can time or anything else kill them off? We have to remember that the fallen angels did not die in the flood, and they are still among us. They will be around as long as Satan is in charge of creating evil. And as far as we know, Satan will be around until the return of Jesus, and only God knows when that will happen.

The single most asked question today in the twenty-first century is, "Regardless of who started or caused God to cut mankind's years of life from huge numbers to any number less than a hundred, what is the one reason why most people cannot live to reach that magic number of 120 years?" The answer is quite simple; it is the same reason why the sons of God mixed and mingled with regular human beings, which caused God to destroy the world. It was the sinful acts of mankind. Today, we have fallen into that the same category as the people in the beginning did. In other words, we cannot save ourselves from short-lived lives for sinning.

If God promised us 120 years, which is down from nine hundred, eight hundred, or six hundred years, it is obvious that he is still sticking by that number. There is nothing we can point to that says God has changed his mind about allowing us to live more than 120 years. Therefore, we are our own worst enemy when it comes to living a moderately long life. Now the question has become, "What is it that we must do to reach the 120-year mark?" First and foremost, we must obey God's commands! Secondly, we must learn how to treat our fellow man right. Admittedly, treating our fellow man right has never been something that the human race has been able to master. We are constantly at war with each other for no apparent reason. Wars have taken the lives of young soldiers who were not even old enough to drink or get a driver's license. And at the end of each war, no one who actually fought and died in battle knew the reason they were fighting.

Of course, we all sing the same old song: "To keep America free or safe!" And then the question becomes, "Free or safe from what or whom?!" In half of the wars that Americans have been involved in, we fought because we were helping other people or nations. They were not to keep America free. For instance, we fought in the North and South Korean War because we wanted help keep South Korea free from being taken over by the North Koreans. Fifty thousand young Americans were slaughtered in the process. Then we have the Vietnam War. This was yet another war situation where the United States tried to free the south from the north. And another five hundred thousand young soldiers died fighting in a war, and most surviving veterans today have no clue as to why they were sent there in the first place.

Of course, I can say that getting involved in these wars was an act of helping our fellow man, which is very noble on our part. But then we have to go back to the beginning and ask why these acts of aggressions on parts of nations were divided into two parts, north and south, in the first place. It is simply because mankind has no sense of reasoning as far as survival is concerned. In other words, mankind was born to learn how to survive in a land that was not created by him as long as the Creator will allow him to survive. These wars were initiated primarily because one side of a nation wanted to own and control the other side of a land that no one rightfully owned in the first place. All wars are fought primarily because of "territorial rights."

Now I come to the other parts of why we cannot take advantage of God's gift of long life. This is called "lifestyle"! The lifestyles of the young, bold, and beautiful are nothing more than a sad excuse for having life in the first place. But to be fair, the lifestyle of people living in the twenty-first century are an "old hat"! In other words, the lifestyles of today have been around centuries. For the average young person born into the world today, yesterday, and probably tomorrow as well, "life is simply one big party!" It is a party that we all hope will last forever. But then reality sets in, and we suddenly realize that the party is over. And when the party is over, what do we do with ourselves then?! Well, for most people, they sit around and wait to die. But that is not what God intended when he said, "My spirit will not remain in human beings forever because they are flesh. They will live only 120 years."

The 120 years are ours for the taking; we just have to learn how to live for 120 years. That, of course, means that we cannot jump-start our lives off with a bang as if there is no tomorrow because there is a tomorrow if we learn how to live today. There is nothing in life that is so urgent that we need to take advantage of every opportunity that comes our way. Most young people want to be on top of everything that pops up in front of them. But they forget or were never told that life does not begin or end with them. There is a tomorrow only if they are around to be a part of it. In other words, to live a long life takes planning from the time we realize that we have lives worth living. And to know that we have lives worth living is to discover that we did not make ourselves, very complex machines that we call "human bodies."

Although God does not and will not guarantee us life or the number of years that each of us will live, it is simply because our life span is pretty much left up to us. However, the guarantee lies in the way we live the only lives that we have been given. If human beings live their lives according to the Commandments that have already been laid out in the Bible, we can be assured to have a long life span. In the Ten Commandments, there is one Commandment that says, "*Honor your father and your mother so that you will live a long time in the land that the Lord your God is going to give you.*" How hard is it to honor our parents? To honor our parents should be like walking in the park. But for many people, it is the worst thing that they can do. And because we show our parents so little respect or regard, God will punish us by shortening our lives.

Needless to say, disrespecting our parents is not the only thing that will keep us from living our lives to the full life spans that God promised. Again, I will take us back to lifestyle: the most important thing that man has simply forgotten is the fact that his body does not belong to him. Our bodies belong to the Creator, and we must give them back to the Maker when our life spans have expired. There is no exchange for a new body when the ones we have get old, worn out, or beat up. We must simply live with what we have until the day we die or if, for some reason, modern medicine cannot make it possible for us to live longer. However, according to the promise of the 120 years that God made to us, we can live a long life in perfect health provided that we live our lives according to God's Commandments.

Now the question that we must all ask ourselves is, "Why is it that we cannot live our lives according to God's commands?" What is so hard about the Ten Commandments that we cannot obey them? Not only that, but why do we find so much pleasure in putting illegal drugs, cigarette smoke, or alcohol in our bodies, knowing beforehand that these things will damage and destroy every organ in the body? Allow me to take this a step further: "Why do we find so much pleasure in eating food that will make us obese and affect every organ in our bodies?" These are only a few of many things that will make it impossible to claim the 120 years that God has promised us.

Besides drugs and alcohol, which rapidly destroy the body of mankind, illicit sex is the next major reason why we as human beings fall short of reaching the magic number of 120 years. In other words, sex can kill the human body faster than a speeding bullet. But we all find reasons to believe that sex is good for the body, which is a made-up philosophy and not one that God gave us. God created sex between human beings as well as between animals for the sole purpose of reproduction and nothing else. Sex that is being used as a pleasure item between human beings is an evil exercise that has caused countless of people to die at an early age. Naturally, we as human beings have always failed to see or understand the evil paradox that lies beneath the beauty of having sex for pleasure.

We as human beings believe that our bodies are ours to do with as we see fit. We also believe that if sex for pleasure was not a part of God's purpose when he included it within the human anatomy, then why make it a pleasurable part of life? Admittedly, I am sure there are many things that God included within the creation of the human being that he probably regretted afterward. But because he gave us all "free will," it became our sinful way to learn and correct our own problems. Therefore, for anyone to reach the 120-year mark, he or she must come to terms with the Commandments of God and learn to obey them.

Furthermore, the Bible tells us that our bodies are "temples of God," which means our bodies are not our own to do as we please with them. When we destroy our bodies by having sex and using other substances that are not intended to be put into the body, we are destroying the image of God. We are the embodiment of God, and whatever we do to harm or destroy our bodies, we also do to harm and destroy the body of God. How is that possible? It is possible because whenever we look at ourselves in a mirror, we are looking at the image of God. In other words, we are God's men and women, or we are little Gods who were created to be a direct reflection of a bigger God, the creator of all things. Naturally, being God's men and women, of course, makes us everything that God himself is, which also puts us a step higher than angels.

Okay, now that we know who we are and how long God had already promised we can live in this world, the rest is totally up to us make it to 120 years. It is not a question of whether we can make it to 120 years, but it is more of what we are willing to do to survive for 120 years. It is not like God is going to actually live our lives for us or come down from his kingdom and hold our hands until we make it there. No, God has given us everything that we need to know to live a long life.

I have written another book about the "seven deadly sins" that all human beings are guilty of committing. These seven deadly things that we commit daily will do more to kill us quicker than we can count to seven. And because the seven deadly sins are so misunderstood or are never considered by most people, I believe that they are worth mentioning again. It is said that the seven deadly sins are transgressions that are fatal to the spiritual process. In other words, if we kill our spirit, we kill our bodies.

Pride is the excessive belief in one's own abilities, which automatically interferes with the individual's ability to recognize the grace of God. In other words, an individual becomes stuck on himself or herself to the point that they believe they are the sole reason for being who they are. And what is even worse is they have become so brainwashed by their own stupidity that they believe there is no power higher than their own powers.

Envy is the desire for others' traits, abilities, or situations. There is no other person like an envious individual who will do almost anything, even commit murder, to have what someone else has. In other words, envy is dangerous, and it is deadly.

Gluttony is an inordinate desire to consume more than that which one requires. And perhaps we have all seen people who, for some strange reason, constantly eat entirely too much food for their own good. In other words, they eat so much food until they become obese. Being obese is never healthy because too much fat in almost all living creatures' bodies will kill them.

Lust is the inordinate craving for the pleasure of the body. For many people in the world, having sex is the only way to live. Having sex is the only way to go and might seem like a good idea at first, but having sex with anybody and everybody can lead us down a path that we cannot return from. Some diseases that can be transmitted from having sex are often deadly.

Anger is manifested in the individual who chooses to spin love, and instead, he or she opts for fury. This condition is also known as wrath. The question is, "If God is all about love, how did man discover the idea of being angry?" It all started with Cain and Abel, when Cain became angry with his brother for no apparent reason and murdered him. The obvious answer as to who invented anger is Satan, the author of wrath and confusion.

Greed is the desire for material wealth or gain, which in most cases is the reason why a person will ignore the realm of the spiritual law.

God is the only real source of wealth. Any gains that are made outside of the blessings of God are a waste because they are easily gained and easily lost. In other words, God gives us power to get wealth.

Sloth is the avoidance of physical and spiritual work. In other words, any individual who would rather lay around and feed off other people is simply lazy. But how did they get this way? People have become this way because they have no desire to do better for themselves by simply working for what they want. Living off the land is good only if we own the land and know how to grow what the land can and will provide us in terms of food and resources. Needless to say, the only way we can accomplish any such living off the land is through God's blessing. However, being guilty of sloth can lead to an early death.

Each one of the seven deadly sins were put in place to let us know that we were given life for a purpose, and that purpose is to serve God. And if we wish to live for 120 years, serving God is the only way for us to get there with clear states of mind and in healthy conditions. Otherwise, like so many before us, we will die long before our time. But regardless of how long we live here on Earth, God has already promised us 120 years, and it is up to us to find the correct solution as to how we can sustain our longevity.

Serving God will lead us in the right direction as to how we can avoid the seven deadly sins and live out to that promise that he has given us.

Chapter 23

THE TRUTH ABOUT HOMOSEXUALITY — My research and deep thoughts concerning this masterpiece, *Telling It Like It Is*, have taken me into many deep corners and dark places where I would have never voiced my opinion on such issues before. Homosexuality is one of those subjects or places where most people dare not tread their pretty little feet in. But as for me, here I am with an opinion like I have never spoken before on the "gay lifestyle." It is nonetheless an ugly lifestyle and one that I believe goes against everything that was put in place during the creation of man and woman.

For me to be correct about my assessment on homosexual behavior, let me first explain what being homosexual really means. According to *Webster's Dictionary*, "homosexual" means or relates to having a sexual orientation toward persons of the same sex or, better yet, sexual activity with another person of the same sex.

Okay, so what is exactly is Webster talking about? Webster is simply saying that the homosexual lifestyle consists of two men or two women having sex with each other. Homosexuality simply means having sex! And there is nothing else that anyone can add or take away from it. In other words, it is just that simple and nothing more. But then I am forced to ask God, "What did you do wrong when you created man and woman that would cause a man to fall in love with another man or that would cause a woman to want another woman?!"

According to the greatest book in the world, which just happens to be the Bible, God planned, schemed, and plotted the perfect world for all human beings. And in doing so, he devised a plan that was so perfect that he would only need to create two human beings in the beginning, which would consist of one man and one woman. And after God had performed his initial creation, the world then become populated with other human beings by men and women having sex and reproducing other human beings in their same likeness.

The question is still ringing in my head: "What was so wrong with God's plan of creating a man and a woman who would then reproduce others to carry on with the plan that was laid out long before them?" In other words, what is it that one man could find so attractive in another man that he would want to have sex with that man? And better yet, what is it that two women could possibly have in common sex-wise that they would want to get involved with each other sexually? On God's drawing board, any two people of the same sex should have nothing in common that would become attractive to each of them sexually. So who changed the game plan that God took so much time putting together? In two words: "Mankind did!"

Without getting too technical, let us look at the physiological makeup of the human body. God created the perfect design for reproduction between male and female. Man was given a penis that was designed to be inserted into a woman's vagina, and when the two came to an emotional climax, the woman would then become pregnant with a child. That child would then grow up and eventually meet a man or woman, and so on the process would continue. But there is no way on Earth this same process can be possible between two men or two women. So what does that tells us? It tells us that mankind decided of his own free will that whatever God had put together, which was perfect for one man and one woman, he would twist it around in such a perverted manner until it seems more like the work of Satan instead of the creation of God.

It has always been my belief that whatever God has put together, no man should be in a position to tear it apart. But lo and behold, there is a world of geeks and freaks who feel that they can disregard whatever plans God intended to be perfect and redesign them to the point where they are actually disgusting to even think about. So who among us as human beings would be bold enough to think that they could change whatever plans God put in place to fit their own perverted ways? It would seem to me that these creatures are the ones who believe that God was wrong when he said to Adam and Eve, "Go forth and multiply!" for there is no way that two men or two women can reproduce, which means God was right, and man is wrong.

There are people who will dare to believe that God made a terrible mistake when he created them as one sex, male or female, but they feel that they should be in another sexual body. In other words, they were born as men but feel that they should be women. Or we have the ones who remain as one sex but perform and/or dress up as another sex. They say God should have made them into the persons that they feel or want to be. When is it that God has ever taken advice from a mere mortal about sex? God did not take advice from his own begotten son Jesus Christ, or he would not have allowed Jesus to die on the cross. But God knows what is best for us all. And admittedly, we do not have a clue as to what God really wants from us or for us. We can only hope that he hears our prayers and pleas when we call his name for help.

Just think for a fraction of a moment: we who believe in God know very well that we cannot change what has already been established as a fact of God. We cannot change the weather, and we can replace neither the sun nor the stars or the moon. We did not decide whether we should be born as males or females; someone else much bigger than all of us made those decisions long before we even entered into the world. Therefore, who are we to tell God who we should or should not be? This is not our call to make! If we decide that we are unhappy with who we are, it is without a doubt that a sex change is not going to solve our problem. There is a real likelihood that we will have a larger problem with trying to be someone we are not. If we change who we are, then we are simply saying to God that the Bible is a lie when it says that he does not make a mistake.

Are we to believe that when God created Adam and Eve and commanded them to go forth and multiply, at the same time, he also created a man who would have sex with another man?! If this is true, then I am forced to believe individuals when they say they were born gay as created by God. But does being born gay mean that a person will have sexual feelings for a man or woman of the same sex? Is it also true that any human being at one time or another in an isolated situation, such as in prison, will have sexual feelings for someone of the same sex? And does that make a man or woman become homosexual because they are in an isolated situation where the opposite sex is not available? If all of this is true, we can assume that all men and women who have been to prison or who are still in prison are homosexuals.

Going back to Adam and Eve, I sincerely doubt that God created anyone to be a homosexual! The reason is quite simple: there is no known purpose on Earth or in life for anyone to become a homosexual. What real purpose besides sexual gratification does homosexuality serve mankind? Naturally, homosexuality is not new to God or mankind. In biblical times, there were perverts who craved to have sexual relations with other men, which means God hated it then, and he hates it today.

The one question that has always escaped my comprehension or understanding is, "What could possibly cause one man to have a sexual desire for another man?" There is no way in a realistic world that two men or two women should desire one another without having a twisted or warped mentality. This type of mentality is no more than slapping God in the face and saying, "I don't like what you have made me! Therefore, I have decided to change what I am and become what I want to be for the simple pleasure of sex." But they are wrong! Two men being together is not an act of having sex; it is a perverted act of two human beings doing what is less than animals.

Today is a new day where the old ways of doing things such as having intercourse with the opposite sex is not enough of an option. Mankind today needs to have a variety of sexual pleasures even if it means knowing that there it is a curse attached to such pleasures. It is a curse simply because it is perverted, it is inhuman, it is unnatural, and it is totally unclean. And anything that is unclean in the eyes of God is as deadly as having a disease.

Once upon a time, I worked a beat where I was in constant contact with a young man who was gay. Personality-wise, he was a great human being, but he loved to be with other men who were also of the gay persuasion. We were friends, and like some people, he wanted to talk to me about his lifestyle. For me, it was more of a curiosity than anything else. I wanted to know what could possibly be so attractive about another man that would make him want to be in bed with one for sex. He said, "Straight guys would never understand the lifestyle of a gay person."

Naturally, I was in total agreement with him because I was not gay, and there is nothing about a man that could entice me to want to have sex with him or any other man. But I was seriously interested in his reason for doing such a thing and becoming a homosexual. While I was working the west side beat, there were several interesting things that shook me to my core concerning so-called "straight men" and those who were openly gay. And my friend Charlie helped me to understand the mystery of what I had witnessed on several occasions.

My conversation with Charlie started with me asking him, "I've seen men who were with women in the early part of the evenings, but they returned later in the night looking for gay men to hang out with. Why is that?"

Charlie smiled as if he was amused by the question. "Like I told you, you would never understand the lifestyle of a gay person unless you are one or you become involved with one. Then you might understand the attraction that other men have for men like me. But since you are in the business of trying to understand what's going on with us, just let me say that we can do things to other men that most women can't do. Why?! It is because we understand what men want, how they want it, and when they want it."

"So would you say the same thing applies for women who understand what other women want, but only women can understand that better than men?" I asked but clearly understood where he would probably go with his response.

"That's precisely what I am saying!" he snapped quickly. "I have several men friends who are married, and I suppose they are happy in their marriages. But when they want to have a sexual relationship with someone who will give them unlimited sexual pleasure, they prefer having it with another man."

"Okay, let's say that I fully understand where you are coming from when you say men understand what other men want much better than women when it comes to sexual pleasures. But you should also understand that this whole idea of sexual pleasure came from the mind of the Creator. He intended for sex to be enjoyed between a man and a woman. Which means you're basically saying that the Creator got it all wrong, am I right?!" I said to Charlie.

"No!" Charlie snapped surprisingly. "I am not saying that God got it all wrong. But you must also understand that the Creator gave us the free will to do what makes us happy and what we love to do. Now if God is a God of love who allows us to make our own decisions, what could possibly be wrong with men making love to other men?!"

"Look, just because we have free will doesn't give us the right to do sinful acts such as having a sexual relationship with the same sex," I tried to explain to Charlie. "If that were the case, we would have free will to commit murder without consequences. But we know it is a violation of God's Commandments. This also means that if God had wanted men having sex with other men, he would have created Adam and Steve instead of Adam and Eve, right?!"

Charlie did not argue the point that I had made. But I knew that he was not a believer in the Bible either. Then he said slowly, "Am I so different from the people who don't believe in God or the Bible? Think about it. The Bible was written by men, not God! And it was those same kinds of men who wrote Bible who think that homosexuality is wrong. It is the same thing as those who said man evolved from an ape instead of being created by God as the Bible says."

Admittedly, Charlie made a valid point in what he was saying. But I was not sold on the idea that homosexuality was a righteous lifestyle as he believed. So I then pressured Charlie further by asking him, "Do you believe that you were born gay, or is this something that you decided to do on your own? In other words, do you believe God created gay people?"

Charlie looked at me and laughed. "Born gay?! Are you asking me if I was born gay? Now I doubt very seriously that you believe that people are born to be gay, right?!"

Then I laughed at him. "Well, to be honest with you, I don't believe people are born gay. I believe it's a lifestyle that you and people like you turn to after you are born into the world. Of course, I've seen very young people act a certain way, and it is obvious from their behavior or the way they carry themselves that they are going to be gay when they are older," I said.

"There you have it! That proves that people are born gay. When you find very young people who don't even know the meaning of being gay yet act in a homosexual manner, how do you explain this type of behavior as not being born gay?!" Charlie asked seriously.

Again, Charlie made his point very clear and effectively. So I decided to make a point that was straight out of the Bible. "You may or may not believe in the Bible, but there is a story about the city of Sodom and Gomorrah when some men showed up at Lot's house and demanded that the two men who had come to destroy city be brought out so they could have sexual relationships with them."

"I have heard the story," Charlie said. "But tell it to me again anyway."

"Okay, you heard the story," I said. "Anyway, Lot went outside and told the men that not to even think of doing such an evil thing because it was against God. He even offered the men his two daughters who had never had sex before. But they wanted the two men who were sent by God to destroy that city. This was because Sodom and Gomorrah had become cities that were entirely too evil to leave standing as they were. Abraham even pleaded with God not to destroy Sodom and Gomorrah, and God responded by telling Abraham that if he could find five righteous people there, he would not destroy them. Well, as you know, Sodom and Gomorrah were totally destroyed along with everyone who lived there except Lot and his two daughters." I then watched Charlie's expression as if he was not totally convinced that the destruction of Sodom and Gomorrah was all about homosexuality and nothing else.

"Okay, your point was well taken," Charlie admitted. "But how do you explain the birth of women who are born with both sex organs? They are called he-shes, you know! And then there is someone who is like myself who was born a man, but there is nothing that I admire or I find attractive about a woman. I prefer being a woman myself! In fact, in a couple of weeks, I am planning to have a sex-change operation, which will make me a complete woman."

Talk about a bombshell being dropped on me. That bit of news was a complete earthquake. "What?! Are you serious?!" I snapped without thinking about my question. Then I looked at Charlie who was a very handsome guy. Finally, I said, "Okay, I can see that!" But it was still hard for me to believe that he was seriously considering becoming a woman.

"You sound as if you didn't see that coming!" Charlie said, laughing.

"See that coming?!" I snapped. "Man, you just hit me over the head with a sledgehammer. But let me ask you this. Why?! I mean, you can have any woman you want in the entire city of Atlanta. In fact, Atlanta has some of the most beautiful women in the world. You are a handsome man who could have the pick of the litter. Why become one of them?!"

"See, that's why I told you that you would never understand the world that I live in unless you become a member of my gay world and my lifestyle," Charlie said, laughing. "Have you ever been involved with a gay man before?"

"No!" I snapped quickly. "Well, not sexually," I admitted. "But there was this one guy when I was in the military, and we used to hang out together. I mean, he was a good-looking guy, and he could pull the chicks with no effort at all. And to be honest with you, I was actually jealous of this guy. And he later became my best friend, and we did a lot of things together. But it was not until he died from the AIDS virus that I knew that he was gay. But I have always asked myself, if he was gay, why was it that I never knew, or why had he never tried to hit on me?"

"It was because he knew that you were not gay, and he didn't want to ruin the relationship that you and he had by letting you know that he was gay," Charlie explained. "You see, we know who are gay from those who are not. Your friend liked you just the way you are, and you were probably not someone he was attracted to."

I was not too sure how to take that one. "Okay, we were the best of friends, but I never even suspected him of being gay. How could he keep such a secret from me?" I asked finally.

"Because you and he never ran in the same circles as he and his gay friends did. However, the question is, how do you think you would have felt about him if you had found out that he was gay before he died?" Charlie asked me seriously.

I sat there for a long while, thinking about the question before saying, "I guess I'd feel crushed like I felt when I discovered the cause of his death and the reason why he had died, which was AIDS that he apparently contracted from another man. Even now, it is still hard for me to wrap my head around the fact that he was gay."

"Well, those are the risks that we all take in becoming gay men, just like there are risks that you take in dealing with women. I am sure there are more sexually transmitted diseases that you catch from women than there have ever been coming from men. So as the old saying goes, we all have to die from something," Charlie said with a laugh. Then he went on to say, "Listen, life can be a real bitch if we are not willing to take chances or risks. Life is worthless if we don't do the things that we really enjoy. I know you feel or think the same way!"

I did not answer the question, and at that point, we concluded our conversation. I left Charlie, feeling a little confused about how I felt about the lifestyle of homosexuality. In other words, we are all human beings living on the same mound of dirt. There is only one human being who has ever worn the title of being perfect, and that was Jesus Christ. And as Charlie had made it so very clear to me, there are people who are actually born to be women but have male sex organs or both. How do we as mere mortals explain that?! Not only that, but how do we explain our own kids who were born to be male or female but show all the tendencies of wanting to be just opposite of who they really are? In two words: "We cannot!"

Six months after my conversation with Charlie, I came in contact with who was now Charlene, after she had the sex-change operation. "Oh my God!" I shouted out loud. For the second time, the guy I knew as Charlie had completely knocked me off my feet. Charlene was simply a beautiful woman, although we did not discuss the details of what had taken place during her transformation from man to woman, and it was better that I did not know. But there was one thing that I knew for certain: any man who did not know Charlie as a man would not believe his eyes to know that what once was a handsome man had now become a gorgeous woman.

With that in mind, and after seeing her with my own two eyes, who am I to say who should be whatever they were born to be until death? Charlie's desire was to be a woman, and his transition to womanhood from manhood was simply a miraculous feat. Maybe this was God's will, and who am I to say otherwise?! I cannot speak for God toward other people's lifestyles. Only my own matters to me.

Chapter 24

THE PRESTON COBB STORY — Twelve angry white men sat as the jury in the murder trial of a fifteen-year-old black male in Monticello, the county seat of Jasper County, Georgia. The young man was Preston Cobb Jr., a ninth-grader who dropped out of school to work on a dairy farm for Coleman Dumas Sr., the man he was accused of murdering. The twelve men who decided the outcome of this trial were R. R. Powell, A. B. Malone, C. L. Gilmore, Burner Lynch, G. B. Turner Jr., L. N. Smith, G. A. Spearman, L. W. Benton, G. S. Ballard, Valvard McMichael, M. E. McElheney, and C. L. Henderson. These twelve men were all old white businessmen and members of the KKK of Jasper County.

Under normal circumstances, this would have been just another case of a black man killing a white man or woman and immediately being sentenced to die on the electric chair. But this was not a just another murder trial where a verdict was reached quickly and where the white folks went back to their normal routine of calling every black face they came across "niggers." No, this was much more than that. This was a young man who was accused of killing his mother's white lover and the man she was housekeeping for.

According to court documents, on June 1, 1961, at approximately five-thirty that afternoon, Preston Cobb Jr. walked to a neighborhood store in Hillsboro, Georgia, to buy a pack of cigarettes. After buying the cigarettes, he began to walk a few miles back to Coleman Dumas Sr.'s house, where his mother had already departed for the day. However, before he committed the murder, he went back to Bud Maddox's store a few miles away and bought some more cigarettes. This time, he returned to the old man's house, where he was not a stranger to the white man. He waited outside of the house for about fifteen to twenty minutes before getting a .22-caliber rifle from the back of Dumas' station wagon, and he sat beside the road a few more minutes.

Then he decided to enter the house through the rear kitchen door, which was already unlocked. But before he went in the kitchen, he placed the rifle by the steps outside that led into the kitchen. And when Preston Cobb walked into the house, the old man looked around and asked him, "What do you want?"

Preston, who was not afraid of the old man, simply said, "Nothing!" Then he walked back outside the house.

Now it was time! He picked up the rifle and went back into the house as Dumas sat in a rocking chair just inside the living room, watching television. Preston Cobb Jr. stood next to the kitchen table, where his view of the white man's back was in plain sight. He aimed the rifle at the back of the man's head and pulled the trigger, killing him instantly. After placing the rifle back outside near the steps, he went back into the house and dragged the man's body out to the station wagon that was parked near the rear door. Preston Cobb was a short, skinny Negro boy who only weighed 140 pounds, and Coleman Dumas Sr. was a six-foot, heavy white man, weighing over two hundred pounds. My question is, "How was Preston Cobb Jr., being so small himself, able to drag this heavy body to the car that was parked outside so easily?"

Preston Cobb then opened the rear of the Ford station wagon and placed the body on top of the spare tire that was in the back of the vehicle. He also placed the rifle in the back of the vehicle alongside the body. He then drove away from the farmhouse and down a dirt road, stopping in a curve where he would not be seen by the neighbors of Coleman Dumas Sr. There, he pulled the body from the vehicle and threw it in a deep ditch. After throwing out everything that belonged to the man whom he had just murdered,

Preston Cobb then drove the station wagon to Bud Maddox's store again to fix a flat tire that had happened while the vehicle was parked at the house.

Upon his arrival at the store, he realized that there was no jack in the car to change the tire. He borrowed a jack from Bud Maddox, the owner of the store, but it didn't fit the vehicle. At that moment, Marshall Tinsley, a close friend of Cobb's, came by the store, and he had a jack that would fit the station wagon. Marshall Tinsley helped Cobb changed the flat tire, and they both drove to the house of Tinsley's aunt, where they would get together for an evening of having fun. With Marshall doing the driving from this point on due to Cobb not having a driver's license, the partying and riding in the dead man's car lasted all night until the next morning.

The next morning on June 2, 1961, they traveled to the Jasper County Training School, a segregated black school, because it was the last day of school before the summer vacation break. There, he and Marshall mingled with several kids and former classmates before their departure for another day of riding and drinking wine and beer. But as they were leaving, at the end of the school driveway, several police officers and deputy sheriffs stopped the now stolen vehicle, arrested Preston and Marshall, and charged them with the murder of Coleman Dumas Sr.

This was the beginning of a murder case gone all wrong. Marshall Tinsley was taken to the city and county jail and was booked for murder while at least three deputies escorted Preston in the back seat of a patrol car to Butts County. There, several white men dressed in law enforcement officer uniforms began to beat Preston with rubber hoses, telling him what to say when the trial began. "You will plead guilty to murdering Coleman Dumas Sr. and stealing his twenty-dollar gold piece as well as his Ford station wagon!" one of the officers screamed at Preston. "Do you understand what I am saying, nigger?!"

At first, Preston would not acknowledge the commands that were given to him, and they continued with the beating. But after several hours of this brutal beating, Preston began to mutter, "Yeah, I understand . . ."

At that point, Preston was then taken to Jones County, where the beating continued and where verbal commands were shouted to him as to what he should say in court. Naturally, the thought came to the law enforcement officers of killing the young black boy and that it would save the county and the good white folks of Jasper County a lot of money and time than it would take to have a trial. But by now, the word was spreading that they had arrested the young black man for the murder of a prominent white man south of the city. Preston turning up dead at the hands of several white police officers and sheriff deputies would not look good on their behalf. And of course, it would spark a lot of questions from the black folks as to what had really happened to an unarmed young black fifteen-year-old teenager.

Naturally, this kind of thinking was a sign of hope that white folks in Jasper County were changing for the better. Because from the early 1900s, Jasper County was known as "Bloody Jasper" to many people outside the county. There had been many rumors floating around as far away as Atlanta that Jasper County, Georgia, was the home station for murdering black men and women for no reason or just because they could, and there was no one with any form of authority to put a stop to it. Therefore, black people were lynched by the hundreds in Jasper County. The last recorded lynching was in 1946, a year after the end of World War II, a war where many black men had served.

By the time the officers arrived in Jones County with Preston, he had been tortured enough to say whatever they wanted him to say. But the beating with the rubber hoses continued. Why the rubber hoses? It was because rubber hoses left no marks or evidence that such brutal tactics had ever taken place. From Jones County, he was taken to Putnam County, where more beatings took place. But now he had been spoon-fed what to say and how to say it. Cobb started off by stating, "When I took Mr. Coleman out of the car, his pocketbook fell from his pocket, and I picked it up and put it in the car. On our way to Macon, we ran out of gas near Round Oak. The twenty-dollar gold piece that Sheriff Ezell got out of my pocket was part of the twenty-eight dollars that I had taken from Mr. Coleman's pocketbook. We bought gas and other things with the other eight dollars that I took."

"Now tell us why you killed Mr. Coleman!" Sheriff Frank Ezell ordered Cobb.

"About two weeks ago, Mr. Coleman and I went fishing. The next day, he asked me, 'Did you eat all the fish?' And I asked him, 'What fish?!' Then he cursed me. And after I had finished feeding the calves, I left and went home. Yesterday, which was June 1, I made up my mind to shoot him. But while I was unloading gravel at the fish pond, Mr. Coleman brought up the subject about me eating all the fish again. And I told him that I didn't eat the fish! That's when he told me that I better be careful how I talk to an old man. He said that he was too old to be playing and that he was going to blow my brains out at any minute. This was about four-thirty that afternoon, and that was when I had made up my mind to kill him. I went to the house and got my brother's pistol, and before I went to Mr. Coleman's house, I left the pistol across the road from his house."

My question is, "If Preston went to his home and took his brother's pistol to kill the old white man, why did he use the rifle that belonged to Coleman Dumas Sr.?" Why not shoot him with the pistol that he had brought to commit the crime with in the first place? However, this question neither came up in the trial nor was ever answered as to what happened to the pistol after he shot the man with the rifle. The testimonies from the officers who investigated the homicide said the shell casings that were found at the murder scene belonged to that of the .22-caliber rifle that belonged to Coleman Dumas Sr. But the gun that Preston Cobb brought from home to commit the murder with was also a .22-caliber pistol. However, there was no ballistic evidence that was used to identify which .22-caliber weapon the shell casings came from. And what happened to the pistol?

Preston Cobb, the defendant, made an open-court admission to members of the jury. This was his statement: "I wanted to tell him that I was sorry, but he kept telling me about how he was going to blow my brains out, and then I got mad. It was then I made up my mind that I was going to kill him. And after I did, I am sorry. I am just fifteen years old. I quit school in the ninth grade. I was mad with Mr. Dumas because he kept telling me he was going to blow my brains out. I was afraid of him before I did it. But on the day I did it, I was not afraid of him. And I shot him with my .22-caliber pistol that fired a long .22-caliber hollow-point bullet. But today, I am sorry for what I did."

It was obvious to me that Preston Cobb Jr. gave an admission of guilt that had been spoon-fed to him by law enforcement officers. But there was one exception, the last part of his admission: "I shot him with the pistol, with a long .22-caliber hollow-point bullet." Why did he make a special effort to mention the type of weapon that was used to kill Coleman Dumas Sr.? Because he assumed that someone would be smart enough to figure out the difference between a .22-caliber pistol that fired a long .22-caliber hollow-point bullet from that of a regular .22-caliber bullet. The rifle was obviously not the murder weapon, but no one ever realized what he was saying.

Later in the trial, Leathy Cobb, the mother of Preston, was called to testify for the defense, but her testimony was probably more damaging than it was helpful for her son. She testified that she never heard the old man threaten her son, although she was standing in the kitchen when the so-called argument took place. She said, "Well, when Preston walked in that morning, Mr. Dumas asked him about the eating of all the fish. And Preston asked him, 'What fish?!' Mr. Dumas cursed him and said, 'You know what fish I'm talking about!' And then he said, 'You'd look like a damn fool if I turned around and dashed this milk in your face.' He said, 'Here, take this milk and carry it out there and give it to the calf.' That was all I heard him say to Preston."

People in the local community questioned if she was trying to say that her son committed the murder without cause. In many ways, they believed that she was trying to protect the old white man's reputation without branding him as a pure white racist. They also believe that the old man had fathered some of her nine children, including Preston. And if Preston did in fact kill the old man, he did so because he had finally discovered the truth: the white man was his father.

I asked the question earlier, "Why did Preston shoot Dumas with the rifle when he had purposely brought a pistol to commit the murder?" The answer, of course, according to the Jasper County Sheriff Frank Ezell, is that Preston used the rifle instead of the pistol because he could get a better shot with the rifle. In other words, by using the rifle, he was sure to hit his target. However, neither weapon was taken to the state crime lab for testing, although a ball-shaped ammunition round was taken from the skull of the dead man. This, of course, meant that the rifle, which contained the ball-shaped ammunition, was used, not the hollow-point round that Preston had mentioned in court in reference to the pistol.

There were twelve white men who sat on the jury, anxiously waiting to find the fifteen-year-old black kid guilty of murdering a white man. And due to the facts of this case held in Jasper County, it was clearly stated,

> *Negroes are and have been, for many years, systematically and arbitrarily excluded from serving on grand juries and petit juries in Jasper County, Georgia.*
>
> *There are Negroes listed upon the tax digest of Jasper County who are landowners, possessing sufficient uprightness, experience, and intelligence to serve on duly and legally selected grand juries and petit juries. The defendant at no time intelligently waived or authorized his counsel appointed by the Honorable Court to waive his constitutional right to be tried by a fair and impartial jury, which was legally composed, and not to be discriminated against because of his race and color in the selection of the grand jury which indicted him or the petit jury by which he was tried.*

In other words, when this case was appealed, it was more than clear that Preston Cobb Jr. was no way fit in age and intelligence to waive his rights to allow twelve angry white men to sit on a jury that found him guilty and sentenced him to die in the electric chair thirty days after the trial. This was a miscarriage of justice to the highest level. However, before this particular case, *at no time in the history of Jasper County had any white lawyer defending a Negro in a criminal case ever legally raised the issue of the rights of any Negro not to be discriminated against because of his race and color as a result of the systematic and arbitrary exclusion of Negroes from serving upon grand juries and petit juries in the County of Jasper, and neither was there such a white attorney in the County of Jasper representing a Negro charged with murder.*

The appeal process for Preston Cobb began when black attorneys such as D. L. Hollowell and Horace Ward came to his rescue from Atlanta. But this was not a normal process of big-city civil rights attorneys filing an appeal for a black kid who, for all intents and purposes, might have been innocent. This was a high-level secret-in-the-middle-of-the-night type of process. These men, along with Leathy Cobb, met in the middle of the night in the basement of a prominent black doctor's home in Monticello to discuss their case. Why? Because if the good white folks of Jasper County had known what was going on, these three or four black people would have disappeared in the middle of the night, and no one would have heard from them again. This kind of thing had gone on in Jasper County for hundreds of years before this case. It was no secret that many black people had run for their lives to escape the long arms of white law.

The argument for an appeal was not based on whether Preston Cobb was innocent or not; it was based on the fact the court had denied him of his rights under the Fourteenth Amendment, which states that all American citizens are to be granted equal protection under the law. But in Preston Cobb's case, he had been denied his constitutional rights. But if he had known that he was going to get the electric chair and die in thirty days, he might not have made the open-court admission of guilt. Nevertheless, he alone knew what would have happened to his mother and his eight other siblings if he had not pleaded guilty. Leathy Cobb knew what was going to happen if the civil rights lawyers had tried to argue his guilt or innocence. The best they could do was to argue the fact that Preston was not old enough or intelligent enough to waive his rights, which his appointed white attorney claimed that he did.

The appeal process lasted for two years as the court continued to deny the motions that were presented. But one afternoon in 1963, Coleman Dumas Jr. was involved in a head-on collision with a dump truck on Highway 11 south, and he was fatally injured in the crash. Before he took his last breath, however, he gave what is known as a "dying declaration" to the truck driver who was not hurt. "Damn! I killed my father, and now I've killed myself." The truck driver was not sure what to make of the statement or what exactly he was referring to. But the investigating deputy sheriffs knew exactly what Coleman Dumas Jr. was talking about as they investigated the accident. They immediately notified the sheriff about the statement.

The truck driver managed to tell his story to a few other people around town, but he was immediately escorted out of town, and he was never heard from again. The civil rights lawyers never heard the truck driver's statement about the son's dying declaration. But that was not end of the story. Marshall Tinsley, who was driving the station wagon on the day the two were arrested, stated that he neither knew anything about the murder nor was ever suspicious as to why Preston was in possession of the white man's vehicle all night and into the next day. It was believed that Marshall had lied in his testimony.

But then it was no secret why Marshall would lie about not having knowledge of the murder; he was only trying to save himself from being an accessory to the crime, which meant that he would be tried for murder as well.

At the trial, Marshall testified that he overheard Preston telling another cellmate that he committed the murder alone. As a result, Marshall was given a free pass to get out of jail and out town as fast as he could and to never come back to Jasper County again. Two days after, the verdict was rendered by the twelve angry white men. Marshall Tinsley left Monticello, and it was twenty-five years later before he showed his face in that area again.

The civil rights lawyers were eventually granted a new trial, and Preston Cobb was found innocent on the grounds that his Fourteenth Amendment rights were violated. The so-called court-appointed attorney was replaced by the black lawyers, who got the case overturned not because Preston was innocent of murder but because he was too young and too stupid to know right from wrong, the court said.

I had the opportunity to meet and talk to Preston many years after he had been released from prison. I learned what had really happened on the day of the murder. Coleman Dumas Jr. and the some of the deputy sheriffs were guilty of stealing and selling the old man's cows in Macon, Georgia. Dumas Jr. gave Preston the keys to the vehicle and the money that he and Marshall had spent that night. But of course, Preston knew all along that Coleman Dumas Jr. had planned to kill his own father. However, everything that the son had planned backfired in the end with his own death. Preston was no more than the "fall guy," an ignorant young kid who would take the blame for murder.

Chapter 25

BLACK PEOPLE WHO WANT TO BE WHITE—we see it being acted out on every stage every day. But most of us never seem to think there is anything wrong with it. And what I am talking about is black people who would rather be white than black. Okay, so what is wrong with wanting to be white? Fifty years ago, when white people fled the inner cities, trying to escape the crime curse that black people had always seemed to generate, many black people thought it was a great idea to follow white people to the suburbs. Black people have always been led to believe that white people have the better neighborhoods. And naturally, in most cases, they do have the better, more expensive neighborhoods. But then again, that is because they are white, and they have always looked out for each other and their financial welfare.

I remember about fifty years ago when black pimps' and hustlers' favorite brand of automobile was the Cadillac. When we saw a shiny Cadillac with all kind of fancy trimmings and big, wide whitewall tires, we did not have to guess the race of the person driving it; we automatically knew he or she was black. Obviously, this trend outraged the General Motors bigshots because in the early 1980s, GM officials announced in a private setting that they were going to make a Cadillac that a "nigger" could not afford. But of course, we now see how that plan worked out. The drug trade made buying more expensive Cadillacs a thing of beauty, and as fast as GM could make Cadillacs and ship them to dealerships, black people with money were buying them.

Needless to say, black people buying Cadillacs do not necessarily want to be white. In fact, back in the days of old, the Cadillac was the symbol of the black man. But somehow, unknowing to black people, the Cadillac suddenly became a staple of white power as well. However, the black people I am referring to who want to be white are those who purposely go out of their way to make white friends. They wear false faces deliberately to try and make white people like them. Yeah, we have a lot of black people who think it is a symbol of success to surround themselves with white friends. And we often wonder, "Why?"

For some black people, this is done to show the world that they do not have a prejudiced bone in their black bodies, as if the same thing can be said for white people. We have had to live with five hundred years of white brutality. They have tortured, slaughtered, butchered, and lynched black people for little to nothing or just because they were black. And now just because we have a right to sit in the same row of seats at movie theaters, eat in the same restaurants, and live in the same neighborhoods as white people do, we are willing to forget every barbaric thing that was done to our ancestors just to be like them. Are we that willing to forgive white people for all the hell that they have put black people through, four hundred fifty years out of the five hundred years we have been in this country? If that is the case, why is it that we cannot forgive our own black brothers and sisters who all came from a slave-ancestry background just like we did?

Today has been a long time coming. The reason why many young blacks love to hang out with whites is because they have no clue what was done to them in the past because of the color of their skin. Yeah, they may have heard a few stories or watched a few slave movies, but until they have experienced what it was really like, then stories and movies are just that. That is the primary reason why black history was forced out of schools. There is an old saying that goes like this: "If you don't know where you have been, you will never know where you are going!" In other words, to correct the future, we have to know what happened in the past. If not, we are doing no more than repeating the same mistakes we made in the past.

So now we are asking ourselves today, "Who stole our black history books?" Who stole the very books that once taught us about who we are and where we came from? Who destroyed all the books about black people?! The answer is very simple and clear: it was white people who made sure that we know very little about who we are. They did the exact same thing back in the days of slavery. They made every effort to keep black people from learning how to read. They knew that to keep a slave a slave, they had to keep him a slave in his mind as well. If a slave ever became free in his mind, the slave master could no longer tell the slave anything and expect for him to believe it. An educated slave could think for himself, which meant he did not need the master to think for him. An educated slave was a dangerous human being, for he could not be led down a blind alley and think that he was going to come back alive.

The twenty-first century has brought about a whole different kind of slave-master mentality with the election of Barack Obama as president of the United States. As I said earlier, this was a trick by a black man who, for once, was smarter than an entire race of white people. It was a genius plan on Barack Obama's behalf, but for the black race as a whole, it became a racial nightmare all over again. We fell asleep at the switch, thinking that we had finally overcome racial prejudice among white people. But in reality, this was no more than a bunch of wolves walking around in sheep's clothing. White people hate blacks now as much as they always have. The only difference now is we have some whites who like to pretend that they are not prejudiced because they believe it shows their godly, human side. But again, in reality, if the wrong button is pushed at the wrong time, the friendly white faces comes off, and the nasty white sheets come on.

The fact of the matter is black people will never be accepted as equals by a vast majority of white people. To say that "all men are created equal" is the biggest lie ever told. That is a lie that man came up with because even in Biblical times, all men and women were not created equally. Men and women who were said to have been God's favorite people had slave men and women. If servants are talked about throughout the Bible, what make us think or believe that modern men are going to make things any better? The same black people who were sold into slavery by the kings and queens of Africa were enslaved by their own black people. In essence, the real facts behind this nonequality situation in America all started with black people in the "homeland of Africa." Black people sold black people to white people as slaves. Go figure!

The bottom line is quite simple if we pay attention to what is going on in the world today. Black people in America will never be completely free or have equal rights as every other race of people in America. The reason again is quite simple: we do not have the money or the power to buy our freedom. The only time black people really matter in America is during election time. And even then, most black people are lured into thinking that their votes do not really matter because they all are looking for something in return. It is a promise that is made in every election cycle, but it is a promise that is never kept. Whose fault is that?! It is the black people's fault primarily because they have failed to hold politicians they helped to get elected accountable. But the black vote is the most powerful weapon that black people have to get what they want. Needless to say, nothing ever happens simply because black people are constantly walking around in dark places, hoping and praying for a miracle instead of doing something about it. Not only that, but black people also have a very difficult time sticking together for a cause.

The largest turnout of black votes was when Barack Obama was elected for president both times. And the only reason why so many blacks voted in those two elections was because they believed that a black man in the White House would make a difference. But we quickly learned that just because a black man was in the White House does not mean a whole lot of things were going to change for black people. Most black people were poor when he was elected the first time and the second time, and they were still poor or poorer when he departed the White House. Therefore, in the grand scheme of things, what difference did a black man make for black people because he became president of the United States? The answer is simply, "*None*!"

The "none" is amplified simply because Barack Obama became president for all the people in America—and not just for black people—like so many thought he would. Obama knew that better than any other black person in America even though he ran on a campaign of "change." It was obvious that he wanted a change from the same old status quo, "You grease my palms, and I'll grease yours!" Throughout the history of America, white people have always been in a position to get things done from the White House all the way down to the statehouses and courthouses. Needless to say, when Barack Obama became the first black president, the white power structure or the white Congress dug their heels in and made a pledge that "as long as Obama's ass is pointed toward the ground, he will never accomplish anything as president."

In spite of all the suffering that black people have gone through, there are still those who would rather be a part of the white race than the one that they were born into. The white world is a world that many black people believe is filled with beauty, money, power, and success. Are they right? By social standards, of course they are! They are right because there is no single reason in America why any white person should be poor. In 1492, Christopher Columbus landed on the shores of America, and from that point until today, white people have robbed, killed, and enslaved other human beings for the sole purpose of gaining wealth and power. Therefore, it has been the trademark of white people to steal or forcefully gain possession of things, people, and property that they desired.

Where there are many black people who believe that they can be a part of the white power structure is a clear case that they have "arrived." What does "arrived" mean? The word "arrived" means that if certain black people can gain a foothold within the white power structure, they will be accepted by white people. What does it take to gain a foothold within the white power structure? The number one thing is that it takes a lot of money. If a black person can make a lot of money, he or she will then gain monetary respect from white people. However, just having money is not enough to get their full attention. The next step is very tricky, of course! Black men are especially guilty of this next step. They have come to believe that having a white woman by their side is the second most important thing that will get the full respect of white people. But is it true?! No, it is a blatant lie!

It is not true for several reasons. And those reasons take us all the way back to the jungles of Africa, where black people were bought and sold into slavery. The white landowners did not steal slaves from the jungle chiefs. They traveled to the African nations and negotiated deals with African leaders for black people who were considered unfit or unwanted by the tribal leaders. These undesirables were sold into slavery by the tribal leaders. Now the question is, "Who should we, as African Americans, be most angry with? White men who paid and enslaved us or the tribal leaders who sold us into slavery?" That is the question!

I often hear some black people complaining about the conditions and the racism in America. They question themselves as to whether or not they should go back the "motherland." Apparently, they have forgotten that it was the motherland that sold them in the first place, and wanting to go back to the place that sold them is non-negotiable. How can we feel welcome in a place that saw us as a bunch of undesirable retards five hundred years ago?

Speaking of black people who want to be white or believe that money will open white doors that being poor cannot open, once upon a time, there was a black man who struck it rich by hitting the lottery. Before becoming an instant millionaire, he lived in a predominantly poor black neighborhood. And immediately after becoming a wealthy man he decided to buy and move his family into a predominantly rich white neighborhood. To him, this was a dream come true. This meant he could live next to some of the richest white families in Atlanta. But he forgot that Atlanta is the same city that General William T. Sherman burned to the ground during the Civil War, which was ultimately the turning point that ended the war and freed the slaves.

Upon his arrival at his new home, which was located next door to a very wealthy white family, he made a gallant effort to meet and show himself and be friendly to his new neighbors. But as racism would have it, his wealthy white neighbors wanted no part of their new black family. In fact, his white neighbors erected a wooden fence that separated the two houses, which had not been a necessity in the past. When the black man saw what was happening, he put forth more effort to meet the white family, but the white family made no attempt to return the favor.

Finally, the rich black man saw the rich white man out on his front lawn, and he immediately approached the white man to introduce himself. "Hi, neighbor, my name is John Doe, and I live next door. I've been trying to meet you and your family for months now. I just want to tell you how glad I am to be your neighbor. Why don't you and your family get together with me and my family and let's all get to know each other?"

The rich white man looked at the rich black man as if he had said a bad word about his wife or his mother. "Look, Mr. John Doe, I know all about you and who you are. I saw you on TV when you won all those millions of dollars. And I heard you say how you were going to move out of the ghetto and into a neighborhood just like this. I felt good for you and your black people. And even now, I am wondering why you didn't stay in your black neighborhood and use your money to build up the place where you were living? Wouldn't your money have served a greater good by helping your own people rather moving into a neighborhood of rich white people who want no part of you and your black family?!"

The black man stood in place, stunned to no end with his mouth opened, for he never expected anything like that to come out of the white man's mouth. "Look, I've spent the last twenty years playing the lottery, trying to become rich so I could afford a place like this in a nice neighborhood like this. And now you're going to stand here and tell me I'm not welcome in this neighborhood because my family and I are black?! Who are you to tell me where to live?"

"Look, don't take this personally! But let me make it very clear to you how this world works as far as black and white people are concerned," the white man said as he placed his hand on the black man's shoulder. "Yeah, you won a whole shitload of money, and you are a very rich man. But to the people who live in this neighborhood, you are no more than another rich nigger!" The white man removed his hand. "You see, that's the problem with your black community as well as the ones who play professional sports and are in the entertainment world. When y'all make a lot of money, the first thing you do is buy a big house in the white neighborhood just to be able to say you are rich. What y'all should do is go back to where you belong and build up your own neighborhoods."

"Go back to where we belong?! This is America, man! We can live anywhere we want to if we can afford it!" John Doe snapped angrily. "What is your problem, man?!"

"My problem is you and all your kind," the rich white man snapped back. "Being rich does not make you white! You were a nigger when you were poor, and you're still a nigger now that you're rich."

The black man stepped back as if he wanted to punch the white man. "I've seen the time when I'd have knocked you to your knees for calling me a nigger. But you know, you're not worth it. All you peckerwood white folks are alike. It doesn't matter if we're rich or poor. All you crackers see is just another nigger!" He turned to walk away.

The white man called out to the black man, "Mr. John Doe, no hard feelings. I just wanted you to know that this is how we feel about you and your kind. If I didn't tell you, someone else will eventually. So welcome to our neighborhood!" The white man turned and went back to what he was doing.

That was apparently a hard reality check for John Doe to deal with. But like many wealthy black people who want to rub elbows with wealthy white people, there are always two conversations as far as whites are concerned: one with the rich black people and a second one with their rich white friends and relatives. But at least this rich white man told John Doe how he felt face-to-face and not behind his back. As the white man mentioned, as for highly paid entertainers and athletes, the only thing they have in common with rich white people is money. Without the money, they are out of mind and out of sight, which makes them a nonfactor.

In a perfect world, we are all one nation and one race of people living on a planet created by one God. This, of course, should mean that the color of a person's skin should not be a determining factor in anything as long as they are qualified to do whatever needs to be done. But in an imperfect world, God has been taken completely out of the equation, and race plays a part in everything that we do in America. However, the world may seem a little different for those who were born after the Vietnam War generation. They are led to believe that race relations are on the back burners as far as racial hatred and prejudice are concerned. But lo and behold, racism is as much alive today as it was a hundred years ago. The only difference today is white people are very good at hiding their true prejudiced feelings.

John Doe spoke to the white man angrily about being called a nigger and what he would have done if he was not rich. The only question that comes to my mind is, "Why is it that black people become bone-chillingly angry when white people say the "N-word" but it is okay for blacks to call each other the N-word? Is there is no different way for black people to say "nigger" than the way that white people say it? I understand that the word is derived from the word Negro, which was created out of hatred by white people toward blacks. But the question is, "Does it have a different meaning when blacks use the word toward each other than when it is used by whites?" Of course it does! However, if we become fighting mad when white people use the N-word, we should become just as angry when our own brothers and sisters say the N-word. Or is it that we live in a world of "double standards"? "We can say it, but they can't!"

Black people cannot play by the same rules as those of white people. The reason is because there are different standards already put in place that we as blacks must abide by, or we do not get the opportunity to play at all. Of course, some blacks believe if they become a part of the white establishment by dating or marrying into the white race, it will level the playing field. But truth be told, white people are making the rules, and the playing fields are always slanted to their side of the tracks, which means we are still playing by their rules.

To act white or want to be white is a game that we cannot play and win. They already know who we are; only black people have forgotten who they are. We can only be the people whom God created us to be. And the only way we will ever make this world work for us is if we build our own communities, families, and businesses. How do we do that?! If we have a talent, a quality, or a product that we can sell to the white man, then by all means, we must utilize our business skills and sell to the highest bidders. Trying to be white or wanting to be white is not an option for us! We must use what we have to get what we want.

·

Chapter 26

HERE'S A TRUE CONFESSION from a stripper/prostitute. Her professional name is Simone, and she is a woman I had the pleasure to meet at a downtown Atlanta sports bar. At first glance, I thought Simone was probably one of Atlanta's most beautiful women. And after a long conversation with her, I finally saw the other side of the woman with a body that a man would pay lots of money just to see naked. And when I told her that I was planning to write *Telling It Like It Is*, she asked me to tell her story as well.

At first, I wondered what made her story so interesting that she would want the world to read about it. And when she whispered in my ear about some of her clients, I became very much interested in telling her story. The following essay is what she brought to me approximately two years ago, but it was not until now that I fully read it in detail, and my mouth dropped open.

Well, here I am! I am at a point in my life where there are no more tricks to save a ho like me. And there is no one to invite me to live with them for some free pussy. . . . So here I am, a forty-three-year-old, homeless, broke, and sleeping on a red recliner at the foot of my mother's bed.

Nearby on the floor was my fourteen-year-old daughter, sleeping on a blow-up mattress. That's when I asked myself, "Simone, how did you fall so low?!" I kept asking myself the same question over and over again. But I still could not give myself an answer as to why. I then said to myself, "Simone, you have always had the finer things in life—a nice ride, a fly-ass crib, and a stack of cash always close by. And before I forget, I had plenty of good dicks to choose from every single day and night if I wanted to be fucked. "Simone, what went so wrong?!" I asked myself softly. And when I answered myself, I said, "I tried to change from being a ho and go straight, and it seems to me that was when all my troubles started."

The beginning of my story goes something like this: when I was a little girl, a skinny little girl who loved wearing a ponytail, I had big nipples for someone so young. My nipples were very big even at the age of twelve. They were so big that they would cause the front of my blouse to sometimes lift up. In fact, they were the size of fifty-cent pieces. I know because I measured them with a coin.

Back then, my favorite outfit was a tight shirt and a pair of ragged jean shorts that was a size too small. But that was my favorite outfit, and I loved it. At the age of twelve, I was pretty much a typical kid who loved standing in front of a mirror and singing any song with a towel wrapped around my head, pretending that I had long hair. And you might say, "Who in their grown-ass right mind would look at a twelve-year-old kid in a sexual manner?" And you would probably say, "No one!" Well, you would be wrong! My whole life changed for the worse when I would catch my own father staring at my young skinny body. Whenever he would walk into the house from wherever he was, I would get a very uncomfortable feeling. But not once did I think that the feeling that I had was because of anything that he was thinking of doing to me.

It all started one Saturday morning when my dad got my three brothers together to go out on his job and clean a parking lot. He told them to hurry and get dressed so they could get an early start. A few minutes later, they were ready to go on the back of Daddy's truck. A few minutes later, they were gone. Me, on the other hand, I was always left at home to do housecleaning because my mother was at work as usual. But on this day, I guess my father had other plans for me because he was gone for about an hour when I heard his truck pull up outside.

At the time, I was cleaning the bathroom when he walked into the house. It was apparent that he knew that I was in the bathroom because he knocked on the door. "Simone, open the door!" he said suddenly.

I responded, "I'll be out in a minute, Marvin!" I never called him Dad; I always called him Marvin.

But again, he said, "Open the door, Simone, okay?!" I thought he might have been in a hurry to use the toilet, so I opened the door, and when I did, he pushed past me and quickly closed the door behind him.

"Marvin, I'm finished, I will get out now," I said to him.

"No, don't leave yet," he almost demanded of me.

"Why?!" I asked sharply.

"Look, I want to do something to properly prepare you for the world," he said.

"Yeah, and what is that, Marvin?!" I asked quickly.

That was when he told me to pull down my pants. And I quickly said, "No! You are my father. Why do you want me to pull down my pants?! You're supposed to protect me from the world. I'm not crazy! I know what you want to do! I am your child, and as my father, you're not supposed to touch me in my private area!"

I guess what I said must have really pissed him off because he picked me up, slammed me against the toilet seat, grabbed my pants and my panties at the same time, and yanked them off violently. I screamed and started to cry, but I knew it would do no good because there was no one else in the house except for me and him.

He violently forced my legs open and began pushing his middle finger up inside my vagina. He did it again and again and then placed his finger in his mouth. Then he lifted up my shirt and began to suck on my breasts as if he was a baby. It was apparent to me that he was so busy doing whatever he wanted to with my young naked body, he never noticed the tears rolling down my face. And in the midst of all his sodomizing and torturing, I became so sick to my stomach that I threw up on him.

He suddenly jumped back and began cursing me, "You nasty little bitch! You clean this shit up, and it better be cleaned up before I get back in here!" He turned and suddenly left me in the bathroom. From that day until I was in my teens, he continued to force himself on me, daring me to tell my mother or he would hurt me very badly.

By the time I was twenty-five years old, I was a well-seasoned whore, and I had learned that men will do anything for a piece of pussy. When I first turned a trick, it was with a man named Marc who owned a little chicken stand on Glenwood Road near the freeway, just outside of Atlanta in Dekalb County. At the time, I was working as a stripper in a club called Booty's VIP. Marc paid two hundred fifty dollars for about five minutes of sex time, which was good money along with the tips that I made for dancing. Then I would work one night a week and make anywhere between two to three hundred dollars a night. And when you add that to working six nights a week, I was making between $1,200 and $1,500 a week on average.

I started working for Booty's, where Michael Hunt was the owner on Peachtree Street in downtown Atlanta, and it was one of the top strip clubs in Atlanta next to the Gold Club on Piedmont Road near Buckhead. The money began to pour in like rain. As I said, Booty's was at the top of its game in terms of being high class. It was very upscale and beautiful with three different dance floors. This is where all the big-money hustlers, players, and drug dealers would come to see some of the most beautiful naked women in Atlanta, and I was one of those women.

The club had valet parking for all the dancers as well as the club's patrons, and we had a "house mother" as well. She was like a real mother to all the girls because she knew that we were young beautiful women who came from broken homes and that we were making a lot of money. Her job was to make sure that we took care of our bodies as well as the money we were bringing in. I quickly became one of the top dancers at the club.

One night in particular was a slow one, and I had worked from noon to midnight. And on this night, I had only made about two hundred dollars, and I needed about two hundred more when my old friend Marc came into the club. My rent was due the next day, and I needed a little extra cash fast. Now Marc was a very clean-cut kind of guy who loved to spend lots of cash for a one-night stand, and I was about to do whatever he wanted for that one night.

He sat in front of the stage where I was performing along with another girl called Strawberry. Strawberry was the kind of dancer that could make men throw their wallets on the stage. She was an amazing woman to watch dance. She could make the muscles in her butt move to the beat of the music. While she was doing her thing, I went over to Marc to get reacquainted with the man who loved to spend cash on strippers. Based upon the way he was gazing at my body, I was sure he was more interested in the one-piece fishnet bodysuit that I was wearing than what Strawberry was doing onstage.

When I reintroduced myself, just in case he had forgotten who I was, I said, "Hello, my name is Simone. We've met once before. So what brings you out tonight?"

"I came out tonight looking for some fun. And yeah, I do remember you," he replied.

"Well, you've come to the right place," I said, smiling. "Can I get you a waitress, or would you like a lap dance in the VIP room?"

"No, but you can find me a dancer who does private parties," he said, smiling as if he wanted me to say I would love to do a private party.

"Private party, huh? What exactly is a private party?" I was curious because up to this point, no one had told me anything about private parties.

"A private party is when a girl leaves the club with a guy and has sex with him for a certain amount of money," he answered. Then he said, "This type of thing is illegal, of course, but if you don't tell, I won't tell either. Come on, I know you've heard of girls having private parties!"

"No, I haven't! But maybe it's because I am new at this type of work. And maybe it's because there is a lot of money involved, and they don't want to share the wealth," I responded with a grin. Then I asked, "Just how much money are we talking about?"

"We're talking about anywhere between three hundred fifty dollars and five hundred dollars a night," he said, smiling. "It's all depends on how good you are."

"Okay, you already know that I'm good, right? But the next question is, is this for all night?!" I asked suspiciously.

"Hell naw! That's for maybe an hour or two. What are you trying to do, fuck a nigger unconscious?! Naw, baby, I'm not into all-nighters. After I'm satisfied, you get your money, and you're on your way," he explained. "Are you game or not?!"

"Hell yeah! For three hundred fifty dollars, I can fuck you into a coma. Shit, I've been dancing all night, and I've only pulled in two hundred dollars. And if you think I'm not going to take you up on three hundred fifty dollars, you're crazy as hell! Let's go!" I hurriedly got dressed while Marc had his big black Mercedes Benz brought around to the front entrance.

Because this was unlike anything that I done before as a dancer, I was quite nervous, but I knew it was something that I had to do if I wanted to pay my rent the next day. And after all, no one would know what I had done, not even our den mother. We did not have to travel far—two streets over to the Sheridan Hotel. I have to admit, Marc was very helpful, and he was good at this sort of thing. When we got into the room, I was even more nervous than I was before. I told him that I wanted to use the bathroom to get ready for him. But the truth of the matter was that I wanted to calm myself down before jumping into bed with this man. As soon as I came out of the bathroom, he handed me the three hundred fifty dollars. I was shocked because I thought for sure that he was going to wait until we had sex first. I said, "What's this, you're paying me first?!"

He said, "Yes, why not? Look, I know you're going to be good. I'm not even worried about that." Then he laughed and said, "Always hide your money before having sex with a guy because he just might try to steal it back when it's all over."

As we engaged in one of the most outrageous nights of sex and just about anything else you can name sexually, it was so good that I wanted to give him his money back. But I knew that I better not do that; my rent was still going to be due the next day. However, the sex was better than any sex toy or any man I had ever come across in my young life. And that night was the beginning of what I would become later in life: a high-priced whore! And from that night on, I was addicted to sex and money because I never got tired of having sex, and I certainly never got tired of making lots of money.

In spite of all the money that I have made in my lifetime, it never dawned on me that I would ever become broke and homeless and live back home with my mother at forty-three years of age. There was a time when I was so good at what I was doing, I was paid to fly to Puerto Rico as well as several other overseas places to dance and fuck and make huge sums of money. But as the old saying goes, "All good things must come to an end." Things at Booty's VIP began to slow after about ten years of operation. This, of course, meant that I had to venture out to other clubs, looking for a dancing spot.

I ended up going to a "hole-in-the-wall" spot out on Empire Street near the airport. But for some reason, the men who frequented that place spent money like it was going out of style. Many nights, I would make over a thousand dollars on just dancing alone. And if I decided to do a private party for someone, I could add on another four or five hundred dollars. In my prime years, I was earning over a hundred thousand dollars a year from dancing and fucking. And many times, I would give thanks to my no-good father who turned his own daughter into a first-class whore and taught me that I had what it takes to make a lot of money just using what God gave me: just my body and not my mind.

I used my body like a machine to fuck as many men as I possibly could for as much money as I possibly could. After going to work at this hole-in-the-hall kind of juke joint, I came to believe that this was the kind of place where certain kind of men were looking for sexual encounters but wanted to stay away from the most popular clubs in downtown Atlanta. I remember such a man. It was on a Thursday afternoon. When I arrived at the club, pulling into the parking lot, I noticed a beautiful brand-new white Lexus GS300. Based on the looks of the car, I knew that he was someone who wanted to spend a lot of money, which made me grab my bags in a hurry and get inside.

As soon as I entered the back entrance, the club owner, James Gresham, told me to hurry and get dressed and that he had someone in the club that he wanted me to meet. It had to have been the guy in the new Lexus, I thought. A few minutes later, I was all dressed up in my costume, smelling real good for whoever was waiting in the club. As soon as I came out of the dressing room, James grabbed me by the hand and escorted me to the VIP room, which was located next to the men's restroom where men would go to get their dicks hard.

When I walked into the VIP room, there was this man waiting there, sitting on the sofa with a newspaper in his hand, pretending to be reading it, I figured. James said to the man, "Hey, Dave, here she is, the one I told you about. She's the best in the house, the cream of the crop! This is Simone!" Then he looked at me and said, "Simone, this is Dave. He's a very special person in this club and in our country. Give him your best!" James turned and left the room.

I had no idea who Dave was and what make him so special. But if James said he was special, so be it! Finally, Dave spoke after taking his time to look me over with a wide shit-eating grin on his face. "Sit down, dear!" And I did as he asked by sitting next to him. Then he said, "I want you to dance for me when the next song comes on." So I waited for the song, but I also noticed that he never moved the newspaper that he was holding from his lap.

A few moments later, the song began to play, and I began to undress while I performed my dance for him. I turned my back to him while I continued to dance, allowing him to see the entire me. And when I turned back around, I was in for a real big shock. I saw why he had been holding the paper in his lap all that time; he suddenly displayed this big-ass dick! I had never seen a dick that big before. I was like, "What in the hell is that you're holding?! Who are you?"

"Oh, James didn't tell you who I am?" he asked me with a surprised look on his face.

"All he said was Dave. And you are Dave who?!" I asked, blushing at the same time.

"I guess I may as well tell you since we are going to have a real good time. My name is Dave Turner, and I'm a U.S. senator," he explained to me, knowing that was not his real name.

"Really?!" I said surprisingly. Now that was a real big shocker, even bigger than his damn dick. "So what do you want from me? Dance, fuck, or what?!"

"I want you to sit on it," he said slowly.

I supposed by the answer he gave me, he must have liked what he saw standing in front of him, completely naked now. But I was not about to sit on that thing without a condom. I asked him, "Where is your condom?! You do have a condom, right?"

"No, I don't have a condom because I don't need one. I am clean. I don't have a disease, and I can't have babies," he said with a straight face.

"Really?! Now what exactly does that mean? And if it means anything, am I supposed to believe you?!" I said quickly.

"Yes! I told you, I am a U.S. senator. My word is my bond. Not only that, but my reputation is at stake. You have nothing to lose. Look, if you do it, I'll give you fifty dollars per song."

"And how many songs do you think you'll last, one? No, I'll tell you what, a hundred dollars a song, limited to five songs whether you last that long or not," I said.

He agreed, and I began my sexual act on him by sitting on that whopper of a dick. The whole time I was on it, I could smell his cheap cologne and a strong odor of mothballs. Not only did he smell like a mothball factory, but he was also constantly moaning and groaning, "Oh baby, you're so good!" A few minutes later into the very first song, he got very quiet, which let me know that he had nutted up. However, when I stood up, he immediately handed me five hundred dollars.

I guess I must have done something really special for a very special man that day, for I became Dave Turner's favorite piece of pussy until I retired from the business. He would come to the club three or four times a week from then on. And we even agreed to raise my fee from five hundred to six hundred dollars a visit, and he never complained about the money, which let me know that my pussy must have been really good to his old ass.

Senator Dave Turner, a U.S. senator from who-knows-where, was a regular at the Dream Girl Club, probably because James Gresham promised never to reveal to the public that he had a thing for hookers in a dance club. But in reality, I can truly tell you that he was nothing more than a big dick, a nasty pervert politician who paid a lot of money for some pussy just like the next trick that walked through the club doors.

Chapter 27

MY ONE-ON-ONE CONVERSATION WITH SIMONE was one that I thought I should have before I could finish my story on her. When I first met Simone, she was sitting at a bar at the Atlanta Stadium in downtown Atlanta, and most men would probably agree that she was beautiful from her head to her feet. However, I would have never guessed that she was a dancer and a prostitute. I just assumed that she was at the game with someone or was just hanging out like a lot of gorgeous women do at professional games in Atlanta. Maybe that is one of the reasons why the Falcons or the Hawks have never won a championship for the city.

After a few meetings with Simone, she finally told me who she was and the kind of business she was in. Naturally, I was shocked because she never approached me in the way she did when she wanted to be paid for sex. And I learned that Simone was her stage name and not her birth name. Her real name, I will not reveal, but her story was very tragic as well as intriguing. She agreed with me that when she decided to give up the business, she would give me her story, which would probably shock a lot of people she knew in the political world.

In my interview, she wanted me to know the beautiful woman who could have had any man of her choosing, but she chose the world's oldest profession: prostitution.

ME: Okay, I read your confession about how you were more or less forced into dancing onstage and prostitution. Whatever happened to your father who raped you as a young girl?

SIMONE: I really don't know. He walked out on my mother a few years after he stopped having sex with me. I hope the bastard is dead or someone chopped his dick off!

ME: And you never told your mother what he did to you in all these years?

SIMONE: No, because she loved the bastard, and she would have taken his word over mine anyway. But as I said in my letter, he was the main reason why I turned to prostitution, and it was because of him that I was able to do the things that I did. I mean, I'm not really sorry about what happened because I made a lot of money for myself.

ME: Now that you're out of the business, and you said you made a lot of money selling your body, do you have any regrets? Or should I say, when you think back on your life, do you ever wish that you had chosen a different path?

SIMONE: Not really! However, I have a sixteen-year-old daughter now, and I am afraid that she is going to follow in my footsteps. And I often ask myself, "How do I tell her not to do what I did?" Because she will end up just as I did: homeless without a penny to my name.

ME: What happened to all the money you made?!

SIMONE: I thought I had it all figured out. I invested into several businesses, not realizing that I was taking a big risk with my money. I even went into the trucking business with a friend of mine, and things went south after three or four years. I should have taken all the money I made out there whoring in those streets and put it all in the banks. But no, I wanted to be a big time investor, and I lost it all.

ME: So now you're homeless, dead broke, and too old to go back to where you were before you lost all your money. How long were you in the business, and how much money do you think you may have made in that time period?

SIMONE: It took me a while to make up my mind to get into the business of whoring. I mean, I had a lot of people telling me that I should use what I had to get what I wanted. In other words, men from all walks of life were paying big money just to see women show their asses onstage. And they would pay even more just to be able to have sex with them. I knew I had a pretty face and a nice body, so I decided to go for it.

ME: You say men from all walks of life. Just what kind of men are you referring to?

SIMONE: You name them, and I screwed them! I had politicians, preachers, lawyers, all of them. There was this one preacher, a very highly respected preacher with a mega-church here in the city. He was a thousand-dollar-a-night customer. Can you imagine, a pastor whom people worship as if he is God himself? But he was paying me a thousand dollars just to play with my pussy. I mean, that's all he was doing, playing with it. [*smiles*]

ME: Do you care to name this preacher or these preachers?

SIMONE: No, I won't do him like that. I may have to call on him again because I'm broke as hell right now!

ME: But you don't think you'll be calling on Senator Turner again do you?

SIMONE: Hell no! I mean, I love his money, but I hated his ass with that big ol' sorry dick he has.

ME: Okay, you're out of the business of tricking, so what's next for you now? Do you plan to marry someone special, or is there someone in your near future?

SIMONE: Why, do you want to get married? [*laugh*] No, I'm kidding. I don't know, and I guess that the biggest question that I have is, "Where does a forty-three-year-old ex-prostitute find a job?" What will I write on my résumé, that I was a prostitute for twenty years and that I made a small fortune but I blew it all on cars, homes, and bad investments? I mean, who's going to hire an ex-hooker?! But then maybe if your book sells a million copies, you can afford to pay me for this interview.

ME: I asked you before, do you know exactly how much money you estimate you made during your prostitution years?

SIMONE: That's right, you did, and I never answered that question, did I? [*laughs*] I suppose I pulled in somewhere between five and seven million dollars over a twenty-year period. And what was so good about it was I didn't pay any taxes, just the people who owned the clubs.

ME: So you're saying that the tax man never showed up at your door looking for a piece of the action? And if he did, you would have given him a piece of the action?! [*laughs*]

SIMONE: Never! The tax man has no idea who I am or who I sold my body to. And my customers don't want to be identified as people who were paying top dollar for sex.

ME: I guess the one question that I want to ask you is, if you had it to do all over again, even with your father doing what he did to you, would you do it?

SIMONE: That's a difficult question to answer. And I really don't know. However, knowing what I know now about men, maybe I wouldn't. I mean, after twenty years of selling my body to a bunch of no-good bastards, I probably wouldn't. But you know, when I think about it, to me, doing what I did was my way of getting even with all the men in this town for what that bastard of a father did to me.

ME: I don't understand. What does that mean?!

SIMONE: It means that all men are no good! All they want from a woman is pussy! They don't care how they get it or who they get it from. The only thing that matters to them is getting some pussy. If you read the Bible, damn near every trouble a man got into was because of a woman. Today, men are still the same as they were back then. Men are the same all over the world.

ME: So giving men what they want most for a price was your way of making men pay for what your father did to you. Is that what you're really saying?!

SIMONE: Yeah, that's exactly what I am saying. However, I had fun doing it, and I would laugh my ass off all the way to the bank. Making money was my payback!

ME: Okay, are you now telling me that you're not broke?

SIMONE: No, I am not telling you that! I am broke, I'm homeless, and I live with my mother. However, I bought the house that my mother is living in.

ME: So in reality, you are not broke, and you're only pretending to be?

SIMONE: If I had money, I would not have given you my story to write. I am hoping that you sell ten million copies of this book so I can get paid. [*laughs*] No, I am not looking for any money from you. But I do hope your book does well.

ME: But you know, this brings up a very interesting question: why did you give me your story, naming only Senator Dave Turner as one of your clients? I am sure that he was not the only big name or the only rich person who would have a lot to lose if you told everyone who they were. So what's really going on here?!

SIMONE: Man! You're very wise for a man. But why would you think that I have something else going on or something to hide by not naming all of my clients?!

ME: I can feel that you're about to drop a bomb on someone or you're putting other people who are primed for blackmailing on notice. You have to remember, I was a cop for a long time. And I also remember that you were one of the two women who were in a white Mercedes at a downtown hotel. And you also went up to the room of a well-known minister in this city. Remember, I know this minister myself. So who is it you're about to take down?

SIMONE: Are you ready to write another book?! [*laughs*] Listen, I didn't spend twenty years having sex with all these high-powered men for nothing. I have tapes and videos of at least ten different men who are worth over a million dollars each. They paid me well because they thought that I wouldn't tell their secrets. However, now that I am at a point where I need money to take care of me and my daughter for the rest of our lives, you can call it blackmail or anything else you want to call it. But the bottom line is quite simple: pay me or be exposed.

ME: This is a dangerous game you're playing. You do know this, don't you?!

SIMONE: What can they do to me, kill me?! All I am going to do is tell the world that there is a boatload of information out there that will blow the lid off for a lot of so-called important people, including your ex-police chief.

ME: Wow! Hold up here. My ex-police chief?! Which one? I had three during in my career. Which one are you talking about?!

SIMONE: You'll know when, who, and where if I have to expose these bastards. Until then, my lips are sealed. However, out of those three chiefs, you can guess which one.

ME: When they read my book, they will know what you have, and you better believe they'll be coming down on you pretty hard!

SIMONE: What about yourself? They will also think that I told you everything about them as well. You're in the line of fire along with me.

ME: Why are you placing me in your line of fire? I am just a writer, that's all. Wait! I get it now. You hate all the men in the world, so you're throwing me in with the bunch, huh?!

SIMONE: No! It's because you are a damn good writer, and *Telling It Like It Is* is a damn good way of letting the world know that I am telling it all in your book. Plus I am helping you to sell ten or twenty million copies. I mean, just think that J. W. Blackwell, the famous author of a very powerful novel, is putting all these so-called important suckers on notice that Simone is going to tell it all if they don't pay me for what I think is worth keeping my mouth shut.

ME: What about Dave Turner? Why didn't you keep his name a secret?

SIMONE: Have you ever heard of collateral damage? Well, he's collateral damage that I am using him to convince the others that the same thing will happen to them if they don't meet my demands.

ME: And what exactly are your demands? I mean, how much money will you be asking for to keep what you have on them a secret?

SIMONE: [*laughs*] Ah, I figure about half a million dollars from each one. I mean, that's a small amount, considering what they will lose if I let the cat out of the bag.

ME: Let me ask you this: do you believe in God?

SIMONE: God, who is that? Oh, you mean the God who allowed my own father to rape me a hundred times? Is that the God you're talking about?!

ME: Yeah, that's the God I am talking about. But are you saying that it was God's fault that your father raped his own daughter?

SIMONE: Whose fault was it if it wasn't God's?! God created the bastard, didn't he?! So yeah, I blame God for what my father did to me. And now I am punishing all men for what God allowed that one bastard to do.

ME: Is it fair to punish all men for what one man did to his own daughter?!

SIMONE: Fair?! There is nothing fair about life. Think about it! We're born into this shitty world to live a few miserable years, doing what we can to survive, and then we die! Ashes to ashes and dust to dust, and that's it! What's so damn fair about being a lump of dirt?!

ME: So in other words, you don't have any fear of going to hell when you die? Not only that, but there is this dude named Satan who was probably the reason why your father became the evil man that he is. Do you ever think about that?

SIMONE: Hell?! You're talking about hell! Do you have any idea what being a fucking prostitute for twenty years is like?! Of course you don't! Yeah, it was a choice that I consciously made of my own free will. But to live in that world, dealing with all kinds of scumbags who look down on you like you're nothing but a piece meat for hire—now that's hell, my friend! Wherever Satan's home is, it can't be any worse than what I have already been through. In other words, I might be able to teach Satan a thing or two. And then on top of that, who in the hell created Satan? Your precious, almighty God did, that's who! And then you want to ask me, do I believe in God?! What in the hell do you think?!

ME: Well, since you put it that way, I'll withdraw the question. [*laughs*] But I think you have lost your faith in God and anything else that has real values attached to it. Honestly, what you're talking about doing is a real danger to you and to your daughter. These people care more about their reputations and money than they care about you and your family. I think you should give this whole idea a second thought before my book is published.

SIMONE: Fuck them! I want you to publish this book with the contents just as I have given it to you. You worry about your book getting out to your readers, and I'll worry about my own safety. Look, that's what makes the world so wonderful and fucked up at the same time. We all have the right to think and believe what we want to. If everybody thought and acted the way God wanted them to think and act, he wouldn't have a need for Satan, would he?!

ME: You know, I have never thought of it like that! But I guess when you think about it that way, you have a good point. So with that in mind, as far as us going to heaven or hell when we die depending on Judgment Day is concerned, that's not something you have even considered, right?

SIMONE: Okay, let me set the record straight for you right now, and you can draw any conclusion that you want to from it. When I was making thousands of dollars a week and sometimes a day, buying whatever I wanted from any stores that I wanted, and traveling all around the world and fucking every kind of man imaginable, that was my heaven. Now I've gotten older, and I am living in my own hell. It's a hell that I made for myself. I am at a point in my life where I don't worry about where this body of dust is going when I die. It is because I have learned that there is no hell that God can put me through that these sons-of-bitches haven't already put me through. Death is the only thing left in my life and probably yours as well.

ME: What about you daughter? How will you explain your life of living in your own heaven and hell to her? How do you even talk to her about that?!

SIMONE: I don't know what I'll say, but I know it won't be easy! However, I'll just have to tell her the truth or, as your book says, "tell it like it is."

ME: Even what her grandfather did to you?! Will you be able to tell her the true story about him, that he was the reason you chose this world of dancing and prostitution?

SIMONE: Tell her, no! Give her your book to read, yes! After that, I'll just have to let the chips fall where they may. Like I said, this is a hell that I created for myself, not for her. She came about because I messed around and fell in love with a no-good bastard! I am glad about that.

ME: I wish you well as you go forward, Simone. Good luck, and may God keep you safe.

SIMONE: Thank you! And as I said before, I hope this book sells many millions because I am looking for my share. [*smiles*]

ME: Well, if my book does what we both are hoping for, I will gladly write you a check.

Two years ago, Simone gave me this interview as well as her confession in writing. Today, I cannot say where she is or what action she has taken in terms of making the people she was connected to aware of her intentions. Is it possible that everything that she was planning to do took a turn for the worse? I cannot say for sure at this time. But I can say this: money and women are mankind's two worst enemies. And I have witnessed and heard of people being wiped off the face of the earth for things far less than what Simone was talking about doing. I have no knowledge as to who these clients she talked about getting even with were. Personally, I did not want to know, for I do not want to become a part of her deadly scheme.

After the publication of this novel, I plan to find Simone by staging an investigation into her disappearance. Hopefully, she is still alive and well. Or she could have just simply gone into hiding. This much, I do know to be true: according to her, many of her clients were very rich, powerful, and politically connected, and more than likely, they could become very dangerous people if pushed to the limit. And apparently, she had everything she needed to shake up a world filled with preachers, politicians, and high-ranking law enforcement officers. Personally, I believed every word she said . . . but only time will tell!

Chapter 28

BLACK LIVES MATTER only to those who believe or assume that police officers across America are killing innocent black men and women. And of course, when we see the videos of such killings and shootings, we only see white police officers taking matters into their own hands in what seems to be an intentional eliminating of black people. Obviously, what we see, we often believe. But what do we believe when we see and hear of hundreds of black men and women who are being murdered in the streets day in and day out by guns that are being held and fired by other black people? Black lives are being put on hold, or they do not seem to matter as much because they are being eliminated by other black people.

This whole idea of "Black Lives Matter" is as serious as a heart attack on one hand, but it is also joke on the other hand. How can anyone take the idea seriously when it only points to one side of the problem or in one direction? If "black lives matter" so much, then they would matter regardless of who are doing the taking of lives. If "black lives matter," they matter regardless of the race, color, or creed of the individuals taking the lives of black people. There cannot be a difference in the color of the perpetrator's skin or the kind of clothing they are wearing or the official capacity they hold. All lives matter in the eyes of God; "thou shalt not kill"!

When we think and talk about whether black lives should matter or not, we need not look any further than Chicago, Illinois. On the first day of January in 2017, over right hundred murders had occurred in that pitiful killing field of a city. By the end of 2016, that grand total had risen way above seven hundred murders in one year. And the question is, "How on God's green earth is it possible that eight hundred people can be murdered in one single city in the United States in one single year?!" There are thirty-five thousand cities and towns in America, and Chicago surpasses every one of them and will be ranked as the "Murder Capital of America."

The brutal truth of all these murders in the city of Chicago is the fact that the vast majority of these murder victims were black people killed by other black people and by neither cops nor white people. Yet when there is a black person killed by a white cop in the streets of America, there are marches, riots, and screams of "Black Lives Matter!" in every inner city in this country. But there are few or no voices heard when black people murder other black people for the same idiotic reasons or for no reason at all. None of these can be claimed as cops killing black people. But as always, there is a serious double standard in the minds of black people when it comes taking responsibility for their own actions. "We can do it, but they can't!"

Due to the latest rash of killings by cops across America, there is a serious lack of trust in police protection as well as police investigations in these black-on-black murders. This, of course, brings up another problem for the police in particular: these senseless crimes are going unsolved because no one is talking to the police about who the suspects are or could be. However, not only do these crimes go unsolved, but they also leave the victim's families without closure or healing after their loved one's untimely departure. Across the board, this is a very sad situation for the families and the police.

Sure, we can say that the cops brought this situation upon themselves, but let us not forget that cops are in the business to catch criminals and solve crimes. And whatever one or two cops might do, whether or not it is sometimes unethical for law enforcement officers altogether, we cannot rightfully condemn all cops for what one or two or three might do. But if black people withhold information that could possibly bring such cases to a court of law, it is impossible for cops to do their jobs properly and effectively.

Let us also not forget that a society or a segment of people in a society that tries to do without the protection of the police is a society that is in serious trouble. This is exactly what is happening in Chicago and many other inner cities across America. The police only go into these areas whenever they have to or when they are called. Otherwise, the police are saying, "Let them niggers kill each other!" The police only show up after to clean up the blood and guts that have been left behind.

Now I ask the question: "Who really cares whether black lives matters or not?" Do black people really care about their black brothers and sisters? Or have they been so indoctrinated by white violence against blacks that they feel that violence against each other is a part of the black heritage? I pose that question simply because if black people really believed the message that they are preaching, they would simply practice the message that they are preaching. As I have said before, we cannot have it both ways; we cannot live in a nation of all people, colors, creeds, and religions and still think that only our lives really matter. Under the Commandments of God, all lives matter. And if we believe that "black lives matter" so much, we must teach our young men and women who are killing each other that black lives matters to black people as well as to white people.

There is an old saying: "If you know better, you will do better." So what does that old phrase mean to the people who have taken the time to adhere to the old phrase? It means there was a time when we as believers took the Bible seriously when it told us, "Thou shalt not kill." But what it does it mean to the people who view taking a human life as no more than stepping on a bug? It means just that! It is because they do not know any better, for no one has taken their precious time to teach them any better. Therefore, we are right back to square one!

When a child is born, he or she is blind to everything that is going on in the world. And for that child to know exactly what is happening around him or her, that child has to be told or taught the correct way. If they are not taught or told the correct way and the wrong way of doing things, the child will assume his or her own way of thinking is the right way, which is the wrong way in most cases. So who exactly is responsible for all the murders that are occurring in Chicago and other major cities across America? They are the same people who birth them into the world, the parents. However, the one major problem that is attached to the parents taking responsibility is they all want to blame the so-called system. What system are they referring to? It is the "welfare system" that automatically creates broken homes.

Regardless of what system they often refer to, it is still the responsibility of every mother and father who engage in a sexual relationship that ultimately produces a baby. They are to raise that child to know the difference between right and wrong. However, it is difficult to expect the parents to raise their children to know right from wrong when they themselves do not know the difference. Obviously, the primary reason why the children who are committing these senseless crimes do not know better is because their parents do not know any better.

There is an old saying: "The proof is in the pudding." In other words, to make it clear that these young people and even some older folks do not know any better, if someone would simply ask the question as to why they had killed another human being, they would not give a logical or coherent answer. And if they tried to give a logical reason why it was necessary to take another human being's life, it would probably sound so idiotic that it seems comical. There is no logical explanation why anyone should willfully kill another human being unless it is in self-defense.

In doing this report, I learned there are people who blame the church for not doing its fair share in helping shape the minds of young people. They say the church is no more than a "money pit" and nothing else. They say the ministers and preachers are doing nothing but making false promises or performing "lip service" to the masses to collect more money. To that, I will agree. And Google has listed the richest ministers known in America for that reason, and I agree. Here are the fourteen richest pastors in America: (1) Kenneth Copeland, who is probably the richest of all and is worth 760 million dollars; (2) Pat Robertson, a staunch Republican who is worth a little less; (3) Benny Hinn; (4) Joel Osteen; (5) Creflo Dollar; (6) Billy Graham; (7) Rick Warren; (8) T. D. Jakes; (9) Juanita Bynum; (10) John Hagee; (11) Paula White; (12) Eddie Long, who is deceased; (13) Noel Jones; and (14) Joyce Myers.

All the million-dollar preachers whom I have named above collected billion dollars from both poor black and white people. And with some of that money, one would think that they could have made a difference in the streets of black America. In Chicago alone, there is a church on every corner with its doors open, collecting tithes and offerings every day of the week and twice on Sundays. And when I look at what is happening in black America's crime-related situations, every black pastor who has a church in the black community should be leading the way in solving these senseless murders. But no, they are not doing anything to put an end to the violence. Instead, they are preaching prosperity, which means that the pastors are the only ones who are reaping the harvest. And the beat goes on in the black communities.

As a former police officer, I know firsthand that violent crimes are nothing new as far as being centrally located in the black communities is concerned. It has always been that way, especially during the 1960s. Due to the fact that the inner cities have always been a breeding ground for violent crimes, the question has always been asked, "Why do black people find it so very necessary to harm and kill each other?" And to this day, no one has been able to give an answer that makes sense or sounds plausible. Why is this statement a simple fact? It is a simple fact because black lives do not matter even to black people. But they expect that black lives should matter to white cops especially.

Telling It Like It Is is a book to set the record straight, plain and simple! "Black Lives Matter" is a joke when it comes to white people. Most white people see the same things that I see. And if the truth be told, black people see it as well. But the problem is that, of course, when it comes to black people speaking the truth, they are often demonized and criticized by other blacks for speaking out. Why is this situation a fact? It is a condition that has characterized black people, dating back to the days of slavery. Some black people think or believe that the "Willie Lynch Letter" is actually true. It is a letter that instructed the slave masters how to break and condition the minds of slaves and that would last for the next five hundred years.

To further clarify my statement, I read an actual statement that was made by a young man who had committed a gruesome murder, and his explanation for his act was the fact that his violent mental condition had been passed down from many generations of brutality on black people that started back in the years of slavery. This is his story to me:

> *Everybody's sitting around, blaming young black men for being angry and violent when they should be blaming the damn white people who brought us to this country as slaves. They taught us everything that we know today, including the God that we serve. The white man killed damn near all the Indians to take control of this country. He killed all the slaves that he could not control. In other words, the white man is a violent human being, and we as black people learned everything that we know from him.*
>
> *Look at the court system! As long as we are killing each other, our time served in prison is very short compared to what we would get if we killed someone white. So in my mind, the Americans' justice system is telling black people that it's okay to commit murder as long as we are not killing white people. Back in the old days, the white man would hang a nigger if we murdered someone white. But if we killed each other, he would laugh and say, "Good boy!"*
>
> *Look, I'm not saying what I did was right, but what I did was handed down to me from the very people who murdered us as if it was a sport. My grandfather once told me that the white man whom he worked for would tell him on Friday, "If you can keep yourself out of the graveyard, I'll keep you out of jail." That tells me that the white man doesn't care about a black man just as long as he can continue to use him for his own monetary gains. All we are good for is to make him money. Look at the drug trade; niggers are killing each other very day over some damn drugs that the white man brings into this country by the boatloads so niggers can sell them to make him money. And they kill each other in the process.*
>
> *Look, we have been brainwashed for four hundred years into believing that one day, we would be a part of this great nation. But instead, we're nothing but a herd of cattle being led to the slaughterhouse to be butchered by our own hands. And you asked me, "Why do we allow it?" And now I am asking you, "What choice do we have?!" We didn't write the laws that we are forced to live by. We didn't create the projects or the ghettos where we are living like a Third World country. We are living in a country where everything is controlled by the white man who brought us here in the first place. The only thing that has changed since the days of slavery is the fact that the white man doesn't hold public lynchings anymore.*

> Look, I'm not making excuses for the wrongs I have done, but when you start looking for answers, look no further than the damn white man because he's the bitch who started this whole violent reaction in this country. He brought violence with him when he came to America and killed all the Indians. He then brought the African people here to do his work, and those who refused to be slaves, he killed as well. So where do we get this violent nature that we have? We got it from the white man, just like we got everything else from him.
>
> So I now sit in prison, probably for the rest of my life if I don't die first by a state-authorized lethal injection, because I was found guilty of killing two white pigs. But I don't regret what I did because white cops are no more than the KKK in uniforms. You should know, you were once a cop yourself, and back in the 1960s, they too were the Klan. "Kill a nigger every chance you get, men!" So there you have it, my story as to why I am in prison for killing two white cops. Black people better wake the fuck up! It's now or never for us.

I cannot argue the points that were made in this man's reasoning for doing bad things. But what I will say is simple and to the point: we are responsible for our own actions. With that being said, I can also say that God must have known long before the creation of mankind that there would be evil people in the world. After all, evil did not begin with today's modern man (if there is such a human being). It started at the beginning of mankind with Cain and Abel, according to the Bible. Therefore, who was it that influenced Cain to kill his brother? Was it the racist white man? I have no clue, unless Satan appeared as the racist white man.

The crime situation in Chicago and every other major city across America, as well the evil throughout the world, is due to the evil in mankind, if we want to blame anyone. Or we can blame God because he is the creator of all things. Not only is God the creator of all things, but he also gave mankind "free will," which, in my opinion, was the worst thing God could have done for mankind and, of course, for many of the angels that were created. My reasoning is quite simple: the angels that now serve and stand by God's throne do not have "free will." That is why they are loyal and dedicated to God's Word, which means every other human creature, as well as the rebellious angels, had the will to think freely. Of course, God gave each and every one of the creative monsters a mind of their own. And eventually, they all turned against the Creator, which, of course, is against their own best interest.

Today, we are faced with a situation that God has been facing since the very beginning of time: how do we turn this violent nature of mankind around? The churches cannot get the job done! Jails and prisons cannot convince people that evil is wrong. And if the thought of God sending them all to hell is not a means of deterrent, what then can be done to stop the violent nature of mankind?! We are the only ones who can control our own violent nature.

Sure, the young man who murdered two white police officers blamed the white man for his behavior, but is that the beginning or the end of violence in the human race? No! God gave Moses the Ten Commandments many years ago, which included, "Thou shalt not kill." It was obvious that even back then, man was a violent creature. However, like so many people have learned down through the years, violence is a means that does not justify the end. Wars have been fought, especially by the American people who hoped that wars were going to be the means that justified a peaceful solution. We have gone through two world wars and many smaller wars trying to find peace among mankind. They have been hopeless and endless efforts.

But I agree with the young man that his violent nature as a black man was an inherited act on behalf of the evil white man because it was he who brought violence to the land of America by killing off the Indians and taking the land that was not rightfully his. Also, through acts of violence, which were a way to make slaves do all the work in this country, the white man then took all the credit for America being the great land that it is today. Yes, as a black man born and raised in this country, I know and understand the statement of the young man who was sentenced to die for murdering two white police officers. But in spite of my agreement, I also know that his action neither justifies his reasoning for murder nor will help those who will follow in his footsteps of violence toward each other.

We as a people must do the right thing for each other. We cannot continue to slaughter our own kind and think that "Black Lives Matter" is going to shed a positive light for others to see. It is never going to happen in our lifetime or in the future. Educating our young people that "black lives matter" to us as much as we want them to matter to other people is the only way. As for now, we have to forget about what white people say or think about us. We have to get our own acts together or "our own house in order" before we can demand respect from any other race of people. And until we can stop killing each other, "Black Lives Matter" will continue to be a joke to the rest of America. To get respect from others, we must first respect ourselves. And to respect ourselves, we have to treat ourselves the way that we want others to treat us.

Chapter 29

WILLIE LYNCH'S "LET'S MAKE A SLAVE" — Whether anyone agrees with the "Willie Lynch Letter" or not, there are many people of color who seem to think of it as a myth. However, there is one thing that no one can deny if they have lived in America long enough to know the history of the African Americans: that our existence in this country was derived from slavery. The Willie Lynch Letter is one of those kinds of stories that some black people wished had never surfaced. Why? Because it brings about a fact that they would forget, never know existed, or wish would simply disappear. However, none of those things are going to happen. And the untold Willie Lynch story hits closer to home than any people of color would like to admit. But now you can be the judge! Here is the Willie Lynch speech of 1712, as it was presented to a group of white Southerners on the bank of the James River:

> *Gentlemen, I greet you on the banks of the James River in the year of one thousand seven hundred and twelve. First, I shall thank you, the gentlemen of the colony of Virginia, for bringing me here. I am here to help you solve some of your problems with slaves. Your invitation reached me on my modest plantation in the West Indies, where I have experimented with some of the newest and oldest*

methods for the control of slaves. Ancient Rome would envy us if they had my program, which you will also have.

As our boat sailed south on the James River, named for our illustrious king whose version of the Bible we cherish, I saw enough to know your problem is not unique. While Rome used cords of wood as crosses for standing human bodies along its old highways in great numbers, you are here using trees and ropes on occasion.

I caught whiff of a dead slave hanging from a tree a couple of miles back. You are not only losing valuable stocks by hangings, but also, you have uprisings, your slaves are running away, your crops are sometimes left in the fields too long for maximum profit, you're suffering occasional fires, and your animals are being killed. Gentlemen, you know what your problems are; I do not need to elaborate on them. I am not here to enumerate your problems. However, I am here to introduce you to a method of solving them.

I am here to tell you that I have a foolproof method for controlling your black slaves. I guarantee every one of you that if it is installed correctly, it will control the slaves for at least five hundred years. My method is simple. Any member of your family or your overseers can use it. I have outlined a number of differences among the slaves, and I take these differences and make them bigger. I use fear, distrust, and envy for control purposes. The methods have worked on my modest plantation in the West Indies, and it will work here and throughout the South. Take this simple little list of differences and think about them.

On top of my list is age, *but it is there only because it starts with an "A." The second one is* color *or* shade, *and there is also:* intelligence; size; sex; plantation; the status of the plantation; the attitude of the owners; whether the slaves live in the valley, on the hill, east, west, north, or south; whether they have fine hair or coarse hair; and whether they are tall or short. *Now you have to list all these differences that I shall give you in an outline of action. However, before I give you the outline of action, I shall assure you that* distrust *is stronger than* trust, *and* envy *is stronger than* adulation, respect, *or* admiration. *The black slaves, after receiving this indoctrination, shall carry this trait and will become self-refueling and self-generating for hundreds or maybe thousands of years.*

Don't forget, you must pitch the older black male versus the young black male and the younger black male against the older black male. You must use the dark-skinned slaves against the *light-skinned slaves. You must also use the female against the male and vice versa. You must also have your white servants and overseers distrust all blacks, but it is necessary that your slaves trust and depend on us. They must love, respect, and trust us no matter what.*

Gentlemen, you must remember that these kits are the keys to control. And you must use them. Have your wives and children learn how to use them; never miss an opportunity to use them. If you use them intensively for one year, the slaves themselves will remain perpetually distrustful. Thank you!

Now the question is and has always been, "What information that was in those so-called 'Making a Slave' kits?" It was a study of the scientific process of man breaking and slave making. It described the rationale and the results of the Anglo Saxons' ideas and methods of ensuring a master/slave relationship.

To make a slave more of a slave, there would have to be a nigger man and a pregnant nigger woman as well as a nigger baby boy. This same principle was used in breaking a horse. The first thing they would do is take the slaves away from their natural state, whereas their natural state would provide them with ways and means of taking care of their own.

The slave masters would break the slaves of their string of dependence on nature and thereby create a state of dependency on their masters to get useful production for their businesses and pleasures.

The Cardinal Principles for Making a Negro a Slave: *For fear that our future generation may not understand the principles of breaking both the horse and the man, we must lay down the art of doing so. If we are to sustain our basic economy, we must break and tie both the man and the beast together. We understand that short-range planning in economics results in periodic chaos, so to avoid turmoil in the economy, it requires us to have depth in long-range comprehensive planning and the articulation of both skills and sharp perception.*

There Are Six Steps to the Cardinal Principles: *(1) both horse and nigger are not good for the economy if they are left in the wild or in their natural state; (2) both horse and nigger must be broken and tied together for orderly production; (3) for the orderly future, special attention must be paid to the black female and her offspring; (4) both female and offspring must be crossbred to produce variety and division of labor; (5) both must be taught to respond to a particular new language; and (6) psychological and physical instructions of containment must be created for both.*

We hold the above six cardinal principles as true and self-evident based on the following discourse concerning the economics of breaking and tying the horse and the nigger together, all inclusive of the six principles laid down above.

Note: Neither principle alone will suffice for good economics. All the principles must be employed for the orderly good of the nation. As Trump said, "Let's make America great again!"

Accordingly, both a wild horse and a wild nigger are dangerous if allowed to remain their natural selves. They both have a tendency after being captured to seek their customary freedom, and in doing so, they might kill you in your sleep. Therefore, you cannot rest while trying to keep a watchful eye on them.

They sleep while awake, and you are awake while they sleep. They are dangerous when they are near the family house, and watching them away from the house requires too much labor. Above all, you cannot get them to work in their natural state. Hence, both the horse and the nigger must be broken; that is to break them from one form of mental life to another by keeping the body and taking the mind. In other words, break their will to resist. Now the breaking process is the same for both the horse and the nigger, only slightly varying in degrees. But as we said before, there is an art in long-range economic planning. You must keep your eyes and thoughts on the female and her offspring of the horse and the nigger.

For example, take the case of the wild horse, a female horse, and an already-infant horse, and compare the breaking process to that of a nigger male in his natural state. With a pregnant nigger woman and her infant offspring, the process is the same for both. Completely break the female horse until she becomes very gentle, whereas you or anybody can ride her in comfort. Breed the mare with the stud until you have the desired offspring. Then you can turn the stud to freedom until you need him again. Train the horse until she will eat out of your hands, and in turn, she will train the infant horse to eat out of your hands as well. And when it comes to training or breaking an uncivilized nigger, you must use the same process but vary in degrees and step up the pressure to do a complete reversal of the mind.

Take the meanest and most restless nigger in the bunch, and strip him of his clothes in front of the remaining males, females, and nigger infants. Tar and feather him then tie each leg to a different horse headed in the opposite direction. Then set the nigger on fire and beat the horses to pull him apart in front of the remaining niggers. The next step is to take a bullwhip and whip the remaining nigger males to the point of death in front of the females and infants. Don't kill them, but put the fear of God in them, for they can be useful for future breeding.

> The Breaking Process of the African Woman: *Take the female, and run a series of tests on her to see if she will submit to your desires willingly. Test her in every way possible because she is the most important factor for good economics. If she shows any signs of resistance in submitting completely to your will, do not hesitate to use the bullwhip on her to extract the last bit of bitch out of her. Take care not to kill her, for in doing so, you spoil good economics. When in complete submission, she will train her offspring in the early years to submit to labor when they become of age.*
>
> *We are reversing the nature by burning and pulling one civilized nigger apart and bullwhipping the other one to the point of death, all in the female's presence.*

Understanding is the best thing. Therefore, we shall go deeper into this area of the subject matter concerning what we have produced here in this breaking process of the female nigger. We have reversed relationships. In her natural, uncivilized state, she would have a strong dependency on the uncivilized nigger male, and she would have a limited protective tendency toward her independent male offspring and would raise the female offspring to be dependent like her. Nature had provided time with this balance.

By her being left alone, unprotected, with the male image destroyed, the ordeal causes her to move from her psychological dependent state to a frozen independent state. In this frozen psychological state of independence, she will raise her male and female offspring in reversed roles. For fear of the young man's life, she will psychologically train him to be mentally weak and dependent but physically strong. Because she has become psychologically independent, she will train her female offspring to be psychologically independent. What do you have now? You have got a nigger woman out front and the nigger man standing behind her, and he is scared. This is the perfect situation for a good night's sleep and sound economics.

> The Negro Marriage Unit: *We breed two nigger males with two nigger females. Then we take the nigger males from them and keep them moving and working. Let's say one of the nigger female bears a nigger female and the other one bears a nigger male; now both nigger females, being without the influence of the nigger male image, are frozen with an independent psychology and will raise their offspring into reverse positions. The one with the female offspring will teach her to be like herself, independent and negotiable. The one with the male offspring, by her being frozen with a subconscious fear for his life, will raise him to be mentally dependent and weak but physically strong, or body over mind. (They are now called "superior athletes" in today's world.) That is good, sound, and long-range comprehensive planning.*

A Letter of Thanks from White America Today

Dear Black Americans,

After all these years and all that we have been through together, we think now is the appropriate time for us to show our gratitude for all that you have done for us. We have chastised you, criticized you, punished you, and in some cases, we have even apologized to you. But we have neither formally nor publicly thanked you for your never-ending allegiance and support to our cause.

This is our open letter of thanks. We will always be in your debt for your labor. You built this country and were responsible for the wealth that we still enjoy today. Upon your backs, laden with the stripes we sometimes had to apply for disciplinary reasons, you carried our nation. We thank you for your diligence and your tenacity. Even when we refused to allow you to even walk on the same sidewalk as us or in our shadows, you followed close behind, believing that someday, we would accept you and treat you like men and women.

We publicly acknowledge black people for raising our children, attending to our sick, and preparing our meals while we were occupied with the trappings of the good life. Even during the time when we found pleasure in your women and the enjoyment in seeing your men lynched, maimed, and burned, some of you continued to watch over us and our belongings. We simply cannot thank you enough. Look, your bravery on the battle fields despite being classified as three-fifths of a man was and still is considered as outstanding today.

We often watched in awe as you went about your prescribed chores and assignments, sometimes laboring in the hot sun for twelve hours a day, to assist us in realizing our dreams of wealth and good fortune. Now that we control at least 90 percent of all the resources and wealth of this great nation, we have black people to thank the most. We can only think of the sacrifices you and your families have made to make it all possible. You were there when it all began, and you are still with us today, protecting us from those black people who have the temerity to speak out against our past transgressions.

Thank you for continuing to bring 95 percent of what you have earned to our businesses. Thanks for buying our Hilfigers, Karans, Nikes, and all the other name brand items that you so adore. Your super-rich athletes, entertainers, intellectuals, and business persons (both legal and illegal) exchange most of their money for our cars, jewelry, homes, and clothing. What a windfall they have provided for us! Wow! That is really, amazingly kind of your black people. Even the less fortunate among you spend all that they have at our neighborhood stores, enabling us to open even more stores. Sure, they complain about us, but they will never do anything to hurt us economically.

Please allow us to thank you for not bogging yourself down with the business of doing business with your own people. We can take care of that by supplying everything that you need. You just keep doing business with us because it is much safer that way. Besides, everything you need and want, we make anyway, even Kente cloth. You just continue to dance, sing, and distrust and hate one another while spending your money with us. Just have yourself a good ol' time, and this time around, we will take care of you. I mean, after all, that is the least that we can do, considering all that you have done for us.

Heck! You deserve it, black people! For all the labor that you have created for our wealth, for resisting the messages of making trouble for us from people like Washington, Delaney, Garvey, Bethune, Tubman, and Truth, and for fighting and dying on our battlefields, we thank you very much! And we really thank you for not reading about the many black warriors that participated in the development of our great country. We also want to thank you for keeping it hidden from your younger generation. Thank you for not bringing such glorious deeds to our attention as well. We appreciate your acquiescence to our political agendas, for abdicating your own economic self-sufficiency, and for working so diligently for the economic well-being of our people. You are real troopers!

Furthermore, even though the Thirteenth, Fourteenth, and Fifteenth Amendments were written for you and many of your relatives who died for the rights therein, you did not resist when we changed those black rights to civil rights and allowed virtually every other group to take advantage of them as well. I mean, that was really big of you to do that. Black people are something else! Your dependence upon us is beyond our imagination, irrespective of what we do to you and the many promises we have made and then broken to you. But this time, we promise we will make it right. Trust us!

I tell you what! You don't need your own hotels. You can continue to stay in ours. You have no need for supermarkets when you can shop at ours twenty-four hours a day. Why should you even think about owning more banks?! You don't have to waste your time and energy trying to break into manufacturing. You have worked hard enough in ours. Relax! Have a party! We'll sell you everything that you need. And when you die, we'll even bury you at a discount. Now how is that for gratitude?!

Finally, the best part of all: since you went far and beyond the pale and turned over your children to us for their education, with what we are teaching them, it is likely that they will continue in a mode similar to the one that you have followed for the past forty-five years (since school desegregation).

When Mr. Lynch walked on the banks of the James River in 1712 and said that he had a formula to make a slave that would last for five hundred years, little did he know or realize the truth in his prediction. Just think, three hundred of those years have already passed, and his prediction is holding true. With three generations of children having already gone through our education system, we can only look forward to at least seventy-five more years of prosperity. Things could not be better for us, and it is all because of you. For all you have done, we thank you from the bottom of our hearts, black Americans! You are the best friends that any group of people could ever have. God bless you, and may your people live long and prosperous!

Sincerely,
All the Other Americans

Chapter 30

WHY ARE THERE POOR WHITE PEOPLE IN AMERICA? In this chapter, I am going to explain the story behind the reason why a certain person was elected president of the United States. It was done by who can be considered mostly poor white people in this country. And I have researched all the facts that allowed the elite white people who came to this country rich remain rich, primarily from the labor of black slaves who shed blood, sweat, and tears, making them millionaires and billionaires. But before the black Africans were brought to this country by way of Jamestown, Virginia, in 1619, plantation owners relied on white indentured servants for cheap labor. These white servants were mostly poor Europeans who traded their freedom for passage to the new American colonies. They were looking for what is now known as the "American dream."

They were given room and board, and after four to seven years of grueling servitude, they were granted their freedom. However, only about 40 percent of those same white slaves lived long enough to see the end of their contract. Colonial law provided the white slaves who made it to the end of their term of service "freedom dues," which was something that was never offered to the black African slaves. Nevertheless, the "freedom dues" were usually one hundred acres of land and a small sum of money as well as a new suit of clothes.

Yet many of these free white servants never received anything simply because they did not know about these grants, and they were swindled out of them by the plantation owners.

Today, we will never hear any mentioning of poor white people being slaves or servants to the elite whites of America. Why? It is because that term or definition was always meant for the African slaves who were brought to America in the 1680s, and the term "indentured servitude" had lost its appeal to the "would-be immigrants" since the British labor market had vastly improved. Therefore, because there was an increase in demand for indentured servants, the idea of going to Africa and buying black slaves to do the work to replace that of the white servants was an idea that would solve the problems of the elite whites in America.

Plantation owners kept all their skilled white servants to supervise the black slaves that were being brought to do the hard labor. Naturally, this idea of skilled and unskilled workers brought the first racial divide among the poor whites and the black slaves. This was brought on because the white elite began to favor the black slaves, for there were way more black slaves to choose from, and it was much cheaper to run plantations with free labor.

To keep many African slaves on hand, the white landowners raped the black females and produced many offspring who were raised to take the place of those who died or were too old to do the work. However, as the African slaves grew in numbers, the plantation owners began to realize that they had a problem. The plantation owners saw the white servants socializing, living, and having babies with the black slaves. They often tried to escape together.

Suddenly, the plantation owners began to see another trend that was taking place; the poor whites and the black slaves were getting along in ways that brought a fear that they might become organized as one group and overtake the plantation owners. The landowners came up with a brilliant idea that created the first incidence of racism between the two groups. Because many of these landowners were also politicians, they began to pass laws that favored the poor whites, which would naturally create a series of conflicts between the white and black slaves.

Again, I must admit that I have never heard of a white person who would admit that the reason they are poor is because they too were once slaves to the master white elite. What laws did the slave masters pass that created separation between the white slaves and the black slaves? They passed laws that said that black slaves could be stripped naked and beaten half to death, whereas the white slaves were never beaten. Obviously, this is where the story of Willie Lynch came into play. Willie Lynch's instructions on how to make slaves of the Africans seem to play a major role in the separation of the black slaves from the white slaves.

Although many poor whites thought that this was their way to achieve the American dream for themselves—working hard to help make better slaves out of the black Africans—they instead saw very little change in their own ways of life. However, with the passing of the new laws, any white slave or white person could beat the black slaves. This, of course, gave whites—the poor ones as well as the rich ones—an elevated status over the African slaves. This way of doing things would take some time, but it would work with future generations.

As time passed, the labor of the black slaves made the wealthy elites richer and richer, and the poor whites got poorer and poorer. Although the poor whites began to believe among themselves that they were gaining equal footing with the elite whites, in reality, it was only an illusion within their own minds.

Time passed, and for the next two hundred years, the elite whites found themselves richer than ever before, and the poor whites found themselves poorer than ever before. But with the election of Abraham Lincoln and his waging war against slavery, the wealthy elite white people saw their way of life of owning black slaves vanishing. It was the North against the South, and because they had successfully accomplished a racial fight between blacks and whites, it would be easy to convince the poor whites to fight in a civil war that would not benefit them at all.

There was an outcry among the elite whites to convince the poor whites that if the "niggers" became free, they would rape their white women, and their white women would have their little black babies. The only way that they could keep the black Africans as slaves and for the poor whites to remain in charge of them was to fight in the Civil War. Naturally, the poor whites bought into the civil war idea, which was no more than a lie because they believed that they were equal to the elite whites just because of their white skin.

The idea of waging a civil war worked for the elite white people because they had convinced the poor whites that it was a war that would benefit them more so than anyone else. But the reality of a war was that it would only benefit the plantation owners. And to abolish slavery would mean that the elite whites would lose their rich way of life. And they needed the poor whites to fight a war that would keep them in their elite world. This was the only reason why a civil war was ever fought in first place. It was to make the rich richer, and they could care less about the poor whites dying in the war. It was all about the economic advantages for the elite white folks.

In my book *Southern Gold*, I told the story about the Southern businessmen and the French government that forked over more than two billion dollars in gold to finance the Civil War that the poor Southern crackers were fighting and dying for the elite whites. Also, the war would maintain the economic freedom of the elite whites. They were willing to send the poor whites to their deaths for them to keep this way of life for themselves.

The idea of poor white people fighting the Civil War worked like someone waving a magic wand in front of their faces. The poor and working-class white men signed up by the thousands to fight a war that they believe would give them equal access to the wealth and success that the elite white people had. On both sides of the Mason–Dixon Line, wealthy white men paid to have themselves exempted from the war. But as the war lingered on, the poor whites who were actually fighting the war finally realized that this was not their war, although they were the ones dying on the battlefields by the hundreds. Finally, someone spoke up by saying, "We're nothing but a bunch of poor white-trash motherfuckers, fighting to make the rich whites richer."

By the end of the war, more than 650,000 poor white men had died for a worthless cause. Although black Africans were freed due to the war, these same ex-slaves were left in a free world that they knew very little about. And many free black Americans died because the North, or the Union Army that fought to free them, abandoned them as well. But the poor whites who fought the war did not fare any better than the ex-slaves. The poor whites and the poor blacks once again found themselves in the same poor conditions that they were in before the war. However, in spite of being white and still poor, they had somehow developed the mindset that they were superior to the poor blacks simply because they were white.

It has been 150 years since the freeing of black African slaves from a condition that was thought of as sometimes being barbaric and ungodly. And being a slave was a condition that God himself would have frowned upon. But wait! Let us go back to our Bibles to see if God really did frown upon the idea of some men being slaves and other men owning slaves.

> Laws for Living: *Then God said to Moses, "These are the laws for living that you will give to the Israelites. If you buy a Hebrew slave, he will serve you for six years. In the seventh year, you are to set him free, and he will have to pay nothing. If the slave's master gives him a wife and she gives birth to sons or daughters, the woman and her children belong to the master. When the slave is set free, only he may leave. But if the slave says, 'I love my master, my wife, and my children, and I don't want to go free,' then the slave's master must take him to God."*

The wording of God's "laws for living" is very similar to that of the slave masters as recent as 150 years ago. And if we listen closely, it is the same coded message that is being spoken by Pres. Donald Trump; his message is pretty much the same today.

Therefore, if we are to believe what the Bible tells us concerning the close relationship between God and Moses, it would seem that even God approved of the Hebrew slaves, which simply means black people. How do we—or should we—argue the point with God? If God approves that there should be slaves and masters in the world, who are we to fight against being slaves or say that God is wrong for the approval of slavery?!

Of course, I know what the general conservations would be like. "That was then, and this is now! When Jesus came into the world, he changed the whole concept of owning slaves. All mankind became responsible for their own bodies and souls. Therefore, owning slaves died along with the Ten Commandments." Did it really?! But if that were the case, where did the elite white people get the idea that owning slaves would make them rich and keeping slaves would continue to make them rich? They got it from the Bible, of course!

As we all know or suspect, the terminology of slave ownership is different between white people and black people. White people are called servants, whereas black people are just called "slaves." But here is the real "kick in the pants": the Bible teaches us about some of God's most beloved characters who are written about in the book—except for Jesus, they all owned slaves. If the Bible called them slaves, they must have been slaves, which means we will continue to be slaves in some form or another as long as the world continue to exist, even as far as asking the question: "How did white people in America become poor?" Obviously, they came to America poor to work for the elite whites. And as a result of coming to America poor, many generations since then still remain poor.

Now the only question remaining to be answered in today's world is, "Are white poor people better off than poor black people?" The truth of the matter is quite simple: poor is poor, regardless of the color of your skin. And if poor white people believe that Donald Trump is the best thing since sliced bread, well, we certainly cannot stop them from believing. After all, that is what the "God concept" is all about: "belief." Therefore, it does not matter whether God is real in the minds of some people because as long as he is real to those who believe, slaves and masters, black poor people and white poor people, are all the same. Like it or not, we are all a part of the same human race!

This is a truth that you will never hear or read anywhere else except right here. And the question now is, as it was in the beginning, "Can you handle the truth?!" God obviously chose a few other people to put the Word out to enlighten the masses, but they all fell by the wayside. So here it is once again! The truth hurts, but it will heal all wounds. A lie kills and destroys!

Chapter 31

THE FINALE OF TELLING IT LIKE IT IS — We have entered a place in this world where the truth does not matter anymore. Telling it like it is is a serious danger to many people, for they do not want to hear the truth. To tell a lie is much easier than to tell the truth. However, I refuse to say things of a non-truthful nature just to satisfy someone else's ego.

With that being said, I want to tell you a story about the America that I live in and have lived in since birth. I was born in the South, where being called a "nigger" by white folks was as common as getting out of bed in the morning. However, being called a nigger was not so bad when I think about the many black people who were lynched and castrated in my small town and countryside for simply looking at a white woman or less. Being called a nigger was an honor!

But here we are in the twenty-first century where America elected its first black president, which should have meant that America is now color blind and that race is a thing of the past. But instead, I see more prejudice and hatred by white Americans today since the days when I grew up having to sit in the balcony to watch a movie because I was not permitted to sit in the lower seating area with white folks. Not only that, but I also remember the days when I was told that I couldn't enter through the front doors of white people's homes simply because I was black. No other reason was necessary; I was black, and I was not fit to enter through the front doors of white people's homes.

Today, I may not have to sit in the balconies or enter through the rear doors or walk on the other side of the street just because of the presence of a white woman on my side of the street, but the hatred is still there in living color so everyone can see. And what is even worse is there are many black people in America who are refusing to see what is standing right in front of them. We still believe that white America needs black people to make America run. America stopped running for black folks when President Clinton signed NAFTA, which sent most of the blue-collar jobs to Mexico and Canada. And yet we called him our first black president!

The truth of matter is that the only decent jobs that are left for black people to do in America are playing sports, performing rap music, and going to jail. We do not have any businesses to call our own; we allowed other races to come to America and open hair products stores, gas stations, and even restaurants in our neighborhoods. But all these businesses cater to black people, whom we have no interest in at all. The question has been for many years, "Why?!" What happened to black businesses in all small towns and large cities? This is a question that we all are asking, but no one has a logical answer.

When I first became a cop in Atlanta in the mid-1960s, there were black businesses all across the city. Auburn Avenue was probably the best known and most famous for black entertainment. Then there was Hunter Street, where the civil rights movement was born. From downtown west to the city limits were black establishments. Further north on Bankhead Highway, from Northside Drive to Fulton Industrial Boulevard, there were black businesses. On the south side, from Grant Park on Georgia Avenue, were black businesses. In other words, black businesses covered mostly the downtown area like dew on a fall morning.

As the 1980s came in and the cocaine boom took over the streets, black businesses began to disappear like smoke in a windstorm. Obviously, we became victims of our own success with a newfound money-making product, "crack cocaine." Young people no longer wanted to set up shop and run legitimate businesses where they did not have to run from the cops every minute of the day. Instead, it was a way of life for the young and the dumb. That same trend has continued today, where young blacks are constantly looking for the quick and easy way to make a dollar.

Then there is "rap music," where young kids are given millions of dollars to rhyme words where most are put to music by artists of the past. The only problem with this idea of making this kind of money is that many of these same rap artists evolved from drug-selling gangs. The mentality of some of these artists hinges on that of drug-related thugs. The old blacks who believed in owning their own businesses fell by the wayside like a rock falling off a cliff.

The question today is, "How do we change the 'thug culture' of the black communities?" And then the question goes on to ask, "How do we bring our kids back from a generation where there is one parent at home to a two-parent family again?" It is a known, undisputed truth that one-parent households are broken. The vast majority of our kids who are in the streets today and are committing 80 percent of the senseless crimes are kids coming from these broken homes. How do we put an end to this cycle of unraised, violent-mentality young people? Obviously, there is no easy solution. But one thing is for sure: black people must take it upon themselves to raise their own children, or the streets and jail cells will do it for them.

We find many black people going to church, searching for answers, but the answers are not in the church; they are at home, where mothers and fathers are taking charge of their own families. When God commanded Adam and Eve to go forth and multiply, he did not mean for them to multiply and to just let their children go astray. Of course, Adam and Eve did just that. Children must be taught right from wrong, or they will gravitate toward the wrong until someone in the law enforcement business shows them where all the people who do wrong end up.

Today, as we move forward with yet another elected president, we all must find a common ground where we all can live in a peaceful society and not have to worry about crime, racism, or political ramification. Let's face it, politicians can pass laws, and cops can enforce those laws, but we as American citizens must obey those laws. We do not necessarily have to like or agree with the laws or even like the people who pass the laws, but we have to abide by the laws until such time that we have those laws change by utilizing our power to vote.

Half the American people today are in an uprising because the president they voted for or thought should have won did not win. And the question is, "What do we do now?" Well, we vote, and we keep voting until we get the right people in the right places to do the jobs right. It is a simple process, but we must be true to our values and our own principles. Donald Trump is not the end of the world, hopefully!

For us American citizens, the only real hope that we have is the Constitution of the United States, which states, "*We the people of the United States, to form a more perfect Union, establish Justice, insure domestic Tranquility, provide for the common defense, promote the general Welfare, and secure the Blessings of Liberty to ourselves and our posterity, do ordain and establish the Constitution for the United States of America.*"

In the real world, I know there is always going to be a difference of opinions simply because people from different walks of life, backgrounds, races, or even religions do not think, act, or even talk alike. But those differences should not keep us from being one nation under God. When the rest of the world is against us, we as a nation come together as one to defend our way of life.

Needless to say—and I am even sad to say it—America was built on racism, as you have already read. But just because your skin color is not the same as mine does not give you the right to deny me the chance to seek the American dream or the American way of life. I am a black man not by choice but because God saw fit to create me black. And as a black man, I help build and protect this nation just as any other races of people did. My black brothers died in World War II, Korea, and Vietnam just as other Americans died. Not only that, but I did not spend thirty-seven years protecting only black people in the city of Atlanta; I risked my life every single day for all the people of this city. And now that I have retired from a job that has killed so many of my friends and coworkers in the line of duty as well as from stress, I am bound by my freedom and duty to express my truth in *Telling It Like It Is*.

As I said from the very beginning, I do not expect for a million people to agree with me or even like me for telling it like it is. But as a God-fearing individual, I believe that the truth will set me free. And if you are offended by what I have written, well, that is God's way of telling you that you have a right to be offended simply because he created you to be offended!

Amendment I to the Constitution of the United States—freedom of speech—gives me the right and the privilege to say and talk about anything or anyone that I choose to talk about as long as I am not falsely accusing them of a crime or conduct. And as a citizen of these United States, I am utilizing my freedom of speech to tell it like it is.

> *Congress shall make no law respecting an establishment of religion, or prohibiting the free exercise thereof; or abridging the freedom of speech, or of the press; or the right of the people peacefully to assemble, and to petition the Government for a redress of grievances.*

In the world that we live in today, we have been so watered down with lies and false accusations that no one knows what the truth is anymore. The churches lie to us, the criminal justice system lies to us, and the politicians are lying to us, which all means that if everybody is lying to us, where do we find the truth? The truth only comes from babies and small children simply because they have not learned how to tell lies.

As I come to the conclusion of my testimony, I am a witness that the greatest lie that was ever told was when Satan convinced the world that he did not exist. How did he do that? He did it by simply telling the world that there is no such thing as an evil spirit. He also did it by convincing people that the Bible is a lie and that God is a fake or a myth to force people to do the right thing. But in reality, how do we know that whatever we see or think we know is real?! After all, God won't show his face, and Satan works from behind closed doors. So that only leaves one solution to the problem: the people! It is up to each one of us to believe or not believe what we see and feel. The truth or whatever we believe is the truth will always stand the test of time. But a lie will fall like rain falling from the sky.

It is my wish that you have enjoyed the stories that you have read. They are all my truths. And I have earned my truths from living a long life that I believe only God could have planned from the day of my birth. Thank you!

Printed in the United States
By Bookmasters